SCIENCE
FOR THE
NEXT
GENERATION

PREPARING FOR THE NEW STANDARDS

William Banko

Marshall L. Grant

Michael E. Jabot

Alan J. McCormack

Thomas O'Brien

National Science Teachers Association

Arlington, Virginia

National Science Teachers Association

Claire Reinburg, Director
Jennifer Horak, Managing Editor
Andrew Cooke, Senior Editor
Wendy Rubin, Associate Editor
Agnes Bannigan, Associate Editor
Amy America, Book Acquisitions Coordinator

ART AND DESIGN
Will Thomas Jr., Director
Joe Butera, Senior Graphic Designer, cover and interior design

PRINTING AND PRODUCTION
Catherine Lorrain, Director

NATIONAL SCIENCE TEACHERS ASSOCIATION
David L. Evans, Executive Director
David Beacom, Publisher

1840 Wilson Blvd., Arlington, VA 22201
www.nsta.org/store
For customer service inquiries, please call 800-277-5300.

NSTA is committed to publishing material that promotes the best in inquiry-based science education. However, conditions of actual use may vary, and the safety procedures and practices described in this book are intended to serve only as a guide. Additional precautionary measures may be required. NSTA and the authors do not warrant or represent that the procedures and practices in this book meet any safety code or standard of federal, state, or local regulations. NSTA and the authors disclaim any liability for personal injury or damage to property arising out of or relating to the use of this book, including any of the recommendations, instructions, or materials contained therein.

Library of Congress Cataloging-in-Publication Data

Banko, William, 1955-
  Science for the next generation : preparing for the new standards / by William Banko, Marshall L. Grant, Michael E. Jabot, Alan J. McCormack, and Thomas O'Brien.
    pages cm
  ISBN 978-1-936959-26-6
  1. Science--Study and teaching (Elementary)--Standards--United States. 2. Science--Study and teaching (Secondary)--Standards--United States. I. Title.
  LB1585.3.B34 2013
  507.1'073--dc23
                    2013003583
Cataloging-in-Publication Data are also available from the Library of Congress for the e-book. The LCCN is 2013017584.
e-ISBN: 978-1-938946-88-2.

CONTENTS

CONTENTS

CONTENTS

V

THE NEW SCIENCE OF LEARNING

VI

THE NEW SCIENCE OF LEARNING IN THE CLASSROOM

VII

LITERACY AND SCIENCE

FOREWORD

Early Science Education

ANSWERING THE QUESTION "WHY?"

Arne Duncan

U.S. Secretary of Education

Children, especially young children, are natural scientists. What parents haven't heard more times than they can remember their two-year-old's insistent question, "Why?" "Why is the sky blue? Why do I have to wear shoes? Why don't cats take baths?" Children's innate curiosity makes them natural scientists almost from birth.

Because children's inquisitiveness and desire to explore is so active in the early years, it is unfortunate to see that some time in elementary school, many kids lose their interest in science. Studies show that even in the early elementary grades, children are forming negative views about science, developing attitudes that can mar their educational careers. In the elementary years, children often say that science is too difficult and even dangerous. While many can easily envision themselves as future firemen, ball players, lawyers, artists, and even presidents, few young children picture themselves becoming chemists or biologists or energy entrepreneurs.

Perhaps young children do not see themselves as future scientists because in the United States students are not introduced to science early enough. Most formal science training takes place in grades 9–12, and this late start is hurting our country and our students. Recent results from the Program for International Student Assessment (PISA), a widely respected test given across the world, indicate that the United States has fallen to 21st place in science. In many of the countries that are ahead of us in science, the subject is taught in schools before the children even learn to read or write. Schools do it by introducing children at a young age to scientific inquiry: to observation, inference, and verification. They do it by integrating science thinking into early lessons in subjects like reading and social studies, even playtime. As children plant school gardens, for example, they learn to measure and observe the effects of the Sun and the rain and the bugs. In our family, we have found that the kids in elementary school are interested in these activities. My own children Claire and Ryan spent hours measuring pepper plants with their mother and me and making predictions about how big the plants would get.

Elementary science lessons can produce powerful results in children because they help them to become comfortable with science. With greater exposure to scientific concepts and to people who practice science in their careers, students can see themselves as scientists today and as the future astronauts, meteorologists, science teachers, and nurses of tomorrow. But more than that, elementary science learning enables students to think critically and begin to solve problems, laying a foundation for learning in all content areas. The kind of discovery learning that is often at the heart of a science lesson helps students to become truly engaged in school and excited about learning.

However, for students to benefit from classrooms built on inquiry and discovery, schools need early childhood teachers who have knowledge of early science learning and strategies that support young children's growth and development in science. Some teachers of higher grades (including middle and high school) also may benefit from professional development to hone their skills in creating science classrooms that are engaging and that model passion and excitement for science and for learning. As states reshape their curricula to ensure that students are ready for college and careers, it also makes sense for states to revisit science standards and align them to a new generation of assessments that test students' knowledge and critical-thinking skills.

More than ever, science learning is critical for our country. President Obama says, "The country that out-educates us today will out-compete us tomorrow." As a country, we need to exponentially expand the number of entrepreneurs, scientists, science teachers, and problem-solvers. We need creative thinkers who can play the lead role in reducing our nation's carbon footprint and our dependence on foreign oil through the use of second-generation biofuels, methane digesters, and energy-efficient tillage methods. We need students who can solve problems that don't yet exist and work on scientific endeavors that we haven't even thought of.

Science is essential in America's success in the knowledge economy of the 21st century. But it's not the only subject that students need to master. All of our young people need a well-rounded curriculum. In order to communicate well, to understand, and to think and inspire others, they need to be engaged readers and lively writers. They need social studies to become informed, participating citizens and mathematics to solve problems across a variety of disciplines. They need to learn social skills and be able to work with others. Students can acquire basic science literacy as they learn to read and write and study social studies and as they work together and do math. They can test theories that they read about in social studies and literature and can keep nature journals, honing writing and science literacy at the same time. What I am suggesting is not that we should supplant student experiences in other core subjects with science instruction but that we become more intentional about including science in an interdisciplinary way in all of these important subjects and about ensuring that our science instruction follows best practices for teaching early learners.

More than anything, we need science teachers to begin introducing our students to science education sooner. As parents, we know that the best way to ensure that our kids are not afraid of the water is to familiarize them with water frequently as soon as possible. So we put them in the baby pool and pour cups of water over their heads. We give them baths nightly and sign them up for swimming lessons. The result of these efforts is that instead of our kids having to get over a fear of water, they never acquire that fear. We need to apply this same approach to teaching science. Science teachers who are skilled in early learning instruction can make a tremendous impact on the life of a child by exposing her to science at an early age so that she doesn't automatically think of it as something that is too hard or boring but as a fun and interesting activity. When a kindergarten student asks, "Why are we testing to see how long it takes to turn cream into butter?" we want another child in the class to reply, "We want to learn where butter comes from, and because it's *fun!*"

BOOK OVERVIEW

Thomas O'Brien, PhD
Professor of Science Education
Binghamton University (SUNY), Graduate School of Education

As elementary school teachers, you have one of the most important, challenging, and rewarding missions of any professional; namely, to help parents and society launch our children into a future that both requires and provides opportunities for lifelong learning. As human cultures have evolved and become both increasingly interdependent and ever more dependent on science, technology, engineering, and mathematics (STEM), the need for and nature of formal education also has evolved. In earlier eras, indoctrinating youth in the traditional beliefs of their elders and informing youth of societal norms, expectations, and predetermined roles were sufficient. The printing press and the subsequent accelerating pace of STEM discoveries and inventions created the need for more formal instruction, especially in the 3 Rs (i.e., reading, writing, and arithmetic). For centuries, theories of learning and models of teaching typically viewed learners as relatively passive, impressionable clay that teachers shaped or as empty vessels to be filled. Thus was wisdom transferred or passed down through the ages. Today, however, a knowledge-based, global economy demands a future-focused, interactive education that reconceives the teacher as a catalyst for learner-active, minds-on construction of understanding. Rather than merely asking learners to reproduce past answers and solutions, the 21st-century educator must inspire learners to inquire and innovate.

Following the earlier release of the *Common Core State Standards* in mathematics and English language arts (which includes literacy in history, social studies, science, and technical subjects) and building on the more recent *A Framework for K–12 Science Education*, the *Next Generation Science Standards* (*NGSS*) invite teachers to be key contributors to an educational revolution. This revolution arises from ongoing and compelling research on how children and adults learn (i.e., a science of learning; see Chapters 8 and 9). The old models of teaching as simply telling and learning as passive sit-and-get listening will not meet the needs of tomorrow's citizens.

For most teacher-readers of this book, science is one of several disciplines that you are expected to teach; for some, it may be your primary area of expertise. Whatever the range of your discipline-based teaching assignment, this book is a resource to help you interpret and implement the vision of the *Framework* and the *NGSS* into your curriculum-instruction-assessment. As teachers, you are like other learners in that your prior knowledge bases and next-step learning needs probably vary. The following overview will help you determine how to approach this book. You can read straight through from the beginning to end. Or you can select the sections that are most immediately relevant to you and navigate the book in a manner analogous to progressive pathways and alternative links in internet-based searches. While some sections are more theoretical and others more pragmatic, keep in mind that "there is nothing so practical as a good theory."

The Foreword (Early Science Education: Answering the Question "Why?"), by U.S. Secretary of Education Arne Duncan, provides a national perspective on the critical role of science in the K–5 curriculum. Elementary teachers are challenged to use interdisciplinary, inquiry-oriented science lessons to build upon and extend children's innate curiosity and set the stage for their lifelong interest in and engagement with the world. The foundation for an informed, scientifically literate citizenry, as well as future scientists and engineers, is laid in the elementary grades by you, the teacher-readers of this book.

Section I, Science: A Human Adventure, is introduced by Nobel Prize–winning physicist and former U.S. Secretary of Energy Steven Chu, who reiterates the theme that preschool children are natural scientists. Dr. Chu also argues that nurturing this innate exploratory orientation in elementary school is essential for economic, energy-related, and environmental reasons. Chapter 1, What Is Science?, expands on this theme of science as an extension of our natural desire to explore our diverse world and discover unifying connections, construct explanatory theories, and invent products and processes that apply what we have learned to solve practical problems. It offers several concrete examples

A knowledge-based, global economy demands a future-focused, interactive education.

of how disciplinary core ideas (e.g., gravity/PS2: Motion and stability: Forces and interactions and PS3: Energy) cut across falsely conceived separate disciplines to reveal the interconnected nature of the universe. The authors suggest that elementary school science should employ an integrated, interdisciplinary approach in which skills of reading and listening, writing and speaking, and visual and mathematical ways of learning and communicating reinforce one another. A brief synopsis of the international, cross-generational contributions to our understanding of our solar system (ESS1: Earth's place in the universe) suggests that the ever-evolving story of science is also a key component of our shared history as humans. Science truly is a human adventure!

Section II, A Framework for K–12 Science Education, opens with an introduction, Science and the Educated Person, by cognitive psychologist Steven Pinker, who argues that science is one of the greatest human accomplishments and an essential component of any educated person's knowledge base. The two chapters that follow help readers see how leadership from the states is ensuring that science is given an appropriate emphasis in school curriculum. Specifically, Chapter 2, High Expectations for All: From the Common Core State Standards to the Next Generation Science Standards, offers a historical overview of the shared vision, political debates, and practical challenges that gave birth to state-led, common standards in English language arts (ELA), mathematics, and science. Chapter 3, From Framework to Next Generation Science

Standards, written by a language arts coordinator, offers a teacher-friendly synopsis of the 383-page document that provides the framework for the *NGSS*. Simple graphics and tables taken from the *NGSS* help teacher-readers see the big picture of how integrating the 8 scientific and engineering principles, 7 crosscutting concepts, and 13 disciplinary core ideas is truly "elementary."

Section III, Using the *Framework* and *NGSS* to Redesign Science Lessons, opens with an introduction, Science at the Center, by a former president of the National Academy of Sciences and current Editor-in-Chief of *Science* (an American Association for the Advancement of Science journal) Bruce Alberts. Dr. Alberts argues for re-envisioning school science as a sense-making activity, rather than an exercise in mindless memorization for fill-in-the-blank worksheets and multiple-choice exams. Elementary science should teach children how to think critically and creatively, make wise decisions, and especially to learn how to learn. Chapter 4, 5E(z) Guidelines for Designing Research-Informed Science Lesson Sequences, develops an extended analogy between the curriculum-instruction-assessment (CIA) work of teachers and the scientific and engineering practices and skills we wish to develop in our students. The BSCS 5E Instructional Model, or Teaching Cycle, of Engage, Explore, Explain, Elaborate, and Evaluate is used both as an organizing frame for the chapter and as an intelligent model for teachers to use when designing CIA units. This chapter serves as a conceptual foundation for the 5E mini-units presented in Chapters 5–7 and for 5E units to be developed later by the teacher-readers.

Section IV, The *Next Generation Science Standards* in the Classroom, opens with an introduction, Connections, by an elementary school principal who shares her enthusiasm for how integrating STEM disciplines and making connections with social studies and literacy is enriching for both students and their teachers. Chapters 5–7, Sample 5E Mini-Units for Grades K–5, presents examples of multi-day mini-units that follow the research-informed teaching cycle of Engage, Explore, Explain, Elaborate, and Evaluate. Teacher-readers can use these samples as models to help them revise their current science units to better emphasize an intentional, inquiry-oriented, constructivist sequence of lessons. Two to three samples (each) are provided for the physical, life, and Earth and space sciences. Short subsection introductions by Nobel Prize–winning brain scientist Eric Kandel and president of a state science teachers association Brian Vorwald divide the second and third subsections and present science-for-citizens arguments for making science a central curricular component of elementary education.

Section V, The New Science of Learning, opens with a brief introduction, Illuminating Minds, that focuses on a child's curiosity and drive to understand as the natural foundation for lasting lifelong learning. Chapter 8, How We Model the Complexities of the World: Learning and Memory, Systems and Function, summarizes the convergence of research from psychology, neuroscience, and other cognitive sciences that overturns earlier, but still prevalent, passive storage and retrieval models of learning and memory. An alternative view that emphasizes concepts such as adaptive malleability, cortical plasticity, and goal-driven meaning-making is presented in conjunction with related, practical pedagogical principles. The unexamined and often erroneous misconstrued metaphors that we have for learning are strong determinants of how we teach. This chapter challenges readers to embrace a research-informed perspective on the nature of learning and teaching that will likely resonate with and reinforce elementary teachers' learner-centered orientation to teaching.

Section VI, The New Science of Learning in the Classroom, opens with an introduction, Science Is Fun, that focuses on the natural joy that we experience when we encounter and explore diverse and sometimes initially discrepant, science phenomena. Learning and teaching science should be considered "FUNdaMENTAL" in that science unites curious questioning minds with the endless wonders of our world. Chapter 9, What Teachers Do to Engage Their Students in Learning, combines classic pedagogical wisdom and current best practices and research on learning to offer broad but pragmatic principles to aid elementary science teachers in aligning their efforts with the *Framework* and *Next Generation Science Standards*.

Section VII, Literacy and Science, opens with an introduction, The Importance of Science in Elementary School, that argues that science is a natural, social extension of the exploratory, hands-on, discovery-oriented world of preschool children and that, as such, builds on and contributes to their overall literacy and learning capabilities. Chapter 10, Science? Literacy? Synergy!, presents a research-informed argument for an inclusive definition of scientific literacy that synergistically integrates reading, writing, and reasoning from texts with inquiry-focused, experience-based science instruction. The elementary grades are an ideal setting to simultaneously develop both general and science-specific literacy skills and knowledge. Readers are directed to field-tested commercial products and given practical examples of how to accomplish the curricular literacy integration that is called for in the *Common Core State Standards* in both English language arts and mathematics.

The concluding chapter, Moving Forward: Science is Elementary!, is written by Alan McCormack, past National Science Teachers Association (NSTA) president and elementary science teaching specialist. Dr. McCormack invites teacher-readers to become active contributors to a Let's Move Forward! initiative that offers the next generation of citizens, our current elementary students, the very best research-informed, standards-based, child- and science-friendly curriculum-instruction-assessment (CIA).

Collectively, the editors and authors invite our readers to use this book (in whatever order you deem most appropriate to your needs and interests) as a resource to become teacher-leaders in the school science reform movement that is being catalyzed by the *Next Generation Science Standards*. In addition, the websites listed by the various authors, plus additional online resources, will be posted on the NSTA website (*www.nsta.org/ScienceForTheNextGen*) where they can be accessed as live links and periodically updated. Working collaboratively with fellow teachers, school administrators, teacher educators, NSTA, state teachers associations, and concerned parents, we can ensure that our children experience a science education that truly prepares them to fully appreciate our world and seek to contribute to a brighter future for their descendants.

I

SCIENCE

A HUMAN ADVENTURE

INTRODUCTION

Teaching Science in Elementary School

TURNING TODAY'S CHILDREN INTO TOMORROW'S LEADERS

Steven Chu, PhD
Former U.S. Secretary of Energy
Nobel Prize in Physics 1997

When we were very young, we were all scientists. We had to make sense of the world through the barrage of what we saw, heard, touched, smelled, and tasted. Each day was filled with a constant stream of experiments. By picking up a baby rattle and dropping it, we saw first-hand the effect of gravity. With additional experiments, we discovered that not all food bounces like a rattle; some of it splatters when it hits the floor. Sometimes, seemingly simple questions lead to great discoveries. Einstein asked himself as a school boy, "If I am holding a mirror in front of me and run at the speed of light, will I still see myself?" The answer to that riddle is a founding postulate of the theory of relativity.

At its core, science is about trying to make sense of the natural world. By teaching science in elementary school, you continue to nurture every child's sense of wonder. Without this early engagement, a youngster's innate scientific curiosity can easily be snuffed out. Equally important, you are teaching our students how to think clearly and critically. Science is a method of gaining understanding independent of the changing whims of fashion. Through a combination of conjecture and observations, you teach our students how to cast explanations into falsifiable theories that can be tested by experiments. They learn that knowledge gained in this way becomes a cumulative wisdom in which the ultimate arbitrator is experiment.

Today, more than ever, we need our citizens to appreciate and understand scientific data and arguments, and that scientific questions are not settled by political debate. Newton's laws cannot be repealed by a majority vote. We also need a new generation of students that will form the corps of future scientists and engineers needed to sustain and strengthen our economic competitiveness. We face unprecedented energy and climate challenges that will require new and bold technical solutions. Indeed, many of the great challenges we will face in this century will require science and innovation to meet them.

CHAPTER 1

What Is Science?

Marshall L. Grant, PhD
Senior Director, Formulation Development, MannKind Corporation

William Banko, MD
President, Knowing Science LLC and Surgical Design Corporation

Dario Capasso, PhD
Department of Physics, City College, City University of New York

Questions about the content and nature of science are essential to framing research-informed elementary science curriculum, instruction, and assessment. Simply put, science is a framework to continually refine, extend, and organize our understanding of our internal and external environments. Common professional practices such as observing events or phenomena, forming and testing hypotheses, and making and testing predictions and tentative explanations underlie all branches of science and engineering. *A Framework for K–12 Science Education* (NRC 2012) and the *Next Generation Science Standards* (*NGSS*) propose that science be presented as an integrated whole rather than as a set of separate topics with disconnected inquiry skills, ideas, and isolated facts. Additionally, these documents argue that students must learn the language of science as a tool to both comprehend and communicate what they learn about science through investigations, oral discussion, prose, and visual and mathematical representations. As such, the content and practices of the *Common Core State Standards, English Language Arts* (*CCSS ELA*) (i.e., reading, writing, speaking, and listening related to both informational texts and investigations with hands-on materials; see Chapter 10) and the *CCSS Mathematics* are intrinsically linked with learning science and meeting the *NGSS*. Moreover, the multidiscipline teaching assignments at the K–5 grade levels makes it possible (even necessary) to teach children in a more integrated, interdisciplinary way that builds on their natural, holistic orientation to learning.

Consider how from infancy, children continually observe and actively explore their environments with all their senses and process the information to make sense of the world. Recent research shows that infants as young as eight months already have expectations of how the world behaves. For example, an infant is shown a basket containing red and white balls and then an adult places the basket so the infant can no longer see its contents. If the adult proceeds to remove only red balls, the infant is perplexed; removing both colors does not elicit the same response in the infant. This suggests the infant's brain does a statistical calculation of expectations (Gopnik 2012), and the baby recognizes that what she is seeing is a bit out of the ordinary (i.e., a discrepant event; see Chapter 4 and O'Brien 2010). Elementary science education should take advantage of this natural, inborn pattern recognition ability to help children further develop their intuitive feel for science.

Not surprisingly, patterns is listed as the first of seven crosscutting concepts in the *Framework* and *NGSS*, which form the foundation for learning science. (See Figure 3.1, p. 40, for a list of the eight scientific and engineering practices, *NGSS* dimension 1, and the seven crosscutting concepts,

NGSS dimension 2, that are discussed in this chapter.) The following discussion will use several examples of scientific practices and concepts to explore the intersection between the nature of science and its pedagogical implications for the elementary grades. Alternatively, if you are anxious to see how the *NGSS* look in action in more fully developed lessons or unit plans, skip ahead to Chapters 5–7 and preview one of the sample 5E mini-units for the grade level you teach, and then return to this chapter and the next three.

Connections—Sorting, Classifying, Grouping—Simple to Complex

Neuroscience tells us that learning is all about connections, both recognizing them in the external world and constructing them within the human brain (see Chapter 8). Science should be presented in an experiential way that actively employs as many senses as possible (i.e., truly "minds-on," more than simply hands-on). Sorting and classification (taxonomy) can be taught at the lower elementary grades using a collection of objects for examination and manipulation. Students or groups of students can sort the objects according to various criteria (e.g., heavy or light, color, size, and so on) to engage the tactile and visual senses. Introduce a new object and ask students to classify it and explain their reasoning to engage the verbal and aural senses. Since social interaction is a required aspect of learning, have students discuss in groups and present to the class various ways to classify the objects.

Science provides a framework to organize data and relationships among the data into patterns. The various ways to organize the objects represent different patterns and the patterns could even be the result of a theoretical calculation or an extrapolation of a series of measurements. The "best" choice of pattern depends on the question being asked. Patterns represent the normal or expected behavior, and deviations are a signal that further study is required. Sorting and classification are also important in their own right and have application in engineering and technology. Google, for example, invests heavily in research to sort, classify, and retrieve files in increasingly sophisticated yet time-efficient ways.

Crosscutting Concepts (*NGSS* Dimension 2): The Foundation for Bridging the Sciences

Classifying objects and ideas into ever finer divisions can lead to a silo effect—biology by itself, chemistry by itself, geology by itself, physics by itself, and so on—in which different concepts and rules seem to apply to each discipline. A major theme of the *NGSS* is that the various disciplines of science are all subject to the same universal physical principles and laws, even if they are manifest in different guises. Consider, for example, gravity or the mutual attraction for a bit of mass with every other bit of mass in the universe. Gravity plays a fundamental role in physics, astronomy, chemistry, Earth science, and life science. How? To answer that question, let's take a quick walk through the immense scales of time, space, system complexity, and stability and change within our universe! (That is, *NGSS* dimension 2, crosscutting concepts 3, 4, and 7.)

Gravity (PS2: Motion and stability: Forces and interactions) is responsible for forming stars from hydrogen and helium (the most abundant and second-most abundant elements in the universe). The hydrogen is fused to form helium nuclei in the stars' cores, and the pressure from the hot plasma balances the tendency of gravity to collapse the star. As the hydrogen is depleted, the star contracts to fuse helium to form carbon.

Carbon, the basis for life on Earth, is a form of stardust. We are literally made from stardust. Massive stars (much larger than the Sun) are compressed under their own gravity to the point where carbon can fuse to form the nuclei of elements up to iron. Fusion of iron accelerates the collapse of stars, leading to supernovas that form heavier elements, which disperse into space as they explode. Gravitational coalescence repeats to form the next generation of stars and their associated planets rich in these heavy elements. Elements, the building blocks of chemistry and of all life (i.e., biology), are therefore a consequence of gravity.

Gravity formed Earth and is at the heart of Earth science. The iron that makes up Earth's core was produced in stars. The inner core is presumably solid iron, while the outer core is predominantly molten iron that is still being heated by radioactive elements generated in the original supernovas. Gravity acts on density differences due to variations in temperature and composition to force molten iron to flow outward from the core (toward the surface) in some regions and flow inward toward the core in others (a form of natural convection similar to what happens in a pan of water warmed on the stove; hot water would not rise if there were no gravity). This motion generates the magnetic field that helps protect Earth from the solar wind and drives the motion of continental plates (plate tectonics).

Earth is the only place in the universe where we know life exists. How does gravity affect life? Beyond providing the elements as the building blocks that make up all organisms and their environments, gravitational attraction between Earth and the Sun keeps us in a stable orbit at a distance that provides a temperature range consistent with liquid water. (Scientists believe that liquid water is essential for life in general, but are certain that

it is essential for *all* life on Earth.) Additionally, Earth's gravity is strong enough to retain relatively light gases, such as nitrogen and oxygen, and maintain an atmosphere thick enough to screen the surface from a lot of solar radiation and most incoming meteors. In contrast, Mars is much colder, and there is little evidence of liquid water. Its weaker gravity retains a thin atmosphere that is primarily composed of carbon dioxide. It is gravity that keeps organisms tethered to Earth's biosphere rather than drifting off into inhospitable outer space.

Finally, gravity provided the motivation for early technology. People have been fighting gravity for a long time. The simple machines—inclined plane, lever, wedge, pulley, screw, and wheel and axle—were all applied to overcome gravity and lift objects. The Romans used the simple machines to build aqueducts to carry water from reservoirs in the mountains or hills to the cities. Once built, the water would flow by gravity without further effort.

One way to unify the various disciplines of science, then, is to see how the same phenomenon (e.g., gravity) affects each discipline. A similar connection can be made between electricity and physics, chemistry, biology, and Earth science. Alternatively, the *Framework* and *NGSS* step back to even larger, more encompassing, crosscutting concepts such as Energy and matter: Flows, cycles, and conservation (crosscutting concept 5). For instance, consider how energy flow and its conversion and conservation enter into and connect the different science disciplines. Specific examples include the conversion of mass to energy through nuclear fusion (occurring in the Sun, thanks to gravity); the radiation from the Sun that warms and lights the Earth; photosynthesis in plants converting the radiation to chemical energy; and consumption of the plants and subsequent metabolism that ultimately converts food energy into heat.

Energy (PS3) is the ability to do work, and much of human technology was developed to convert chemical energy into mechanical energy. The steam engine, invented by James Watt in 1775, was the first practical system to use the chemical energy of fossil fuels (coal) to perform a mechanical task, such as pumping water from flooded coal mines. The steam engine revolutionized manufacturing and as it became possible to build portable steam engines, also changed transportation forever. Steamships replaced sailing vessels and together with steam locomotives, significantly increased trade, communication, and travel between far-flung parts of the world.

The equivalence of heat and work was demonstrated by James Prescott Joule (1818–1889) who showed that mechanically stirring water could increase its temperature. This led to the development of the first law of thermodynamics: the conservation of energy. Once the equivalence was established, it became clear that while mechanical work could be converted completely into heat, heat could not be completely converted into work. This is a consequence of the second law of thermodynamics and is what makes perpetual motion machines impossible. Of course, the second law applies to everything and can seem mind-boggling on occasion, but it comes into play every day and at least one aspect of it (irreversibility) can be easily understood by elementary students.

The second law is associated with entropy, a measure of irreversibility and disorder in the universe. Physicists call entropy "time's arrow" because it can only increase or stay the same, never decrease. Given two pictures, before and after an event, if you can tell which one came first, the event is irreversible without the addition of energy. Back in the day when teachers showed movies in class, the students would always ask to see the movie run backward. The class would laugh as balls rolled uphill, water cascaded up the waterfall, or the flame would go out to reveal the unused match. Why was this so funny? Because these events do not happen in real life; each one violates the second law of thermodynamics.

There are some commonplace examples of the one-way nature of time and the concept of irreversibility that can be demonstrated in class and provide some sense of normal behavior. Heat flows from warmer regions to colder regions, and two objects of different temperatures in contact with each other will cool or warm by transferring heat to each other until they reach a final temperature. If two objects in contact are initially at the same temperature, one does not spontaneously become warmer and the other cooler. Mixing is another irreversible process that can be demonstrated in class. Once you stir the milk into the coffee (or food coloring into water), it does not spontaneously separate. And, for good measure, broken eggs do not spontaneously become whole again. If your elementary students understand that these are all one-way processes, then they are on their way to developing an intuitive understanding of the world (and doing thermodynamics), long before the processes are formally introduced at the high school level.

Sensory Input—Seeing, Feeling, and Measuring for Yourself

How can we expand elementary students' sensory awareness and intuition to include more scientifically valid concepts? Largely by providing a means for students to experience science through phenomena where they can test ideas. For example, suppose that someone suggested that the food coloring would separate if you waited long enough. The student could mix the food coloring into the water and place it in a sealed container (to prevent spillage and evaporation) and make observations over the next several days. With each passing day, the spontaneous separation of the food coloring from the water would seem less likely until the student decides it may never happen. Did the experiment prove the mixture would never separate? Strictly speaking, no, but it did confirm it was highly unlikely and may have satisfied the student's curiosity. Actually, from experimental evidence alone, it is extremely difficult to prove that something never happens without research-informed theoretical arguments (scientific and engineering practices 6–7). The point is that with relatively little effort, students can conduct experiments to provide viable, tentative answers to their own questions.

Children continually process their environment through their senses and social interactions, so it makes sense to present science along the same lines. Returning to the theme of sorting and classifying, we can begin in the early grades with binary comparison of objects in which the students determine which of two objects is larger or smaller, heavier or lighter simply by holding each object. Students can present their results to others who can confirm them, thereby building consensus and providing social reinforcement and encouragement. As the objects become more and more similar, it is more difficult to determine which one is larger or heavier. For that, we need measurement. The choice of measuring unit (pencils, paper clips, inches, grams) is completely arbitrary, but it is important that everyone agree to use the same unit because results obtained by different people can then be compared directly without having to repeat the measurement. (In practice, it is possible to use different sets of units if the conversions between them are known.

Still, NASA lost the Mars Climate Orbiter in 1999 because of confusion between English and metric units.) Once the unit is agreed, the students can measure objects in parallel, and the group as a whole can rank them. An exercise like this not only provides experience in integrating individual results but also demonstrates how productivity can be increased by standardization and provides social interaction as the group reaches consensus.

Communication: *CCSS ELA* and *NGSS* Synergy

One benefit of using measurement is the ability to share results. It is impossible to reach a consensus of what is true without a body of results that have been presented and independently confirmed. Scientific results in isolation do not tell us much; the communication, dissemination, and verification of scientific results (scientific and engineering practice 8) tell all. The presentation of results is just as important as the experiment itself, even if people do not find that part fun. Elementary students can present their results in four forms depending on their level: (1) a live demonstration for the group or class followed by replication by another student; (2) a video demonstration followed by replication by another student; (3) a presentation involving pictures on a blackboard, art easel, or interactive whiteboard; or (4) an audio recording or written summary in which the student describes the experiment so that another student can reproduce it. We have emphasized replication by others because results must be reproducible to be considered scientifically valid.

Scientific groups communicate through presentations and publications. The ability to read and listen with comprehension and write and speak with clarity is essential for science. (Even some professionals are not so good at this.) Each discipline tends to use its own vocabulary in which words or terms have specific meanings that can be different from their meanings in the outside world or even in another scientific discipline. Grade-appropriate fiction, nonfiction, and informational texts related to scientific topics are available even for kindergartners. Reading selections to the class complements science lessons and shows students that science is about everyday objects and phenomena, not something that is experienced only in school or a science lab. Older students can read the books on their own and write book reports or complete exercises to reinforce the concepts. Scientific vocabulary can be included in regular spelling lists. (See Chapter 10 for links to a number of research-informed, integrated science and ELA curriculum projects.)

To converse fluently in science, one must also read and interpret a wide variety of visual information such as schematic drawings, images from microscopy, bar graphs, scatter plots, and even surface plots. Combinations of drawings and text or captions are routinely used to present experimental apparatuses or illustrate important physical features. A useful drawing finds the right balance between detail and generality. Digital images from a microscope camera can be helpful, especially for highlighting biological or structural features of interest. Graphs, however, are at the heart of understanding and presenting scientific data and lead us to another kind of connection in the real world that should be reflected in school curriculum.

A Word About Math and the CCSS Mathematics

The *Framework* and *NGSS* documents call for the inclusion of engineering, technology, and applications of science that align with the growing popularity of STEM education in which mathematics helps serve as the bridging discipline. The mathe-

matics component of STEM is really applied mathematics, by which we mean that the numbers are associated with quantities and units (feet, meters, grams, and so on) or entities (cows, cars, blocks, and so on). What's more, there is directionality in many science problems so negative numbers are encountered often. The answer to the question, "How far did the block slide?" can never be "four" but could be "4 cm" or even "−4 cm."

Geometry may be the most useful branch of mathematics in elementary school. With geometry, you can represent shapes, location, distance, and direction either at full scale or in a scale drawing. As one of the older branches of mathematics, geometry has a long history of applications to Earth and space sciences, from Eratosthenes' calculation of the circumference of the Earth (even then, in 240 BCE they knew the Earth was round) to Johannes Kepler's determination (in 1609) that the planets are in elliptical orbits around the Sun, through the distortion by gravity of Euclidean space into Einstein's space-time continuum (in 1916).

Mathematics is a concise, precise means to express the behavior of both natural and manufactured systems. One thing to point out is that sometimes certain physical behavior may be presented as a law of science when, in fact, it is an approximation—perhaps an incredibly good one—that can be solved readily with standard techniques. Even when the equations describing the science are exact, some terms may remain unknown, and significant approximations must often be made so that they can be solved for real-world applications. Table 1.1 depicts the eight core mathematical practices of the *Common Core State Standards, Mathematics* with emphasis added to show their correlation with science. Integrating science and mathematics (as well as ELA) is facilitated at the K–5 grades since most commonly the same classroom teachers teach all subjects.

TABLE 1.1
STANDARDS FOR MATHEMATICAL PRACTICE

1. *Make sense of problems* and persevere in solving them.

2. *Reason* abstractly and quantitatively.

3. Construct *viable arguments and critique* the reasoning of others.

4. *Model* with mathematics … apply … to *solve problems arising in everyday life, society, and the workplace*.

5. *Use appropriate tools strategically* … pencil and paper, concrete models, a ruler, a protractor, a calculator, a spreadsheet …

6. Attend to precision … careful about *specifying units of measure* and labeling axes to clarify the correspondence with quantities in a problem.

7. Look for and make use of structure.

8. Look for and *express regularity* in repeated reasoning.

Source: Common Core State Standards, Mathematics, *www.corestandards.org/Math*

Mathematics was absolutely critical in the following final example of the nature of science and its importance in elementary (K–5) schools.

Earth's Place in the Universe (ESS1): A Historical Case Study of the Scientific Process and Models

Our theory of the solar system serves as a classic example of how scientific understanding unfolds across human history through the development, refinement, and periodic dethroning of once dominant models (i.e., developing and using models is the *NGSS* scientific and engineering practice 2). Stonehenge and other early observatories attest to a longstanding interest in the seasons and the stars (often driven by practical agricultural and navigational needs). Sumerians documented their observations. The Babylonian astronomers incorporated those data with their own, recognized the periodicity of many astronomical phenomena, and applied mathematics to predict the daylight hours, rising and setting of stars, and lunar eclipses. The Greeks constructed an "Earth-centered" model of the cosmos with ideal geometric forms: The spherical Earth was stationary while the planets in the heavenly sphere moved along circles. This model was refined into the Ptolemaic system by moving the center of the planets' orbits away from Earth and adding small circular loops (or epicycles) to planetary orbits (approximately 147 BCE). Then, in a span of approximately 150 years, Copernicus revolutionized the field with the heliocentric model (in 1543), Kepler determined the planetary orbits were actually ellipses rather than circles (in 1609), and Newton demonstrated the elliptical orbits were a consequence of an inverse-square gravitational attraction between planet and Sun (in 1687). Two hundred years later, Einstein's general theory of relativity resolved the final discrepancies (in 1916).

While this rendition of the story is true in general, the transition from one theory to the next was not smooth, and there are some interesting side notes. For example, in the third century BCE, Aristarchus of Samos proposed a heliocentric model that displaced the Earth from the center of the cosmos and explained astronomical phenomena just as well as the Ptolemaic system. Today, we say, "Yes, of course the Sun is the center of the solar system," but the heliocentric model was not embraced by the majority of the Greek (or later) scholars. Why not? First, there was a cultural bias against the idea—why should the Earth not be the center of the universe? Second, the heliocentric model was not initially obviously superior to the Ptolemaic model because the accuracy of the observations at that time was insufficient to distinguish between the two.

In *De Revolutionibus Orbium Coelestium* ("On the Revolutions of the Celestial Orbs"), Copernicus argued for a heliocentric system (with circles and epicycles) and provided new mathematical constructs for astronomical calculations. One of the consequences of the new model was that the solar system was much larger than had been previously assumed and the distances to the fixed stars were beyond imagination. The heliocentric aspect of the theory was mostly ignored or denied outright because, again, it seemed to conflict with everyday experience and common sense of the time. That did not stop astronomers from adapting the mathematical treatments for use in geocentric models to make more accurate calculations. Tycho Brahe made measurements (approximately 1570s) that were much more frequent and accurate than those of his predecessors and documented numerous discrepancies between data and the predictions of the Earth-centered model. Nevertheless, Brahe opposed the heliocentric model on philosophical grounds. He crafted a hybrid model in which Earth was at the center, the Sun orbited Earth, and the planets orbited the Sun. Finally, by careful analysis of Brahe's data, Kepler was able to explain the orbits of the planets as ellipses (not circles) with the Sun at one focus and without recourse to epicycles. Kepler was a supporter of the Copernican system, so that may be why he was able to focus on the eccentricity of planetary orbits.

The story of astronomy reflects all eight of the *Framework* and *NGSS*'s dimension 1: scientific and engineering practices: (1) asking questions (for science) and defining problems (for engineering);

(2) developing and using models; (3) planning and carrying out investigations; (4) analyzing and interpreting data; (5) using mathematics and computational thinking; (6) constructing explanations (for science) and designing solutions (for engineering); (7) engaging in argument from evidence; and (8) obtaining, evaluating, and communicating information. The brief synopsis of this particular historical case study makes the process of science appear linear, with progress coming in small incremental steps as the models are refined. This is often not the case. At any given time, there may be competing incompatible hypotheses and models that seem to explain the same phenomena. All the refinements to the cycles and epicycles, for example, improved the predictions but were ultimately a dead end because the Copernican/Newtonian model of the solar system eventually displaced the once-dominant Ptolemaic system.

In the End, It Comes Down to Elementary Teachers

The *Next Generation Science Standards* call for students to think, apply universal principles, and draw on concepts across disciplines to solve problems and innovate. To that, we add the communication of scientific ideas and results in as many ways as possible and in as many real-world contexts as possible so that children do not think science is abstract and distinct from everyday life.

Even the best standards, curricula, and assessments will not succeed without high-quality instruction by teachers who are caring, capable, engaged, and enthusiastic. A single teacher can make a big difference. Children have come home excited about science when the teacher is connected, but uninterested when the teacher is indifferent. It is not easy being an elementary school teacher, and change is not easy either. New curricula, instruction, and assessment demand extra effort on the part of teacher-as-learners and leaders. The subsequent chapters of this book focus on the developmental history of the *Framework* and *NGSS* (Chapters 2 and 3), the 5E teaching cycle and mini-units (Chapters 4–7), research synopses on children's learning and literacy (Chapters 8 and 10), and the importance of engaging children in their own learning (Chapter 9). Collectively, these chapters serve as references as teachers design or adapt lessons to meet the promise of the *Next Generation Science Standards* for all students.

References

Achieve Inc. 2013. *Next generation science standards*. *www.nextgenscience.org*.

Gopnik, A. 2012. Scientific thinking in young children: Theoretical advances, empirical research, and policy implications. *Science* 337: 1623–1627.

National Governors Association Center for Best Practices (NGAC) and the Council of Chief State School Officers (CCSSO). Common Core State Standards Initiative. 2010. *Common core state standards for mathematics. www.corestandards. org/Math*.

National Research Council (NRC). 2012. *A framework for K–12 science education: Practices, crosscutting concepts, and core ideas*. Washington, DC: National Academies Press.

O'Brien, T. 2010. *Brain-powered science: Teaching and learning with discrepant events*. Arlington, VA: NSTA Press.

II

A FRAMEWORK FOR K–12 SCIENCE EDUCATION

INTRODUCTION

Science and the Educated Person

Steven Pinker, PhD

Professor of Psychology, Harvard University

Author, *The Language Instinct* and *How the Mind Works*

An education in science does more than prepare students for technologically sophisticated jobs. It also shapes them as human beings and with them, our culture and civilization.

For one thing, it is an astonishing fact about our species that we have come to understand as much as we do about how the world works. We can say much about the history of the universe and our planet, the forces that make it tick, the stuff we're made of, the origin of living things, and the machinery of life, including our own mental life. All this is a magnificent accomplishment, and we have a responsibility to nurture and perpetuate it for the same reason that we have a responsibility to perpetuate an appreciation of great accomplishments in the arts. A failure to do so would be a display of disrespect for our ancestors and heirs, and a philistine indifference to the magnificent achievements that the human mind is capable of.

Also, the picture of humanity's place in nature that has emerged from scientific inquiry has profound consequences for our understanding of the human condition. The discoveries of science have cascading effects, many unforeseeable, on how we view ourselves and the world in which we live: For example, that our planet is an undistinguished speck in an inconceivably vast cosmos; that all the hope and ingenuity in the world can't create energy or use it without loss; that our species has existed for a tiny fraction of the history of the Earth; that humans are primates; that the mind is the activity of an organ that runs by physiological processes; that there are methods for ascertaining the truth that can force us to conclusions that violate common sense, sometimes radically so, at scales very large and very small; that precious and widely held beliefs, when subjected to empirical tests, are often cruelly falsified. A person for whom this understanding is not second nature cannot be said to be educated.

CHAPTER 2

High Expectations for All

FROM THE COMMON CORE STATE STANDARDS TO THE NEXT GENERATION SCIENCE STANDARDS[1]

Robert Rothman
Alliance for Excellent Education

The *Next Generation Science Standards* (*NGSS*), released in the spring of 2013, represent a significant milestone in American education history. Unlike in the past, when each state developed its own standards, with widely varying levels of rigor and quality, the *NGSS* were internationally benchmarked to reflect the expectations of the highest-performing nations and are intended to be adopted by many states.

The science standards follow closely on the heels of the *Common Core State Standards* (*CCSS*) in English language arts (ELA) and mathematics, which have been adopted by 45 states, the District of Columbia, and the Department of Defense Education Activity. Like the science standards, the *CCSS* were intended to be common across states—hence the name—and to be internationally benchmarked. The *CCSS* were also intended to spell out the knowledge and skills all students need to learn in order to be prepared for first-year college and career-training courses.

The wide acceptance of the two sets of standards represents a substantial step for the United States. Nearly two decades ago, attempts to create standards in core subjects prompted fierce political battles and derailed national efforts to define what students should know and be able to do. While these arguments, along with others over states' rights, did not go away, the *CCSS* and the *NGSS*

have been able to attain a degree of consensus that has eluded standards advocates for years.

To be sure, as even the most passionate supporters of the standards will acknowledge, standards themselves do not transform schools. The record of the past two decades, in which states developed and adopted standards only to see schools make modest improvements, is a testament to the challenges ahead.

Yet there is a great deal of optimism about the standards and a belief that they will help produce a transformation in American education. There is a tremendous amount of work under way to develop assessments and curricular materials, and to prepare teachers to teach to the new standards.

How did this happen? How did states agree to set the same high expectations for student learning, just a few short years after the idea of national standards imploded? This chapter will describe the history of the standards movement over the past two decades, examine how a small group of state leaders and reform advocates led a revised effort to create common standards, and look ahead to the challenges states face in putting the new system in place.

The Rise of Standards

The movement to set standards for student performance emerged in the late 1980s. Earlier that decade, the report *A Nation at Risk* warned of a

---

1. Adapted from Rothman (2011).

"rising tide of mediocrity" and led states to ratchet up expectations for students, largely by increasing course requirements in high school. Although there was some concern that increasing expectations could harm students who were unable to meet them, a growing number of educators began to express the belief that high standards could apply to every student. Invoking the mantra "all children can learn," educators developed standards that they expected all students to meet. This represented a profound change in American education. In contrast to traditional practice, in which some students learned at high levels while most learned basic skills, the new standards were aimed at making sure that all students, regardless of their backgrounds or life aspirations, would have the same educational opportunities.

Although a few states had begun to set standards that defined what students should know and be able to do, the standards movement took hold at the national level. In 1986 the National Council of Teachers of Mathematics (NCTM), the professional association of mathematics teachers based in Reston, Virginia, just outside Washington, D.C., named a 26-member panel to craft "a coherent vision of what it means to be mathematically literate in a world that relies on calculators and computers to carry out mathematical procedures, and in a world where mathematics is rapidly growing and is extensively being applied in diverse fields" (NCTM 1989, p. 1).

The mathematics council's report, *Curriculum and Assessment Standards for School Mathematics*, was released in March 1989. The document was noteworthy for two reasons. First, it was intended to represent a consensus view of what should be taught in school mathematics to every student in every school in the United States. In other words, the standards specified the knowledge and skills students should know and be able to do, as well

as measures for schools to evaluate their own programs.

The NCTM standards were also significant because in many ways they represented a sharp departure from conventional mathematics programs in use at the time. They placed a greater emphasis on the ability of students to solve problems and demonstrate their understanding of mathematics and less emphasis on the ability to plug numbers into calculations and use formulas. They also recommended the use of calculators and computers as aids to problem solving. These recommendations would ultimately prove controversial, throwing the idea of national standards into question.

Nevertheless, the NCTM standards were enormously influential, at least initially, both in schools and with other subject matter organizations representing English, science, and social studies teachers. By one estimate, the NCTM standards were used as a model by 40 states in revising curricula and helped inform the redesign of tests, such as the National Assessment of Educational Progress (NAEP) (Ravitch 1995). The document also helped inspire other subject matter organizations to consider the knowledge and skills that were essential in their disciplines.

Working on a parallel track, the American Association for the Advancement of Science (AAAS) also convened a panel to consider what all students should know in science, mathematics, and technology. The 26-member panel released its report, called *Science for All Americans*, in March 1989, and the association formed an effort, known as Project 2061—named for the date of the predicted return of Halley's Comet—to implement the plan, beginning in six school districts.

Like the NCTM document, *Science for All Americans* aimed to outline the knowledge, skills, and habits of minds all students needed to develop, not just those with academic or career interests in scientific fields. It called for less emphasis on memorization of facts and more on conceptual understanding. It also stressed the connections among scientific disciplines rather than compartmentalizing the traditional subjects of Earth science, life sciences, physical sciences, and so forth. However, the document did not spell out expectations for students at different grade levels, or even grade spans, as the NCTM document did. Rather, it outlined the knowledge and skills all students would be expected to leave high school with. As the document stated, "The reader should not expect to find recommendations in this report on what should be taught in any particular course or at any grade level. The report deals only with learning goals—what students should remember, understand, and be able to do after they have left school as a residue of their total school experience—and not with how to organize the curriculum to achieve them." (Rutherford and Ahlgren 1989, pp. xii–xiii). Phase II of Project 2061, beginning with the pilots in six school districts, was intended to develop a curriculum that would lead to the attainment of the learning goals spelled out in *Science for All Americans*.

To begin that process, AAAS produced a separate document, called *Benchmarks for Science Literacy* (AAAS 1993), which outlined learning goals for students at the end of grades 2, 5, 8, and 12 that would lead toward attainment of the goals outlined in *Science for All Americans*. *Benchmarks* is not a curriculum, but it was aimed at providing guidance to teachers and curriculum specialists in creating a program of study that would enable students to reach the learning goals spelled out in the document.

The idea of national standards—and national tests—developed increasing support from a wide range of quarters. So in June 1991, Congress passed legislation creating a commission to study the "desirability and feasibility" of national standards and assessments before moving forward to developing them.

The commission, known as the National Council on Education Standards and Tests (NCEST), represented what one member, Chester E. Finn Jr., called a typical Washington "Noah's Ark" panel: it included two senators, two House members, two governors, the presidents of the two national teacher unions, superintendents, testing experts, and teachers. The council released its report in January 1992 and issued a ringing endorsement of standards, stating that high standards and assessments tied to them can promote educational equity, preserve democracy, enhance the civic culture, and improve economic competitiveness. The panel stated:

> In the absence of well-defined and demanding standards, education in the United States has gravitated toward *de facto* national minimum expectations. Except for students who are planning to attend selective four-year colleges, current education standards focus on low-level reading and arithmetic skills and on small amounts of factual material in other content areas. Consumers of education in this country have settled for far less than they should and for far less than their counterparts in other developed nations. (NCEST 1992, p. 2–3)

The council also noted that standards alone are insufficient, and that tests influence what is taught. However, the council stopped short of recommending a single national test to measure performance against the standards. Instead, the council proposed a voluntary "system of assessments" that would consist of multiple measures of performance, not a single test. The system would include both individual student assessments and large-scale samples, like the NAEP. The assessments could eventually be used for high-stakes purposes, such as high school graduation or college entry, as well as for system accountability, the report concluded.

To oversee the development and implementation of the standards and assessments, the council proposed the creation of a national entity, called the National Education Standards and Assessment Council, which would work with the National Education Goals Panel to certify the standards and criteria for assessments as "world class." This proposal proved hotly controversial, as we shall see.

National Standards Move Forward

The Bush administration did not wait for NCEST's report to embrace the idea of national standards. The administration issued grants to subject matter organizations and researchers to develop standards in a wide range of content areas, including history, English language arts, science, geography, foreign languages, the arts, and civics. The goal, according to Diane Ravitch, who was assistant U.S. secretary of education at the time and who led the effort, was to "encourage professional fields to shape a consensus about what students should know and be able to do. Eventually, the standards would make their own way into the schools (or not) by virtue of their quality, as the NCTM standards have, and not

because of the coercive power of government to impose them" (Ravitch 1995, p. 29).

The science standards were a good example of the principle Ravitch espoused. The project began in 1991, when the president of the National Science Teachers Association (NSTA) wrote to the president of the National Academy of Sciences to ask the National Research Council (NRC), the operating arm of the academy, to lead the development of standards in science. This idea drew wide support from scientific associations, the federal government, and the National Education Goals Panel. With funding from the U.S. Department of Education and the National Science Foundation (NSF), the NRC took on the project.

To carry it out, the NRC established the National Committee on Science Education Standards and Assessment, which formed an advisory committee that included representatives of major scientific and science education organizations. The NRC committee met for 18 months and solicited advice from more than 150 individuals and organizations before releasing a "predraft" of the standards in 1994 for review by focus groups. The committee then revised the document and released a draft in December 1994, which was distributed to more than 18,000 individuals and 250 groups. Based on their comments, the committee released the final version, entitled *National Science Education Standards* (*NSES*), in 1996 (NRC).

The *NSES* were more comprehensive than many of the content standards documents produced by other subject matter groups. In addition to outlining the content students should be expected to learn, the document also lays out standards for teachers, professional development, assessment, science programs, and systems. These standards, the document states, were undergirded by a set of principles:

- Science is for all students.

- Learning science is an active process.

- School science reflects the intellectual and cultural traditions that characterize the practice of contemporary science.

- Improving science education is part of systemic education reform.

The *NSES* proposed standards for student learning in three grade spans: K–4, 5–8, and 9–12. The document was careful to emphasize that it was not a curriculum and that there were many ways of organizing a curriculum that would enable students to attain the standards. However, the document was also clear that there is certain content all students should learn, including the often-controversial topic of evolution.

Despite Ravitch's belief that the quality of standards, rather than politics, would determine their influence, political debates helped derail national standards for U.S. history, and the vehemence of the debate put the idea of national standards in jeopardy. History is invariably a contentious topic, since it usually sparks debate over different perspectives in a diverse nation on the role of prominent individuals and events. The standards, developed by the National Center for History in the Schools at the University of California, Los Angeles, were no exception. The day before the document was set to be released, Lynne Cheney (the wife of Secretary of Defense and later Vice President Dick Cheney), who as chairman of the National Endowment for the Humanities had sponsored the history standards project, took to the op-ed page of the *Wall Street Journal* to denounce it in scathing terms. In an article entitled "The End of History," Cheney lambasted the proposed standards for placing too little emphasis on historical figures like Robert

E. Lee and the Wright brothers and too much emphasis on individuals like Harriet Tubman and events like McCarthyism. The implication was that the standards were a monument to political correctness, rather than an objective definition of what students should learn about the past.

Cheney's article was somewhat misleading because the references she cited were in teaching examples that accompanied the standards, rather than the standards themselves. And the standards were subsequently revised, earning plaudits from Ravitch and others. Nevertheless, Cheney's criticism hit a nerve, and the U.S. Senate voted 99 to 1 to denounce them. Although the vote was nonbinding and thus did not carry the force of law, the Senate action took much of the wind out of the standards' sails.

Congressional opposition also scuttled an agency intended to oversee the development and implementation of standards. In its report, NCEST had recommended the creation of such an agency to certify standards. Although this certification process would have no force of law, it would represent a kind of "good Housekeeping seal of approval." In 1994, the Goals 2000: Educate America Act authorized the creation of a version of this entity, called the National Education Standards and Improvement Council (NESIC). However, this provision came under fire from Republicans, who called the proposed council a "national school board." The following year, after Republicans took control of the House and Senate, Congress repealed the provision before members were even appointed.

The political battles over the history standards, and over NESIC, led some observers to contend that national standards were dead. However, some of the national efforts had an impact on educational practice. As noted earlier, the NCTM standards influenced national tests and curriculum in 40 states. And the science education standards have been widely accepted and have had an influence on curriculum materials and professional development across the country. Their effect on teaching practice and on student achievement has been less evident, at least so far (Lauer et al. 2005).

In addition, New Standards, a private organization created by the National Center on Education and the Economy and the Learning Research and Development Center at the University of Pittsburgh, also developed a widely praised set of national standards in English language arts, mathematics, and "applied learning." Several large school districts, including New York City and Pittsburgh, adopted these standards.

Action Moves to the States

While the national debates raged, most of the standards-setting action took place at the state and local levels. States and districts continued to select curriculum materials and develop assessments, and states increasingly developed standards to guide those decisions in the 1990s. In 1996, 15 states had developed standards; by 2000, 49 states (all but Iowa) had done so.

Science standards, while not mandated by federal law, were also adopted by states. In some cases, controversies over the issue of evolution broke out. In Kansas, notably, the state board of education in 1999 approved a set of science standards that omitted the word *evolution* entirely, provoking a national outcry. The National Academy of Sciences and the AAAS, organizations whose science standards formed the basis of the Kansas standards, revoked their copyright, disallowing the state from using its materials. In the 2000 election, five members of the state school board were voted out of office, and the new board

in 2001 issued a new set of science standards that reinstated the concept.

Last Try for a National Test

While the standards work continued at the state level, President Clinton, at least, held out some residual hope for national standards. At a summit in 1996 convened by the National Governors Association and the IBM Corporation, Clinton stated his belief that "being promoted ought to mean more or less the same thing in Pasadena, California, that it does in Palisades, New York. In a global society, it ought to mean more or less the same thing" (Ravitch 1996).

To carry out that idea, Clinton made a bid to create a national test. In his 1997 State of the Union Address, Clinton proposed creating tests in fourth-grade reading and eighth-grade mathematics that would be available nationally, but voluntary. The reading test would be based on NAEP, and the mathematics test would be based on the Third International Mathematics and Science Study. (U.S. eighth graders performed below the average of 41 nations in that study; students from 20 nations outperformed U.S. students.) The idea, as Clinton explained, would be to measure students in any part of the country against national standards. "We must start with the elemental principle that there should be national standards of excellence in education," Clinton said in a February 5 speech at Augusta State University. "Algebra is the same in Georgia as it is in Utah" (Hoff 1997).

Although some educators and public officials expressed support for the plan, the voluntary national test quickly ran into a buzz saw of bipartisan opposition. Chester E. Finn Jr., the former assistant U.S. secretary of education who was then the president of the Thomas B. Fordham Foundation, predicted as much when he quipped that no one would like national testing because Republicans don't like "national" and Democrats don't like "testing."

The opposition proved too much. Congress in 1998 agreed to allow the National Assessment Governing Board and its contractors to continue development of the test, but prohibited field-testing or pilot testing of test items. The plan eventually withered away.

No Child Left Behind

Standards and testing at the state level, meanwhile, continued apace. And once again, this activity was spurred by incentives and support from the federal government.

Shortly after taking office in 2001, President George W. Bush proposed No Child Left Behind (NCLB), his plan for reauthorizing the Elementary and Secondary Education Act. NCLB, which Bush signed at an Ohio school in January 2002, built on the standards-based system established by the 1994 Improving America's Schools Act (IASA). But NCLB's emphasis on tests and test results was much stronger than the earlier law's. While IASA required testing in at least three grades, NCLB required states to institute tests in every grade, from third grade through eighth grade, and once in high school. And the consequences placed on test results were much more severe. Under the law, all states were required to set a definition of *proficiency* based on reading and mathematics test scores and set a goal that all students would be proficient by 2014, the year that students who entered school when the law was signed would graduate from high school. States would also set annual targets toward that goal, both for schools as a whole and for groups of students within schools (such as African Americans, Hispanics, students with disabilities, and English language learners), and all groups would have to meet the

targets in order for a school to make adequate yearly progress (AYP). Schools that failed to make AYP for two consecutive years would be subject to sanctions, which would intensify over time if schools continued to fall below the bar.

NCLB did have a strong impact on the emerging drive for common standards. Several provisions of the law, and the ways in which they were implemented, helped fuel that drive.

First, the law's requirement that each state set its own definition of proficiency quickly made clear that the word *proficiency* lacked a common meaning and that states varied widely in what they expected of students. This problem was particularly evident because of another provision of the law: the requirement that each state participate in the National Assessment of Educational Progress (NAEP). The results showed wide discrepancies between the proportion of students who were proficient on state tests, compared with the proportion of students who were proficient on NAEP. In some cases, the discrepancies were quite stark: In Tennessee, for example, 87% of fourth graders were proficient on the state test in mathematics in 2005, compared with 28% who were proficient on NAEP. In Massachusetts, on the other hand, 40% of fourth graders were proficient on the state test in mathematics in 2005, compared with 41% on NAEP.

Why should judgments about students and school performance depend on the state in which a student happened to live? That was the question that advocates of national standards began to ask.

Similarly, researchers also found that the content students were expected to know varied widely from state to state. A 2008 study by Andrew Porter and his colleagues at the University of Pennsylvania examined state content standards in mathematics and compared them with one another and with the NCTM standards. The study found very little commonality among the states, suggesting that there is no de facto national standard. Moreover, the study found, there was more similarity in different grades' standards within a state than there was between states. That is, a student was more likely to encounter the same content moving from, say, fourth grade to fifth grade in Arizona than she would if she moved from Arizona to California in the middle of fourth grade (NRC 2008).

Porter's study pointed out a weakness in many state standards, especially in mathematics: They did not expect students to master a topic and move on to topics in a progression toward expertise. But it also raised the question that President Clinton had asked a decade before: Why should algebra be different in Georgia than it is in Utah?

In addition to the questions about the content and performance standards, educators and policy makers also began to ask questions about the assessments that were put in place in the wake of NCLB. Because of the law's requirements for tests in every grade from third to eighth and once in high school, a number of states scrapped ambitious testing programs that had been developed in the 1990s that would have been too expensive to maintain in every grade level. For example, Maryland had had in place a sophisticated test, known as the Maryland School Performance Assessment Program (MSPAP), which asked students to work in groups to complete projects, among other tasks. In order to implement the program, the state employed a matrix sampling design, much like NAEP's, in which students in different schools completed different tasks; the results were combined to produce scores at the school and district levels, but not at the individual student level. But after NCLB became law, Maryland replaced MSPAP with a more conventional test that measured a narrower range of student abilities and produced individual student scores. Overall, 15 states—educating 42% of U.S. students—used tests that were completely multiple-choice in 2005 and 2006 (Toch 2006).

The Renewed Search for Common Standards

These concerns about standards and tests helped fuel a renewed interest in common standards that would be high for all students, and in June 2006 former Governor James B. Hunt Jr. of North Carolina pulled together a small group of education leaders in Raleigh, North Carolina, to begin considering the issue.

To follow up, Hunt enlisted another former governor, Bob Wise of West Virginia, the president of the Alliance for Excellent Education, a Washington, D.C.-based policy and advocacy group, to continue the conversation in the nation's capital. In September 2006, Wise hosted a meeting in Washington, D.C., on the topic, bringing together some of the leaders of national education policy organizations, such as the Aspen Institute, the Education Trust, and the Thomas B. Fordham Institute—groups that are active in developing education policy at the national level—to talk about whether to pursue the idea of developing national standards.

Although these meetings were held behind closed doors, they signaled that, less than 10 years after President Clinton's proposal for voluntary national tests went down in flames, the concept of national standards had not perished in the ashes. What was different this time?

To participants in the discussions, there were several factors that made the idea more palatable—and pressing—than it had been in the 1990s. One was the evidence that state standards varied widely and that many states appeared to have set low expectations for students.

Perhaps as a result, there were large gaps in student performance. A 2004 study by ACT, the Iowa City, Iowa-based organization that produces the widely used college-admissions test, attempted to quantify how large the gaps were. The study found that only 26% of high school graduates who had taken the ACT—students who indicated their intention to go to college—earned scores high enough to have a good chance of success in a college-level Biology course, 40% were prepared for college-level algebra, and 68% were prepared for a college English composition course. The proportion of racial and ethnic minority students ready for college was far lower. And, the study found, because the expectations for the workplace are essentially the same as those for college, large numbers of students graduating high school were not prepared to enter the job market either (ACT 2004).

At the same time, there was a growing recognition that state boundaries were becoming increasingly irrelevant in an increasingly global economy. Thomas Friedman's widely influential book, *The World Is Flat*, (Friedman 2005) showed that the spread of fiber-optic cable made it possible for companies to outsource a wide range of tasks that had previously been performed within national borders, such as tax preparation and technical support for computers. Thus, U.S. students, no matter where they lived, were now competing in a global economic market with students from Shanghai, Bangalore, and Osaka. The idea that each state could set its own expectations for what students should know and be able to do seemed anachronistic.

Moreover, international assessments continued to show that U.S. students were performing well below the level of students in other countries. In 1999, eighth graders in 14 nations outperformed those in the United States in mathematics and science on the Third International Mathematics

and Science Study (TIMSS) (Gonzales et al. 2000). In 2003, U.S. 15-year-olds performed below the average of students in industrialized nations in mathematics literacy; students in 20 of the 28 participating countries outperformed U.S. students on the Programme for International Student Assessment (PISA), a test administered by the Paris-based Organisation for Economic Cooperation and Development (Lemke et al. 2004).

The evidence from international studies showed that one of the key factors in the success of high-performing countries was the fact that they had a common benchmark for student performance. In other words, high-performing nations had national standards for students, rather than allowing regions or states within their borders to set expectations that varied widely.

In addition to former governors Hunt and Wise, a number of prominent individuals and organizations had already been discussing the idea of national or common educational standards, and doing so out loud. For example, in 2005, the Center for American Progress issued a report pointing out the disparities in state standards and concluded, "Today, state testing results really tell the public little about how schools are performing and progressing. But the establishment and implementation of national standards and the testing and reporting of student achievement in two or three core subjects like reading, math, and science would provide the public with a much more accurate picture of how United States' students are progressing nationally and state-by-state" (Brown and Rocha 2005, p. 4).

The same year, the *New York Times* published an article by Ravitch arguing for national standards, and *Education Week* held an online chat on the topic. In March 2006, Education Sector, a Washington, D.C.-based policy organization, held a debate on national standards, and in September 2006, the Thomas B. Fordham Foundation issued a report outlining four scenarios for the creation of national standards. In recognition of the quixotic nature of the idea, the Fordham report was entitled "To Dream the Impossible Dream," the theme song from the musical, *Man of La Mancha*.

An influential commission convened by Carnegie Corporation of New York and the Institute for Advanced Study at Princeton University also issued a ringing call for common standards—in this case, in mathematics and science, specifically. The commission stated, "The time has come for the nation to adopt more academically rigorous common standards defining what mathematics and science education ought to look like for all Americans. The Commission believes that math and science standards should be fewer, clearer, and higher and that they should articulate our best understanding of what all students need to know and be able to do in order to succeed in college, thrive in the workforce, and participate in civic life." (Carnegie Corporation of New York and Institute for Advanced Study 2009, p. 20).

Common standards would serve as a "strong platform" on which states could redesign and upgrade their instructional programs, the commission stated. The standards would inform the development of stronger curriculum and course sequences, improved curriculum materials, and better teacher preparation and professional development, the commission stated.

The commission stated that the standards should be developed collaboratively by the states, rather than by the federal government, and that they should be linked closely with new, high-quality assessments and more effective forms of accountability. Common assessments would encourage and reward effective instruction, the report noted, and could reduce costs and make possible comparative information on performance and international benchmarking.

Toward the Common Core

The organizations that former Governors Hunt and Wise first convened to consider common standards continued to meet throughout 2006 and 2007 to discuss the feasibility of the idea. The discussions dragged on for many months, as participants debated the roles the various organizations would play and who would take the lead. Wise compared the deliberations to the Paris peace talks aimed at ending the Vietnam War, at which negotiators argued for months over the shape of the bargaining table.

Two additional organizations—the Council of Chief State School Officers (CCSSO) and the National Governors Association (NGA)—came to the table and made possible a solution. These two associations had been moving toward support for common standards. They agreed with the need for upgrading their state standards by adopting the idea of internationally benchmarked standards for college and career readiness, but they recognized that they lacked the resources to develop such standards on their own. By coming together and pooling their funds, they could attract the nation's best researchers and subject matter experts and produce standards that were better than any state could develop by itself.

Mindful of the previous defeat of national standards in the 1990s, the organizations debating the standards effort—Achieve, the Alliance for Excellent Education, the CCSSO, the Hunt Institute, and the NGA—agreed that the project would only succeed if it was led by states; a national effort, especially one that carried the aroma of federal involvement, was doomed to failure. But states coming together to develop standards could succeed. Thus, the CCSSO and the NGA assumed leadership of the effort.

To gauge state support, governors' education policy advisers and chiefs convened at a meeting arranged by the NGA and CCSSO at the Chicago Airport Hilton in April 2009. The support was overwhelming. The state leaders agreed that variations in expectations for student performance were no longer acceptable, and that they should work together to develop common standards. The chiefs' group and the governors' association then drew up a memorandum of agreement, which would commit states to participate in the process of developing state standards. By signing the agreement, states would agree to take part in "a state-led process that will draw on evidence and lead to development and adoption of a common core of state standards (common core) in English language arts and mathematics for grades K–12" (CCSSO and NGAC 2009, p. 1). As part of the agreement, the states also committed to supporting the development of common assessments to measure progress toward the standards.

To indicate their commitment, governors and chief state school officers (and in some cases, state board of education chairmen) had to sign the memorandum. The governors of Alaska and Texas refused to participate, but in the end, 48 states agreed to take part in the venture. The organizations formed teams to draft standards, received—and responded to—extensive public feedback, and released a final version of the standards on June 2, 2010. Within a month, more than half the states adopted the standards, and by the end of the year, two-thirds of the states had done so. As of 2012, 46 states, the District of Columbia, and the Department of Defense Education Activity had adopted the *Common Core State Standards*.

Toward *Next Generation Science Standards*

The *Next Generation Science Standards* built on many of the pillars that created the Common Core State Standards (*CCSS*). As noted above, *The Opportunity Equation*, the report issued by a commission established by Carnegie Corporation of New York and the Institute for Advanced Study (IAS), argued that "the time has come" for common standards in science. The commission noted that the *CCSS* in English language arts and mathematics were under development, and that science educators could take advantage of the momentum gained through this initiative.

The report also suggested a number of reasons why standards in science were necessary. First, the report noted, standards that were fewer, clearer, and higher would counteract the tendency in American schools to teach a long list of topics without much depth. (A paper commissioned by the commission, entitled "Math and Science Standards that are Fewer, Clearer, Higher to Raise Achievement at All Levels" exerted a strong influence on the *CCSS*, and its two authors became lead writers of the standards.) A report by the NRC had found that the science curriculum in kindergarten through eighth grade was in many cases a "mile wide and an inch deep" (NRC 2007). The NSES might have accelerated this tendency, the Carnegie-IAS report noted.

At the same time, the report stated, the science curriculum tended to overemphasize the facts of science, and placed too little emphasis on conceptual understanding and the nature of science as a way of thinking. "Our emphasis should therefore be on enabling students to develop the competencies that characterize scientific thinking and a more thorough understanding of the foundational concepts and theories that provide a baseline of scientific literacy and serve as building blocks for further studies," the report states (Carnegie-IAS 2009, p. 26).

As a first step in revising the standards, the NRC convened a meeting of its Board on Science Education in the summer of 2009 to consider a revision of the *NSES*. The meeting, sponsored by the NSF, explored a number of problems with the existing standards and reasons for revision.

One important development that needed to be addressed was the advances in the science of learning that had taken place in the decade since the *NSES* were released. These advances were documented in *How People Learn*, an NRC report released in 1999, three years after the science standards were issued.

How People Learn found that students need more than an array of facts or a set of general problem-solving skills in order to develop deep understanding of a domain. Rather, the report stated, "expertise requires well-organized knowledge of concepts, principles, and procedures of inquiry" (Bransford, Brown, and Cocking 1999, p. 228). In science, that requires helping students overcome deeply rooted misconceptions and pointing them toward coherent and broad understandings of concepts.

The NRC board also found that the implementation of the science standards had been uneven. There was considerable variation among the states, and thus the quality of the science education students received depended on where they lived. That pointed to the need for a new statement that would be more coherent and able to be implemented in a more uniform way.

The board also found, as *The Opportunity Equation* had pointed out, that the teaching of science tended to place too much emphasis on science facts, rather than conceptual understanding or scientific inquiry. That occurred in part, the board concluded, because the standards did

not sufficiently address learning progressions, or the steps that lead students toward a deep understanding of scientific concepts. New standards would be needed.

First, Get the Science Right

To begin the process of setting standards, Carnegie Corporation of New York, one of the organizers of the commission that issued *The Opportunity Equation*, agreed to fund the effort and to conduct it in two parts. First, Carnegie funded the NRC to put together a committee to develop a framework for the standards. The involvement of the NRC, which agreed to work in partnership with AAAS and NSTA, was aimed at "getting the science right," according to participants. They wanted to ensure that the standards rested on firm footing and would have credibility in the field. The involvement of the other science groups helped ensure that the product represented a single consensus document that the entire science community could stand behind.

For the second part of the process, the development of grade-by-grade standards based on the framework, Carnegie turned to Achieve, a Washington, D.C.-based organization that had played a key role in the development of the *CCSS* in ELA and mathematics. Achieve had close ties with state leaders, who could ensure that the standards were grounded in the standards states already had developed and could help ease adoption.

To develop the framework, the NRC convened a 28-member committee that consisted of working scientists, including two Nobel Prize winners; cognitive scientists; science educators; standards experts; and policy researchers. The chair was Helen R. Quinn, a professor emerita at the Stanford Linear Accelerator National Laboratory. The committee also formed design teams in four areas: physical science, life science, Earth/

space science, and engineering. These design teams were responsible for developing a framework in each disciplinary area.

Unlike many NRC committees, which try to forge a scientific consensus without outside influence, the Committee on a Conceptual Framework for New K–12 Science Education Standards deliberately sought feedback and incorporated it into their discussions. The committee produced a draft and released it for public comment in July 2010. During the three-week comment period, more than 2,000 people responded to an online survey; two dozen organizations also held focus groups with 400 participants, and individuals and organizations submitted written comments. The committee examined these responses in two subsequent meetings and made substantial revisions to the draft. A summary of the feedback the committee received and the revisions made in response to it is included in the committee's report.

The final report was released on July 19, 2011 (and published as the book *A Framework for K–12 Science Education* in 2012). It laid out a three-part framework for science education standards: scientific and engineering practices, crosscutting concepts, and disciplinary core ideas in the physical sciences, life sciences, Earth and space sciences, and engineering. The committee stated that these three dimensions should be integrated into standards, assessment, curriculum, and instruction.

The scientific and engineering practices represent the ways of doing science and engineering. They include

1. asking questions (for science) and defining problems (for engineering);

2. developing and using models;

3. planning and carrying out investigations;

4. analyzing and interpreting data;

5. using mathematics and computational thinking;

6. constructing explanations (for science) and designing solutions (for engineering);

7. engaging in argument from evidence; and

8. obtaining, evaluating, and communicating information.

The second dimension, crosscutting concepts, was aimed at identifying the key ideas that are represented in many scientific and engineering disciplines. The goal of including them, the *Framework* states, is to "help provide students with an organizational framework for connecting knowledge from the various disciplines into a coherent and scientifically based view of the world" (NRC 2012, p. 3).

The seven crosscutting concepts are

1. patterns;

2. cause and effect: mechanism and explanation;

3. scale, proportion, and quantity;

4. systems and system models;

5. energy and matter: flows, cycles, and conservation;

6. structure and function; and

7. stability and change.

The third dimension includes the core ideas of each discipline. Reflecting the goal of *The Opportunity Equation* for fewer, clearer, higher standards, the *Framework* identifies only two to four core ideas for each discipline: four in physical sciences (matter and its interactions; motion and stability: forces and interactions; energy; and waves and their applications in technologies for information transfer); four in life sciences (from molecules to organisms: structures and processes;

ecosystems: interactions, energy, and dynamics; heredity: inheritance and variation of traits; and biological evolution: unity and diversity); three in Earth and space sciences (Earth's place in the universe; Earth's systems; and Earth and human activity); and two in engineering (engineering design and links among engineering, technology, science, and society). Unlike the practices and crosscutting concepts, which are generic across all grade levels, the disciplinary core ideas are identified for particular grade levels: grade 2, 5, 8, and 12. Those specific expectations are intended to show that students at different grade levels are expected to build on their prior knowledge and understand more complex concepts.

A State-Led Process

Once the *Framework* was released, the process of developing the standards shifted to Achieve. Building on the successful experience of the *CCSS*, Achieve designed a process to put states in the lead. First, the organization recruited a state science supervisor, Stephen Pruitt from Georgia, to direct the effort. Then the organization enlisted state partners to serve as lead states. While the organization intended to provide opportunities for all states to provide feedback, the lead states would take the role of guiding the standards writers and develop models for adoption and implementation of the standards.

Achieve asked states to apply to become lead partners. The application asked states to give serious consideration to adopting the standards, to participate in multistate meetings around adoption and implementation, and to form a broad-based committee of 35 to 100 people to review the drafts, all at state expense. The application would have to be signed by the chief state school officer and state board chair, and states would have to make public their participation in the process.

Although about a half dozen states were expected to seek to become lead partners, the idea became popular, and 26 states ended up choosing to take part in that role.

Once the lead states were identified, the project's leaders worked with science and science education organizations to choose standards writers. In the end, 41 writers were selected. They included teachers, curriculum specialists, science educators, and scientists and engineers. Unlike the writers of the *CCSS*, however, the science standards writers did not have to start from scratch. With the NRC *Framework* (2012) as their guidepost, they were able to dive right in and determine the progression of knowledge and skills students would have to demonstrate through the end of high school.

The writers agreed to develop an "architecture" for the standards that would guide how they would be implemented in classrooms and assessed. First, each standard would begin with a performance expectation—that is, how students should be able to demonstrate that they have met the standard. The language of the performance expectations would be taken directly from the NRC *Framework* (2012); for example, rather than say that students should "explain" a given concept, they would have to "construct an argument" for it.

The writers also agreed that each standard would show each of the three dimensions of the *Framework*—the practices, the crosscutting concepts, and the core ideas. In that way, test developers, curriculum developers, and teachers would be expected to integrate the dimensions as they put together assessments and instructional programs around the standards.

The standards writers also agreed to link each science standard directly to relevant standards from the *CCSS ELA* and *Mathematics*. Such links would accomplish several goals. First, they would show to teachers ways in which they could integrate their instruction and help students meet standards from multiple subject areas—how teaching science concepts could also enable students to demonstrate their reading and writing abilities, for example. In addition, the links would also help ensure that the science standards reflect the knowledge and skills students would be expected to have at a particular grade level. It would make little sense to develop a science standard that expects students to have mathematics abilities beyond those expected for a certain grade level.

While the standards were intended for each grade level, the writers recognized that the structure of science education differs widely around the country. In the elementary grades, schools generally teach integrated science each year. But in middle school, about a third of districts teach science that way, and a third teaches a discrete science course in each grade. (Another third allows local options.) For that reason, the standards would be presented for the entire grade 6 through grade 8 band, although the standards writers intend to offer suggested pathways. Similarly, the standards are expected to be presented for all of high school, with suggested pathways depending on how a state or district structures its science curriculum. The *CCSS Mathematics* provides a similar structure for high schools.

Because the standards were intended to be state led, Achieve and its partners designed numerous opportunities for state stakeholders to provide input into the process. As noted above, the lead states were expected to name groups of people who would serve as initial reviewers of drafts. These groups would be shown the drafts before they were released publicly and have opportunities to offer suggestions.

The leaders also set up a process for extensive public feedback. A first draft was released online May 11, 2012; within 15 minutes, the website shut down because as many as 10,000 users logged on to the site at the same time. It reopened shortly afterward, and over the three-week comment period, more than 126,000 people visited the site. (That number does not include the many individuals who visited and issued comments as a group.) In addition, some states that were not lead states, such as Wisconsin, set up "listening sessions" to gather feedback.

The project leaders intend to categorize the comments and revise the draft based on them, and to issue a public document that explains the comments they received and how they dealt with them, just as the NRC committee had done. The group issued a second draft for public comment in January 2013 and made a second round of revisions. A final version of the *NGSS* was released in April 2013.

High Expectations for All

The *CCSS ELA* and *Mathematics* and the *NGSS* represent a sea change in American education. The United States was the first country to open access to schools to virtually all young people. Beginning in the 1990s, states began to become explicit about what that education should be by developing standards for student performance. Now, states have agreed to common expectations for students in key subject areas and have defined those expectations as what students need to know and be able to do to succeed in college and careers and to be comparable to those of the highest performing nations.

As difficult as it was to imagine the nation getting to this point, particularly after the heated battles over national standards in the 1990s, it is difficult now to imagine the nation proceeding another way. States have seen that working together produces a better set of standards than any state could develop on its own, and they have shown a willingness to publicly declare their support for high expectations for all students.

As significant an achievement as the development of common standards has been, it is only the first step toward improvement in classroom practice and, ultimately, student learning. States, districts, and schools now must take the difficult steps of developing and implementing new assessments that measure student performance against the standards, developing and securing curriculum materials that will support instruction around the standards, and helping teachers understand the expectations and preparing them to teach in ways that will enable students to reach them. These are difficult steps. But the foundation—the standards that spell out what all students need to know and be able to do—has already been laid.

References

Achieve Inc. 2013. *Next generation science standards.* www.nextgenscience.org.

ACT. 2004. *Crisis at the core: Preparing all students for college and work.* Iowa City, IA: ACT. *www.act. org/research/policymakers/pdf/crisis_report.pdf.*

American Association for the Advancement of Science (AAAS). 1993. *Benchmarks for science literacy.* New York: Oxford University Press.

American Association for the Advancement of Science (AAAS). 1989. *Science for all Americans.* New York: Oxford University Press.

Anderson, N. *Washington Post.* 2010. Governors, State School Superintendents to Propose Common Academic Standards. March 10.

Bransford, J., A. Brown, and R. Cocking, eds. 1999. *How people learn: Brain, mind, experience, and school.* Washington, DC: National Academies Press.

Brown, C., and E. Rocha. 2005. *The case for national standards, accountability, and fiscal equity.* Washington, DC: Center for American Progress.

Carnegie Corporation of New York and Institute for Advanced Study (Carnegie-IAS). 2009. *The opportunity equation.* New York: Carnegie Corporation of New York.

Coleman, D., and J. Zimba. 2007. *Math and science standards that are fewer, clearer, and higher to raise achievement at all levels.* New York and Princeton, NJ: Carnegie Corporation of New York–Institute for Advanced Study (Carnegie-IAS) Commission on Mathematics and Science Education.

Council of Chief State School Officers (CCSSO) and National Governors Association Center for Best Practices (NGAC). 2009. Common Core Standards memorandum of agreement. *www. edweek.org/media/commonstandardsmoa.doc.*

Friedman, T. L. 2005. *The world is flat: A brief history of the twenty-first century.* New York: Farrar, Straus, and Giroux.

Gonzales, P., C. Calsyn, L. Jocelyn, K. Mak, D. Kastberg, S. Arafeh, T. Williams, and W. Tsen. 2000. *Pursuing excellence: Comparisons of eighth grade mathematics and science achievement from a U.S. perspective.* Washington, DC: U.S. Department of Education, National Center for Education Statistics.

Hoff, D. J. *Education Week.* 1997. Clinton Gives Top Billing to Education Plan. February 12.

Lauer, P. A., D. Snow, M. Martin-Glenn, R. J. Van Buhler, K. Stoutemyre, and R. Snow-Renner. 2005. *The influence of standards on K–12 teaching and student learning: A research synthesis.* Aurora, CO: McREL.

Lemke, M., A. Sen, E. Pahlke, L. Partelow, D. Miller, T. Williams, D. Kastberg, and L. Jocelyn. 2004. *Outcomes of learning in mathematics literacy and problem solving: PISA 2003 results from the U.S.*

Perspective. Washington, DC: U.S. Department of Education, National Center for Education Statistics.

National Assessment of Educational Progress (NAEP). *http://nces.ed.gov/nationsreportcard*.

National Commission on Excellence in Education. 1983. *A nation at risk: The Imperative of educational reform.* Washington, DC: U.S. Government Printing Office.

National Council on Education Standards and Testing. 1992. *Raising standards for American education*. Washington, DC: U.S. Department of Education.

National Council of Teachers of Mathematics (NCTM). 1989. *Curriculum and evaluation standards for school mathematics*. Reston, VA: NCTM.

National Governors Association Center for Best Practices (NGAC) and the Council of Chief State School Officers (CCSSO). 2010. *Common core state standards*. Washington, DC: NGAC and CCSSO.

National Research Council (NRC). 1996. *National science education standards*. Washington, DC: National Academies Press.

National Research Council (NRC). 2007. *Taking science to school: Learning and teaching science in grades K–8*. Washington, DC: National Academies Press.

National Research Council (NRC). 2008. *Common standards for K–12 education? Considering the evidence.* Summary of a workshop series. Washington, DC: National Academies Press.

National Research Council (NRC). 2012. *A framework for K–12 science education: Practices, crosscutting concepts, and core ideas*. Washington, DC: National Academies Press.

Program for International Student Assessment (PISA). *http://nces.ed.gov/surveys/pisa*.

Ravitch, D. 1995. *National standards in American education: A citizen's guide*. Washington, DC: Brookings Institution.

Ravitch, D. 1996. *50 states, 50 standards: The continuing need for national voluntary standards in education*. Washington, DC: Brookings Institution.

Rothman, R. 2011. *Something in common: The common core standards and the next chapter in American education*. Cambridge, MA: Harvard Education Press.

Rutherford, F. J., and A. Ahlgren. 1989. *Science for all Americans*. New York: Oxford University Press.

Toch, T. 2006. *Margins of error: The education testing industry in the No Child Left Behind era*. Washington, DC: Education Sector.

Trends in International Mathematics and Science Study (TIMSS). *http://nces.ed.gov/timss*.

CHAPTER 3

From *Framework* to *Next Generation Science Standards*

Lesley Quattrone

Former K–12 Language Arts Coordinator, West Clermont Local Schools (Cincinnati, Ohio) and Greenwich Public Schools (Greenwich, Connecticut)

Science Education Today

A teacher's work is never done. Educators have barely digested the *Common Core State Standards* (*CCSS*), *English Language Arts* and *Mathematics*, and now the *Next Generation Science Standards* (*NGSS*) are rolling their way. Why can't teachers wait until they are comfortable integrating the former into their practice before tackling the latter? Why are they called upon to reform science instruction, too? Are there possible synergies between the *CCSS* and the *NGSS*? (See Chapter 10.) What is the urgency? A look at previous efforts at science education reform, student achievement data, and contemporary global issues will provide some answers.

Efforts to reform science education in American schools are not new. They have come in waves since 1957, when Russia trumped U. S. space efforts by launching Sputnik 1, the first satellite to enter the Earth's orbit. The most recent, national-level initiative to improve science education occurred in 1996, when the National Research Council (NRC) published the *National Science Education Standards* (*NSES*). Most states took these standards as the jumping off point for reforms in their science curriculum, assessment, and professional development. However, despite decades of efforts to improve K–12 science education, American students continue to produce lackluster results on national

and international tests designed to gauge their knowledge of science and their ability to apply scientific concepts. On the 2006 administration of the Programme for International Student Assessment (PISA) science test, an instrument that measures students' capacity to apply scientific concepts in a real-world context, American 15-year-old students placed 21st out of 30 developed countries; in the 2009 administration of the same test, they placed 23rd. Most recently, the results of a special 2011 administration of the National Assessment of Educational Progress (NAEP) test on science mastery offered little cause for celebration. Administered to a representative sample of eighth graders from all 50 states, the scores indicate a minor improvement over 2009 results, but less than one-third of those students scored at the proficient level (Sparks 2012, p. 6).

Boosting student achievement in science has been an especially challenging problem at the elementary level. The reasons are many. Among them is that the elementary classroom is a crowded place, not just with students but also with subjects. Particularly since the advent of No Child Left Behind (NCLB), English language arts (ELA) and mathematics have taken big chunks of the school day, with science, social studies, and other subjects left to jockey for whatever time remains. Compounding the problem is the fact that many K–5 teachers feel ill-prepared to teach basic science. Just as importantly, some educators have historically believed that basic science is too abstract for young learners. Additionally, the science curriculum is frequently perceived as "one mile wide and an inch deep," filled with topics but light on the connective tissue that relates those topics to one another. In early elementary grades, for example, students often learn facts about plants and animals, but the curriculum does not provide them with sufficient context to understand how those facts interact in real-world, natural environments.

Clearly, the time is right for another reform of K–12 science education, and not solely because of American students' subpar performance on science tests or lack of implementation of previous reforms. Most states have recently adopted *Common Core State Standards* in English language arts (*CCSS ELA*) and mathematics (*CCSS Mathematics*). It makes sense for science to ride that wave. The previous NSES standards were never truly "national" in their adoption, and they are now more than 15 years old. Much has happened since 1996. Scientific knowledge has expanded exponentially, with engineering and technology playing a larger role in investigations, analyses, and innovations. Research on how youngsters learn and how teachers can most effectively scaffold their learning has burgeoned (see Chapter 8). Finally, many of our most pressing contemporary problems—especially those related to the economy, energy, environment, and health—require that citizens have an understanding of science, technology, engineering, and mathematics (STEM) in order to participate in discussions about solutions. It has become essential to increase scientific literacy in this country now.

A New Conceptual Framework for K–12 Science Education

To address the weaknesses in American science education, the NRC in 2012 released a major, research-informed report—*A Framework for K–12 Science Education: Practices, Crosscutting Concepts, and Core Ideas*. The *Framework* provides a vision for K–12 science and engineering education. Funded by the Carnegie Corporation of New York, this document responds to the criticism that K–12 science education is "one mile wide and an inch deep" and attempts to redress other weaknesses in current science education. Just as the *CCSS* pared down the unrealistic number of standards in English language arts and math to what is essential for a deep understanding, the *Framework* has taken as its mantra "fewer, higher, clearer" standards.

The *Framework* envisions a K–12 science and engineering education in which "students, over multiple years of school, actively engage in science and engineering practices and apply crosscutting concepts to deepen their understanding of the core ideas in these fields. The learning experiences provided for students should engage them with fundamental questions about the world and with how scientists have investigated and found answers to those questions. Throughout the K–12 grades, students should have the opportunity to carry out scientific investigations and engineering design projects related to the disciplinary core ideas" (NRC 2012, pp. 8–9).

This vision builds on previous work outlined in the *NSES* (NRC 1996) and the *Benchmarks for Science Literacy* (AAAS 1993), but the definition of and means to achieve the goal of scientific literacy has been refined. First, the *Framework* insists on an integrated approach to science and engineering education in which content is inextricably bound up with practices that characterize the work of real scientists and engineers. Second, it supports the idea that learning is developmental and therefore students should delve into content in a developmentally appropriate way across the K–12 continuum. Third, to avoid superficial and fragmented knowledge, the *Framework* seeks to limit content knowledge to 13 disciplinary core ideas distributed across four domains: physical sciences (4); life sciences (4); Earth and space sciences (3); and engineering, technology and applications of science (2).

The principles on which the *Framework's* vision for K–12 science education rest are operationally defined in terms of three dimensions—practices, crosscutting concepts, and disciplinary core ideas—that collectively provide the foundation for curriculum, instruction, assessment, and professional development (see Figure 3.1, p. 40). The first of these—dimension 1—defines the more generic term *inquiry learning* as a set of eight scientific and engineering practices. These eight practices counter the misconception that there is one scientific method with a set number of linearly sequenced steps. Students do not learn these practices by simply watching a teacher demonstrate them or by merely reading about them in a textbook. Doing and learning science require that students actively engage in the work of real scientists and engineers. For example, they ask questions, develop models as tools, participate in investigations, gather and analyze data, learn how to construct arguments from evidence, and communicate their findings. In a coherent approach to science education, students learn that science and engineering are collaborative endeavors. Past iterations of science standards have identified these practices as skills without explicitly tying them to content. The *Framework* envisions these practices as the mechanisms by which students deepen their understanding of how the world works.

The practices outlined in dimension 1 engage students in the actual doing of science. Dimension 2 complements these practices with seven crosscutting concepts that have broad explanatory power across all scientific disciplines. These themes are common to physical, life, Earth and space sciences, and engineering. Once students understand that these concepts represent science as a way of knowing about the world, they will be less likely to view various topics in science as disconnected, fragmented pieces of knowledge. For instance, the first two concepts—patterns and cause and effect—are basic to all science. Noticing patterns leads to asking questions about phenomena, including causation. Students will not necessarily discover these themes on their own. It is up to teachers to make these connections explicit for their classes. For example, the theme of structure and function is just as important to the mechanics of bicycle design as it is to the study of plant and animal life.

Dimensions 1 and 2 describe how students best learn science and the themes that constitute a scientific way of knowing about the world. Dimension 3, disciplinary core ideas, consists of what is traditionally thought of as the content of science. Today, we live in an information age, and most of that information is just a click away on the internet. Scientific knowledge in particular is expanding at an exponential rate. It is simply not possible to cover all of science within the boundaries of grades K–12. The authors of the *Framework* note that the role of science education is "not to teach 'all the facts' but rather to prepare students with sufficient core knowledge so they can later acquire additional information on their own" (NRC 2012, p. 31). Figure 3.2 (p. 41) outlines the four domains of dimension 3. Taken together, dimensions 1, 2, and 3 constituted the foundation for the development of the *NGSS* that have been

FIGURE 3.1. THE *FRAMEWORK*

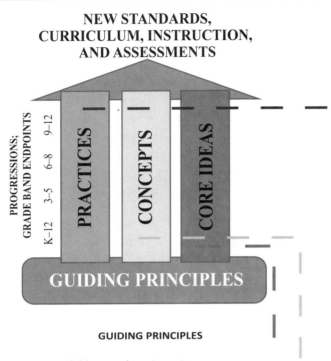

GUIDING PRINCIPLES

- Children are born investigators
- Focusing on core ideas and practices
- Understanding develops over time
- Science and engineering require both knowledge and practice
- Connecting to students' interests and experiences
- Promoting equity

DIMENSION 1

Science and Engineering Practices

- Asking questions and defining problems
- Developing and using models
- Planning and carrying out investigations
- Analyzing and interpreting data
- Using mathematics and computational thinking
- Constructing explanations and designing solutions
- Engaging in argument from evidence
- Obtaining, evaluating, and communicating information

DIMENSION 2

Crosscutting Concepts

- Patterns
- Cause and effect: mechanism and explanation
- Scale, proportion, and quantity
- Systems and system models
- Energy and matter: flows, cycles, and conservation
- Structure and function
- Stability and change

DIMENSION 3

Disciplinary Core Ideas

- Physical Sciences
- Life Sciences
- Earth and Space Sciences
- Engineering, Technology, and Applications of Science

designed to guide curriculum, instruction, assessment, and professional development over the next decade.

While these three dimensions provide the structure for the *NGSS*, another important element of the *Framework's* vision for science education—learning progressions—provides sequencing within that structure across the K–12 grades. Students develop facility with the eight practices outlined in dimension 1 through learning progressions that identify the developmentally appropriate standards for the elementary school (K–5 with grades 2 and 5 as endpoints), middle school (grade 8 as an endpoint), and high school (grade 12 as an endpoint) levels. For instance, a first grader may use a drawing or a photograph as a model of a real-world phenomenon while a high school student expresses his understanding with an elegant mathematical formula. While learning progressions are less clear-cut in the crosscutting concepts of dimension 2, they still apply. Young children, for example, come to school already recognizing some patterns (e.g., day and night; seasons; objects fall down, not up). They can recognize observable characteristics of matter and identify similarities and differences that lead to classification of living and nonliving things. By the time students are in high school, they can recognize that classifications based on visible characteristics may need to change when the same phenomena are studied at the macro and micro levels.

The concept of learning progressions achieves its fullest expression in disciplinary core ideas of dimension 3. For each of the 13 disciplinary core ideas, the *Framework* authors used checkpoints to define what students should know and be able to do at the end of grades 2, 5, 8, and 12. Taken as a

FIGURE 3.2. DIMENSION 3: DISCIPLINARY CORE IDEAS

Physical Sciences
PS1: Matter and its interactions
PS2: Motion and stability: Forces and interactions
PS3: Energy
PS4: Waves and their applications in technology for information transfer

Life Sciences
LS1: From molecules to organisms: Structures and processes
LS2: Ecosystems: Interactions, energy, and dynamics
LS3: Heredity: Inheritance and variation of traits
LS4: Biological evolution: Unity and diversity

Earth and Space Sciences
ESS1: Earth's place in space
ESS2: Earth's systems
ESS3: Earth and human activity

Engineering, Technology, and Applications of Science
ETS1: Engineering design
ETS2: Links among engineering, technology, science, and society

group, these endpoints suggest how each of the core ideas can be developed over the K–12 continuum to provide a road map for curriculum development. In general, the grade cluster endpoints focus initially on what is directly observable and within the experience of K–5 youngsters and move to increasingly sophisticated, theoretically informed understandings and investigations by grades 9–12. Figure 3.3 on page 42 provides a sample of endpoints by grade-level clusters for one of the life science core ideas—LS1.A: Structure and Function.

Next Generation Science Standards (NGSS)

Twenty-six states collectively committed to improving science curriculum and instruction led the development of the *NGSS* in conjunction with the National Academy of Sciences, the National Science Teachers Association (NSTA), and the American Association for the Advancement of Science (AAAS). Achieve managed the process. Using the three dimensions (practices, crosscutting concepts, disciplinary core ideas) and the learning progressions outlined in *A Framework for K–12 Science Education*, teams of writers (over half of whom were practicing teachers) constructed standards that outlined performance expectations for students at each individual elementary level (grades K–5) and for the middle school (grades 6–8) and high school (grades 9–12) bands. The first draft of these standards was released in May 2012 for public comment. A second draft that utilized public reaction to the first draft was released in

FIGURE 3.3. ENDPOINT CLUSTERS

Life Sciences LS1.A: Structure and Function— How do the structures of organisms enable life's functions?

A Framework for K–12 Science Education: Practices, Crosscutting Concepts, and Core Ideas

BY THE END OF GRADE 2	BY THE END OF GRADE 5
• All organisms have external parts. • Animals use body parts to see, hear, grasp, move, defend, eat, and breathe. • Plant parts (roots, stems, leaves, flowers, fruits) help them survive, grow, and reproduce.	• Plants and animals have internal and external structures that serve essential functions of growth, survival, behavior, and reproduction.

BY THE END OF GRADE 8	BY THE END OF GRADE 12
• All living things are made up of cells in many different configurations. • All cells need a living environment and ways to take in food and water and dispose of waste. • Within cells specialized structures fulfill these functions. • The cell mambrane controls what enters and leaves the cell. • Cells work together to form tissues and organs that serve particular functions.	• The essential functions of life require chemical reactions within systems of specialized cells. • All cells contain genetic information in the form of DNA. • Genes shape the formation of molecules called proteins that carry out the work of cells. • Multicellular organisms are arranged hierarchically. • Organisms have feedback mechanisms that help them regulate or adapt to conditions essential for survival (temperature, food, water).

January 2013, and the final *Next Generation Science Standards* was published in April 2013.

What is the nature of the *Next Generation Science Standards* (*NGSS*) and what do they look like? How are they different from previous standards?

- They are performance expectations that integrate the three dimensions described in the *Framework*. They do not separate content or concepts from inquiry practices.

- They reflect real world interconnectedness within and between science and engineering.

- They focus on both understanding and application of content.

- They recognize the importance of reading, writing, speaking, and listening in science (i.e., this is made explicit in the *CCSS ELA* connections feature)

- While they may provide some guidelines for curriculum developers, they are not in and of themselves curriculum materials.

- They connect to the *CCSS Mathematics* (again via the *CCSS* connections feature).

The *NGSS* are ambitious and intended for all students, with the aim of changing both what and how science is taught in American schools. For teachers in those of the 26 sponsoring states that voluntarily adopted the *NGSS* (and in other states that might use the *NGSS* as a foundation for updating and revising their own state standards), implementing the standards will require substantive changes in the scope and sequence of curriculum, changes in instructional strategies, and the development and use of curriculum-embedded assessments. (See Chapters 4–7 for discussion on and examples of the 5E teaching cycle approach as a model for this new direction.) All of this is challenging and will require an investment of teachers' time and energy for both professional and curricular development work. Yet, the return on investment in terms of the excitement on our elementary students' faces and our own engagement with science will be substantial. Moreover, as our middle and high school colleagues collaborate on this joint mission, our nation will reap substantial dividends in terms of improvements in economic, energy, environmental, individual health, and social well-being metrics. Laying the foundation for all high school graduates to become scientifically literate and fully ready to meet the challenges of college, career, and civic obligations and opportunities is our privilege and responsibility as elementary teachers.

References

Achieve Inc. 2013. *Next generation science standards.* www.nextgenscience.org

American Association for the Advancement of Science (AAAS). 1993. *Benchmarks for science literacy.* New York: Oxford University Press.

National Research Council (NRC). 1996. *National science education standards.* Washington, DC: National Academies Press.

National Research Council (NRC). 2012. *A framework for K–12 science education: Practices, crosscutting concepts, and core ideas.* Washington, DC: National Academies Press.

Sparks, S. D. *Education Week.* 2012. Eighth Grade Scores Inch Upward on National Science Assessment. May 16.

USING THE FRAMEWORK AND NGSS TO REDESIGN SCIENCE LESSONS

INTRODUCTION

Science at the Center

Bruce Alberts, PhD

Professor Emeritus, University of California, Department of Biochemistry and Biophysics

Editor-in-Chief, AAAS *Science* Magazine

Any education that prepares students for life in our complex, rapidly changing modern societies must be very different from the preparation for a quiz show such as *Jeopardy!* or for the types of multiple-choice examinations commonly used to test for factual recall. The internet can bring us most such facts in seconds, but along with social networks it also connects us to huge amounts of misinformation—much of it designed to get our money or our vote. With each passing year, it becomes ever more critical that our education systems prepare the next generation to learn how to learn, which requires an ability to think logically and skillfully argue from evidence with the tools of a scientist. This is why *A Framework for K–12 Science Education: Practices, Crosscutting Concepts, and Core Ideas* (NRC 2012) and the *Next Generation Science Standards* (*NGSS*) place great emphasis on actively engaging students, from the earliest age, with science and engineering practices. We urgently need to step back from a model of the teacher as the source of all knowledge, as well as from any sense that education centers on learning all the right answers. Inviting young students to explore school science as it is envisioned in the *Framework* lies at the heart of such a change.

I gained this important insight when my daughter, a science teacher, took time off from her profession to raise a family. During this period, she served as a volunteer teacher of science in her children's elementary school. As an initial lesson for second graders who had never before been exposed to science, she provided each student with four different types of soil; her lesson then began by asking each of them to carefully examine each type and write down what they observed. She was surprised to find that the class was paralyzed, with very few students willing to write. Further exploration revealed the reason: These students believed that the point of schooling was to learn correct answers. They had not yet been taught anything about soils, and not knowing the correct way to describe any of the soil samples, they were afraid to write anything at all. Later, after a few weeks of hands-on science experiences, the students became eager to produce their own observations about the natural world. This experience has helped to convince me of the enormous importance of including such inquiry activities for students in the earliest years of schooling, continuing throughout their many years of further education.

It has been repeatedly observed that, when taught appropriately, science becomes the favorite subject in school for young children. How sad it is then to observe the distaste for science on the part of so many middle school students. This rejection of science is unsurprising when one considers the dry textbook learning, fill-in-the-blanks word memorization that presently constitutes science education in too many classrooms. Consider a story told to me by a dismayed parent, whose young child recently returned from an encounter with school science with the following insight: "Now I get it, science is just like spelling. You just need to memorize it and it doesn't make any sense."

Here is my bottom line: It is critical that we work to redefine what the term *science education* means to most students. As clearly demonstrated in Chapter 4 "5E(z) Guidelines for Designing Research-Informed Science Lesson Sequences," we know what works in classrooms to excite children about science and to enable them to progress as adults who know how to make wise judgments for themselves, their families, and their nation.

And science can then usefully move to the center of schooling, with the type of science education described in the *Framework* and *NGSS* also serving as the basis for gaining reading, writing and communication skills—thereby enlivening the broader field of education (see Chapter 10 of this book and Pearson, Moje, and Greenleaf 2010).

References

National Research Council (NRC). 2012. *A framework for K–12 science education: Practices, crosscutting concepts, and core ideas*. Washington, DC: National Academies Press.

Pearson, D. P., E. Moje, and C. Greenleaf. 2010. Literacy and science: Each in the service of the other. *Science* 328: 459–463.

CHAPTER 4

5E(z) Guidelines for Designing Research-Informed Science Lesson Sequences

Thomas O'Brien, PhD
Professor of Science Education
Binghamton University (SUNY), Graduate School of Education

Commercial textbooks, science activity books, and internet resources offer elementary teachers a plethora of science activities that claim to be "inquiry based" (NSTA 2004). Although far fewer activities meet all the S_2EE_2R criteria of being Safe, Simple, Economical (time and money), Enjoyable, Effective, and Relevant (O'Brien 2010, p. 343), a number of quality elementary science methods books are available to assist teachers in separating the wheat from the chaff (e.g., Friedl and Yourst Koontz 2004; Martin 2011; Martin et al. 2005). Overworked elementary teachers do not have to invest their limited time in creating, field-testing, and revising their own science activities from scratch. Instead, individual teachers and teacher teams can invest their precious time in exploring how to synergistically sequence a series of such activities to align with not only the *Next Generation Science Standards* (*NGSS*) but also research-informed, developmentally appropriate learning progressions. In this way, the whole science unit can become greater than the sum of its parts (i.e., the individual lessons).

Well-designed science curriculum-instruction-assessment (CIA) is like a carefully crafted book or book series in which each chapter or book in the series builds on and extends the previous one. High-quality writing (and intelligent CIA sequences) draw the reader (or student) into an ever deepening and broadening world of understanding, which both builds on and challenges their prior understandings. Great books and CIA units also create a need-to-know that propels the reader (or student) by the power of intrinsic motivation (Banilower et al. 2010; see also Chapter 8 of this book). Interestingly, this same kind of self-reinforcing feedback loop motivates scientists and engineers to keep pushing against the boundary of the known, exploring the endless frontier of new discoveries and inventions. And this is not surprising, since "science is fundamentally a social enterprise … . [T]he way that scientists operate in the real world is remarkably similar to how students operate in effective science classrooms" (Michaels, Shouse, and Schweingruber 2008, pp. 5–6).

Research-informed science lesson sequences (i.e., integrated CIA mini-units) support learning as a process of conceptual change and meaning-making where students are regularly engaged with the eight scientific and engineering practices identified in Chapter 3 of *A Framework for Science Education, K–12* (NRC 2012). Planning, implementing, and revising CIA units requires teachers to follow an analogous set of inquiry-driven practices. The following discussion integrates ideas from the *Framework* (NRC 2012) and the *BSCS 5E Instructional Model* (Bybee et al. 2006), or Teaching Cycle by drawing an extended analogy between the work of scientists and engineers and the CIA work of teachers.

The 5E Teaching Cycle of Engage, Explore, Explain, Elaborate, and Evaluate is an instructional model for designing a series of experientially rich lessons that are conceptually linked and developmentally sequenced to support the ongoing, progressive refinement in student understanding as it develops over time (Bybee 2002). As such, it is especially effective in designing mini-units of five or more lessons in which at least one lesson is devoted to each phase of the 5E Teaching Cycle (O'Brien 2010). But depending on the learning objectives and available time, adjacent phases can be combined into shorter time frames. The underlying logic of the teaching cycle is that individual lessons only make sense in light of how they build on previous lessons and how they create the cognitive need and scaffolding for subsequent lessons. Both the individual and the collective human understanding of science are built on (and in some cases reconstruct flaws in) the foundation of prior conceptions, including resistant-to-change misconceptions (Mintzes, Wandersee, and Novak 1998; O'Brien 2011a). Similarly, intelligent CIA is designed around a cycle of learning experiences with diagnostic, formative, and summative assessments embedded in an instructional sequence that is aligned with the curriculum objectives (NSTA 2001; O'Brien 2010 and 2011b).

Let's consider, then, five steps that teachers can use to better sequence science learning experiences and how these steps are analogous to the eight scientific and engineering (S&E) practices:

1. **Engage:** Both science and science teaching begin with asking questions (science) or defining problems (engineering) [S&E Practice 1] that need to be answered or solved about some observed phenomenon or system (e.g., "I wonder what, where, when, how, or

why … ?"). As such, intelligent K–5 CIA rests on the fact that like scientists and engineers, "[c]hildren are born investigators … [who] have surprisingly sophisticated ways of thinking about the real world, based in part on their direct experiences with the physical environment" (NRC 2012, p. 24).

The *Framework* (NRC 2012) frames the problem or challenge of K–12 science education as the progressive development of students' ability to "actively engage in scientific and engineering practices and apply crosscutting concepts to deepen their understanding of the core ideas" (pp. 8–9). In defining the latter, the *Framework* addresses two common deficiencies of conventional, textbook-based science curricula: (1) a mile-wide, inch-deep scope versus a more limited, developmentally appropriate set of 13 disciplinary core ideas in the physical, life, and Earth and space sciences; and (2) a failure to give sufficient attention to the recommendation that "classroom learning experiences in science need to connect with [students'] own interests and experiences" (NRC 2012, p. 28) and integrate engineering, technology, and applications of science (NRC 2012) to communicate relevance and salience.

Facilitating students' understanding of these three dimensions of science education requires teachers to recognize that every scientific concept, principle, or theory in their local district and state curriculum, was initially (and continues to serve as) an answer or solution to one or more real-world relevant questions or problems. Furthermore, "[i]n order for problems to be effective for supporting learning, they must be meaningful both from the standpoint of the discipline and from the standpoint of the learner … if students fail to see the problem as meaningful, there is little chance that they will engage in the range of productive science practices that result in student learning" (Michaels, Shouse, and Schweingruber 2008, pp. 127–128).

CIA units make scientific questions or problems meaningful to students by beginning with activities that engage them with one or more "FUNomena" to activate their natural curiosity, focus their attention, and generate a need-to-know motivation (O'Brien 2010). In contrast, conventional instruction begins with teacher and textbook-based, premature answers and solutions, rather than with rich, pregnant problems that have the potential to develop improved student understandings. Stating curricular objectives in the form of questions-to-be-answered leads teachers to consider a range of differentiated instructional strategies to engage students with the question(s) (Gregory and Hammerman 2008; O'Brien 2011b, Appendix A). Minds-on, discrepant event-type demonstrations; hands-on explorations with surprising outcomes (O'Brien 2010, 2011a, and 2011b); and multimedia-based invitations to inquiry and puzzle-like reading passages (e.g., Scholastic's *Magic School Bus* books and DVDs and Dan Sobel's *Encyclopedia Brown* short stories) all serve the purpose of raising questions. The questions that students generate from experiencing such FUNomena (with teacher prompting and assistance as needed) challenge them to activate relevant prior knowledge and to consider whether they might need a "cognitive upgrade." Student- and teacher-generated questions also provide a diagnostic assessment of students' prior knowledge that is analogous to a second, important aspect of science and engineering.

2. **Explore:** In framing researchable questions and planning and carrying out Exploratory investigations [S&E Practice 3], scientists

and engineers attempt to make explicit their prior conceptions and assumptions about the system being studied. Given the adaptive malleable nature and cortical plasticity of the human brain (see Chapter 8) and the integrated, systems-based complexity of nature, the fields of science and engineering develop and use models [S&E Practice 2] that are forever subject to reconstruction, renovation, and expansion. Both our individual and discipline-wide prior conceptions contain a mix of valid conceptual models that need to be recovered and built on; misconceptions that need to be uncovered and displaced (e.g., Driver et al. 1994; Duit 2009); and conceptual holes that need to be discovered and filled. While no individual or series of investigations can ever absolutely prove the validity of a given hypothesis, they can provide data that either support or contradict it. Investigations attempt to test and extend the limits of prior understanding (i.e., theory-driven challenges to our comfort zones) and are often motivated by puzzles, discrepant data, or anomalies (i.e., things that don't seem to work as we think they should). Thus problem finding is a desired goal and "miss-takes" are viewed as catalysts for further research. Scientists and engineers have a habit of mind that causes them to look critically and creatively at both unanswered questions and unquestioned answers about how things work. Their research is systematic, with intentionally designed and articulated plans for data collection and analysis in light of a given hypothesis. But their plans are also flexible and adaptive to new, unanticipated barriers or serendipitous occurrences (e.g., Pasteur's "chance favors the prepared mind").

Similarly, teachers bring a set of tacit beliefs and assumptions about the nature of science, teaching, and learning to their curricular planning. Documents such as the *Framework*, the *NGSS*, and this book are designed to challenge teachers to consider the unquestioned answers of their prior beliefs and practices. For instance, a "common but limited approach to sequencing investigations has been to teach the content related to the investigation first, and afterward do the investigation in order to validate the content" (Michaels, Shouse, and Schweingruber 2008, p. 129). Laboratory exercises that follow, rather than explorations that precede, teacher and textbook-based explanations have been cited as a primary reason for the failure of laboratory-based learning to achieve its full potential (NSTA 2007; Singer, Hilton, and Schweingruber 2006). Accordingly, the 5E Model intentionally places the Explore phase immediately after the Engage phase to continue the Engage phase's emphasis on "FUNomena first, facts follow/Wow and wonder before words" (O'Brien 2010, 2011a and b). However, it is important to note that typically "students are not sent off on an unguided exploration of a phenomenon or question, but are presented with intentionally sequenced and supported experiences framed in a sustained investigation of a central problem" (Michaels, Shouse, and Schweingruber 2008, p. 129). Simply having students participate hands-on does not guarantee minds-on cognitive processing.

Guided, inquiry-based investigations that ask students to p̲redict, o̲bserve, e̲xplain (POE) help ensure that student hands-on explorations are "FUNdaMENTAL" in two senses of the word (O'Brien 2011b, p. xviii). First, they involve both emotionally engaging play and minds-on, mentally engaging cognitive processing. Second, they develop students' facility with using funda-

mental science and engineering practices, cross-cutting concepts, and core ideas (i.e., the three dimensions of the *Framework*). During the Explore phase, the teacher plays the role of the "guide on the side" (rather than "sage on the stage"), helping small cooperative learning groups of two to four students carry out hands-on activities (and/or computer-based simulations) and record and organize their observations. Teachers also model and assess student lab skills (for safety skills, see Kwan and Texley 2002; NSTA 2007) and actively scaffold and monitor student learning with probing questions without providing premature answers. Explore phase investigations are analogous to a farmer who hoes a field to dislodge weeds and rocks (i.e., activates and challenges misconceptions) and provides fertilizer that prepares the soil (i.e., experiential grounding of conceptual precursors) to support new seeds (i.e., scientific concepts). Student explorations also lead the way to a third phase of the 5E Model and additional scientific and engineering practices.

3. **Explain:** Scientists and engineers regularly analyze and interpret data [S&E Practice 4] obtained from their investigations, often using mathematics and computational thinking [S&E Practice 5], and engage in argument from evidence [S&E Practice 7] to construct explanations (science) and design solutions (engineering) [S&E Practice 6].

Similarly, students who have gained empirical evidence in the Engage and Explore phases are challenged in the Explain phase to develop, discuss, and debate evidence-based explanations for the FUNomena they've experienced. During the Explain phase, teachers challenge the students to make sense of data gathered from the Engage and Explore phases. At least part of the story hidden in the data can be revealed by inviting students to make evidence-based arguments in which they propose and critique both complementary and competing claims with an eye to collaboratively constructing the best ideas (rather than winning an argument in the traditional combative sense of the term). Teachers can use modeling and explicit instruction to teach students strategies such as restating what a peer has said to check for understanding; asking clarifying, analytical questions that probe the connections between claims and the evidence gathered (and allowing sufficient wait time for thoughtful answers); and piggybacking off the ideas (and data) of peers to generate creative synthesis. Teaching students how to have productive, collegial conversations models what scientists and engineers do in the course of their work and what concerned citizens should do as participants in a democracy (see Bergman's discussion of Socratic seminars in Chapter 9).

During the Explain phase, teachers may introduce age-appropriate mathematics; individual and group readings and related writing activities from textbooks, tradebooks, science magazines, and so on; physical models and analogies that help make abstract ideas more concrete (Gilbert and Ireton 2003; Harrison and Coll 2008); and multimedia presentations and simulations that help bridge the gap between students' original ideas and scientifically valid conceptions. The key is that the teacher helps students construct sensible (i.e., sense-based and logical) explanations versus over-relying on either the teacher or textbook as the absolute source of the authoritative answer irrespective of the data collected. If the latter is necessary to save an activity, it is likely that the teacher used a poor-quality activity or introduced a concept beyond the specific grade band of the students (K–2, 3–5 or 6–8). Of course, after productive student discussions based on their data has gone as far as possible, teachers will

need to formally introduce scientific concepts, principles, and terminology. But even during the Explain phase, teachers' words and actions are less about indoctrinating or informing students about the right answer and more about instructing and inspiring them to individually and collectively reconstruct their prior ideas in light of new, compelling, empirical evidence. Learning science is a process of continual conceptual change based on evidence (NRC 2007).

Equity and excellence are achieved as an outcome of teaching students the importance of respecting different views; playing devil's advocates with their own ideas; and working collaboratively toward the best answers based on empirical evidence, logical argument, and skeptical review (NRC 1996). This ever-evolving narrative of discovery is very different from the rhetoric of conclusions approach to learning science. Inquiry-based, constructivist-oriented science instruction has the added benefit of accurately portraying how we know what we know in science. Thus students learn through direct experience about the nature of science as a way of knowing that is similar to yet distinct from other disciplines (NSTA 2000). More broadly, "exemplary science education can offer a rich context for developing many 21st-century skills, such as critical thinking, problem solving, and information literacy, especially when instruction addresses the nature of science and promotes use of science practices. These skills not only contribute to the development of a well-prepared workforce of the future but also give individuals life skills that help them succeed" (NSTA 2011, p. 1).

Students' ability to obtain, evaluate and communicate information [S&E Practice 8] and engage in collaborative discussions about claims, evidence, and reasoning provides formative assessment data. This data informs the teacher's subsequent actions that may require modification of her/his prior assumptions about students' abilities and how to best serve their learning needs. Learning-to-read/reading-to-learn; learning-to-write/writing-to-learn; and drawing and graphical organizer-based activities (e.g., concept mapping and graphs) are especially powerful when students have a need to construct explanations for FUNomena they've experienced in the two previous phases. True scientific literacy requires explicit attention to students' general English language arts (ELA) literacy skills, science-specific literacy demands, and the synergy between the two. (For more background on the science-literacy connection, see AAAS 2010; Douglas and Worth 2006; Saul 2004; Thier 2002; Wellington and Osborne 2001; and Chapter 10). Although the *Framework* tells us that "every science or engineering lesson is in part a language lesson" (NRC 2012, p. 76), learning to use the written and spoken language of science (including mathematics) is necessary but not sufficient for learning science. The real power in science (and the real test of learning) comes when students can use their revised conceptions to accurately predict, observe, and explain new FUNomena related to those they've experienced in the first three phases of the 5E Model. This application and extension occurs in the fourth phase of the 5E Model.

4. **Elaborate:** The generalizability and power of scientists' and engineers' refined explanations and solutions are put to the test when they are applied to related but seemingly new or different contexts. In contrast to popular misunderstanding about the nature of science, scientific theories are inherently parsimonious (NRC 2012, p. 48). That is, a limited set of broadly applicable crosscutting concepts (7) and disciplinary core ideas (13) are tightly interconnected to provide powerful explanatory and exploratory tools. Combined, these big ideas both account for the known and provide a compass or GPS to lead us into previously uncharted waters by triangulating from known points of reference.

Similarly, in the Elaboration phase, teachers introduce new activities in which students are challenged to apply and extend what they've learned in seemingly different but related contexts. Real-world applications and new challenges, problems, or tasks solidify and broaden students' understanding about the implications of what they've learned. These applications also provide another opportunity for students to experience the "Eureka, I got it!" effect. During this phase, all the lessons learned from the previous activities should be brought together and synergistically integrated into a sensible whole that is greater than the sum of the parts. The formative assessment aspect of the Elaboration phase provides additional cognitive scaffolding and lets both the students and teachers know whether the students are ready for the final summative evaluation phase.

5. **Evaluate:** The final test of the work of scientists and engineers occurs when they submit their results for publication in journals or their product designs for patent review, a process in which peers judge the quality and originality of the scientists' or engineers' work. Because of this public reporting requirement, future research and practice build on and improve the past. Subsequent research may fill in missing pieces of the puzzle, extend previous ideas into new applications (i.e., expand the field of view of the puzzle), or occasionally require reconceptualization of

what was thought to be true, which in light of additional testing, isn't so. In any case, science and engineering are progressive human endeavors because their practitioners build on prior work (i.e., Isaac Newton's "standing on the shoulders of giants") *and* are subject to subsequent revision (see, for example, Chapter 1).

Summative assessment of student work in the fifth and final Evaluation phase can take a variety of forms beyond conventional pencil-and-paper tests. Individuals and teams of students can demonstrate their learning via a wide variety of means such as constructing models, displays, graphic organizers, or artwork with linked oral presentations for their classmates; completing a related at-home experiment; and composing written reports to their teacher, letters to their parents or younger siblings or classes, or science songs or poems for posting on a real or virtual bulletin board (Harris Freedman 1999). Regardless of the means, formal summative evaluation should inspire student interest in further scientific investigations and inform their teachers of their readiness to move forward to new topics. Thus, the end of one 5E Teaching Cycle is really the launching pad to the next one, just as the published work of scientists and engineers serves as a catalyst for further research.

The *Framework* and *NGSS* call for the development of learning progressions (NRC 2007) that scaffold student understanding of scientific and engineering practices, crosscutting concepts, and disciplinary core ideas across the K–12 grades. The *Common Core State Standards* (*CCSS*), *English Language Arts* and *CCSS, Mathematics* (NGAC and CCSSO 2010; see also Chapter 2 of this book) further challenge teachers, curriculum developers, and textbook publishers to consider how to

articulate and integrate these core disciplines with elementary science (NSTA 2002). This kind of horizontally integrated (i.e., across subjects at the same grade level) and vertically articulated (i.e., within subjects across grade levels), spiral curricular scope and sequence goes beyond the time, abilities, and resources of individual teachers (and most school districts) to develop. However, as researchers continue to identify more precisely the learning progressions that relate to the three dimensions of the *Framework*, teachers and school districts will be challenged to field-test and improve these ongoing works-in-progress.

Effective science teaching requires teachers and schools to practice what they preach with respect to engaging in scientific and engineering practices to inform their teaching and take their practice to progressively higher levels. Effective teachers use lessons learned from the design, implementation, and evaluation of integrated curriculum-instruction-assessment (CIA) units to not only enrich their students' understanding but also to expand their own science content and pedagogical content knowledge (Cochran 1997). Furthermore, analogous to scientists, teachers exchange the wisdom of practice across professional collaborative networks that extend beyond the confines of their individual classrooms (or learning laboratories) and schools (NSTA 2010).

Learning to integrate the science and engineering practices and the 5E Teaching Cycle unit design is as easy as ABC. As a start, this book invites its teacher-readers to

1. **A**ctively align their individual science curriculum-instruction-assessment practices in light of the research-informed, "less is more" orientation of the *Next Generation Science Standards* (*NGSS*) (i.e., explore a reduced number of more central, age-appropriate

concepts in greater depth). Instead of waiting for your district to purchase the "next generation" of science textbooks, you can use the sample 5E teaching cycle units in Chapters 5–7 as models for how to sequence consecutive science lessons (obtained from a variety of book and internet sources) into constructivist mini-units;

2. **B**uild better-coordinated science programs with their districts' fellow K–5 teachers (and, at the upper elementary level, their grades 6–8 colleagues) to achieve the developmentally appropriate learning progressions called for by the *NGSS*. Talented teachers can accomplish this despite outdated science textbooks, tests, and technologies, but it will require redistributing some topics across the grades and paring down the number of topics taught; and

3. Creatively collaborate with science teaching colleagues within and beyond their school, district, and state. Most state-level science teaching professional associations coordinate with geographically distributed sections within their state and with the National Science Teachers Association (NSTA). Being a member of a professional network provides ongoing opportunities to exchange wonderful ideas and best practices for teaching children science and to become a part of an epidemic of excellence in elementary science education! Together, an interdependent *we* can synergistically achieve more than an isolated, independent *me*. Remember, networks make it "E (z)" to produce a higher quantity and quality of "net work" that reflects the FUNdaMENTAL nature of science.

References

American Association for the Advancement of Science (AAAS). 2010. Science, language, and literacy. *Science* 328 (5977): 393–532.

Achieve Inc. 2013. *Next generation science standards. www.nextgenscience.org*

Banilower, R., K. Cohen, J. Pasley, and I. Weis. 2010. *Effective science instruction: What does research tell us?* 2nd ed. Portsmouth, NH: RMC Research Corp., Center on Instruction. *www.centeroninstruction.org/ effective-science-instruction-what-does-research- tell-us---second-edition.*

Bybee, R. W., ed. 2002. *Learning science and the science of learning*. Arlington, VA: NSTA Press and Science Educators' Essay Collection.

Bybee, R. W., J. A. Taylor, A. Gardner, P. Van Scotter, J. Carlson Powell, A. Westbrook, and N. Landes. 2006. *BSCS 5E Instructional Model: Origins and effectiveness*. Colorado Springs, CO: Biological Sciences Curriculum Study (BSCS). *www.bscs. org/clinical-study-bscs-5es*

Cochran, K. F. 1997. Pedagogical content knowledge: Teacher's integration of subject matter, pedagogy, students, and learning environments. Brief. *Research Matters to the Science Teacher.* No. 9702. National Association in Research in Science Teaching. *www.narst.org/publications/ research/pck.cfm*

Douglas, R., and K. Worth, eds. 2006. *Linking science and literacy in the K–8 classroom*. Arlington, VA: NSTA Press.

Driver, R., A. Squires, P. Rushworth, and V. Wood-Robinson. 1994. *Making sense of secondary science: Research into children's ideas*. New York: Routledge.

Duit, R. 2009. Bibliography "STCSE" (Students' and Teachers' Conceptions and Science Education). *www.ipn.uni-kiel.de/aktuell/stcse/stcse.html.*

Friedl, A. E., and T. Yourst Koontz. 2004. *Teaching science to children: Inquiry approach.* 6th ed. Boston, MA: McGraw-Hill.

Gilbert, S. W., and S. W. Ireton. 2003. *Understanding models in Earth and space science.* Arlington, VA: NSTA Press.

Gregory, G. H., and E. Hammerman. 2008. *Differentiated instructional strategies for science, grades K–8.* Thousand Oaks, CA: Corwin.

Harris Freedman, R. L. 1999. Science and writing connections. White Plains, NY: Dale Seymour.

Harrison, A. G., and R. K. Coll, eds. 2008. *Using analogies in middle and secondary science classrooms: The FAR guide—An interesting way to teach with analogies.* Thousand Oaks, CA: Corwin.

Kwan, T., and J. Texley. 2002. *Exploring safely: A guide for elementary teachers.* Arlington, VA: NSTA Press.

Martin, D. J. 2011. *Elementary science methods: A constructivist approach.* 6th ed. Belmont, CA: Wadsworth.

Martin, R., C. Sexton, T. Franklin, and J. Gerlovich. 2005. *Teaching science for all children: An inquiry approach* (with "video explorations" video workshop CD-ROM). 4th ed. Boston, MA: Allyn and Bacon.

Michaels, S., A. W. Shouse, and H. A. Schweingruber. 2008. *Ready, set, science! Putting research to work in K–8 science classrooms.* Washington, DC: National Academies Press.

Mintzes, J. J., J. H. Wandersee, and J. D. Novak, eds. 1998. *Teaching science for understanding: A human constructivist view.* New York: Academic Press.

National Governors Association Center for Best Practices (NGAC) and the Council of Chief State School Officers (CCSSO). 2010. *Common core state standards (English language arts and mathematics standards).* Washington, DC: NGA and CCSSO.

National Research Council (NRC). 1996. *National science education standards.* Washington, DC: National Academies Press.

National Research Council (NRC). 2007. *Taking science to school: Learning and teaching science in grades K–8.* Washington, DC: National Academies Press.

National Research Council (NRC). 2012. *A framework for K–12 science education: Practices, crosscutting concepts, and core ideas.* Washington, DC: National Academies Press.

O' Brien, T. 2010. *Brain-powered science: Teaching and learning with discrepant events.* Arlington, VA: NSTA Press.

O'Brien, T. 2011a. *Even more brain-powered science: Teaching and learning with discrepant events.* Arlington, VA: NSTA Press.

O' Brien, T. 2011b. *More brain-powered science: Teaching and learning with discrepant events.* Arlington, VA: NSTA Press.

Saul, E. W., ed. 2004. *Crossing borders in literacy and science instruction: Perspectives on theory and practice.* Newark, DE: International Reading Association and Arlington, VA: NSTA Press.

Singer, S. R., M. L. Hilton, and H. A. Schweingruber. 2006. *America's lab report: Investigations in high school science.* Washington, DC: National Academies Press.

Thier, M. 2002. *The new science literacy: Using language skills to help students learn science.* Portsmouth, NH: Heinemann.

Wellington, J., and J. Osborne. 2001. *Language and literacy in science education.* Philadelphia: Open University Press.

Resources From the National Science Teachers Association

NSTA Position Statements

2000. Nature of science:
www.nsta.org/about/positions/natureofscience.aspx

2001. Assessment:
www.nsta.org/about/positions/assessment.aspx

2002. Elementary school science:
www.nsta.org/about/positions/elementary.aspx

2004*:* Scientific inquiry:
www.nsta.org/about/positions/inquiry.aspx

2007. The integral role of laboratory investigations in science instruction:
www.nsta.org/about/positions/laboratory.aspx

2007. Liability of science educators for laboratory safety: *www.nsta.org/about/positions/liability. aspx*

2010. Principles of professionalism for science educators:
www.nsta.org/about/positions/professionalism.aspx

2011. Quality science education and 21st century skills:
www.nsta.org/about/positions/21stcentury.aspx

Brain-Powered Science
www.nsta.org/publications/press/brainpowered. aspx. See also the extensive list of internet-based resources at *www.nsta.org/publications/press/ extras.*

IV

THE *NEXT GENERATION* SCIENCE STANDARDS IN THE CLASSROOM

SAMPLE 5E MINI-UNITS FOR GRADES K–5

CHAPTER 5

Physical Sciences

INTRODUCTION

CONNECTIONS

Patricia B. Molloy

Principal, Jackson Avenue School (Mineola, New York)

It is a very exciting time to be involved in science education in elementary schools as we promote and implement the *Next Generation Science Standards* (*NGSS*) from kindergarten to grade 12. The *NGSS* support the critical need to teach and integrate science, technology, engineering, and math (STEM) as soon as a child begins formal schooling. As educators, we have learned that students learn best when they are able to make meaningful connections and understand the interrelations among the topics that they are learning. Connecting classroom teaching to children's interests and day-to-day lives facilitates deep and memorable learning.

Children are born fascinated with the world around them. They immediately begin using their senses to investigate their world: experimenting, building, tinkering, and disassembling to learn the function of an object, how it is made, and what happens if. … They ask questions and soon begin to define problems and search for solutions. How many times have we watched a child making a paper airplane increase the distance and duration of the plane's flight by adjusting the wings and tail and redistributing the plane's weight? Students who have built other structures at home or in school with Legos, craft sticks, tissues, paper clips, or blocks have probably followed the three core ideas of engineering design (i.e., define and delimit an engineering problem, develop possible solutions, optimize the design solution), without being cognizant of the sophistication and organization of their actions and processes. Through *NGSS*, our students will now learn the vocabulary associated with their engineering experiences.

As educators, we must nurture and develop children's innate skills of curiosity, exploration, observation, open-mindedness, creativity, and problem solving. The movement toward integrating science, technology, engineering, and math, while recognizing the natural connections to social studies and literacy, is exhilarating and enriching for both students and educators alike.

Part IV provides sample 5E teaching cycle mini-units that integrate the three dimensions of *A Framework for K–12 Science Education* and the *NGSS* with a teaching cycle that progressively invites students to Engage, Explore, Explain, Elaborate, Evaluate. The content of the units is drawn from the core disciplinary ideas (physical sciences, life sciences, and Earth and space sciences). Children ask questions and use scientific and engineering practices as they seek answers to those questions. And through crosscutting concepts that bridge many fields of science, children will begin to see the relationships among them.

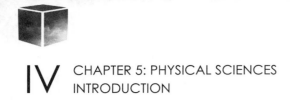
Critically examine these sample 5E mini-units as models to help you learn how to develop more constructivist, multiday lesson sequences—that is, to design mini-units in which students' progressive interactions with phenomena and discovery of scientific practices and principles are center stage. Designing and improving mini-units places teachers in roles that are analogous to scientists and engineers. It will also afford you the opportunity to learn with and from your students.

A. What's All the Noise About?

THE SCIENCE OF SOUND

Helen Pashley, PhD
Consultant
Putnam/Northern Westchester Board of Cooperative Educational Services (BOCES)

Recommended Level

Grade 1

Topic Focus

Physical Science

Disciplinary Core Idea

PS4: Waves and their application in technologies for information transfer

Time Frame

Engage Phase
30 minutes (Activity 1)

Explore Phase
90 minutes (Activity 2)

Explain Phase
60 minutes (Activity 3)

Elaborate Phase
60–90 minutes (Activity 4A and/or 4B)

Evaluate Phase
30–90 minutes (Activity 5A and/or 5B)

Objectives

As a result of these experiences, students will be able to

- explore the connections between sound, vibration, and matter;

- collect and communicate evidence that sound causes vibrations, and vibrations cause sound in a material medium (solid, liquid, or gas);

- apply understanding of these concepts to explain otherwise discrepant events;

- manipulate materials to change the pitch and volume of sound; and

- demonstrate, through solving an engineering problem, that sound waves can convey information over a distance and be muffled by use of insulating materials.

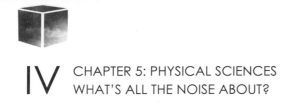
TABLE 5A.1. CORRELATION TO THE *NEXT GENERATION SCIENCE STANDARDS*

1. Waves: Light and sound[1]		
1-PS4-1. Plan and conduct investigations to provide evidence that vibrating materials can make sound and that sound can make materials vibrate.		
1-PS4-4. Use tools and materials to design and build a device that uses light or sound to solve the problem of communicating over a distance.[1]		

Scientific and Engineering Practices (Dimension 1)	Disciplinary Core Ideas (Dimension 3)	Crosscutting Concepts (Dimension 2)
1. Asking questions (for science) and defining problems (for engineering)	PS4: Waves and their applications in technologies for information transfer	1. Patterns
2. Developing and using models	PS4.A: Wave properties * Sound can make matter vibrate, and vibrating matter can make sound.	2. Cause and effect: Mechanism and explanation
3. Planning and carrying out investigations	PS4.C: Information technologies and instrumentation * People use a variety of devices to communicate (send and receive information) over long distances.	
4. Analyzing and interpreting data		

[1] This mini-unit does not address all portions of the standard as written; the relevant elements are underlined.

Note: PS = Physical sciences; ETS = Engineering, technology, and applications of science

Continued

Table 5A.1. (continued)

Scientific and Engineering Practices (Dimension 1)	Disciplinary Core Ideas (Dimension 3)	Crosscutting Concepts (Dimension 2)
6. Constructing explanations (for science) and designing solutions (for engineering)	ETS1: Engineering design ETS1.A: Defining and delimiting an engineering problem ETS1.B: Developing possible solutions	6. Structure and function
7. Engaging in argument from evidence		
8. Obtaining, evaluating, and communicating information		

Common Core State Standards Connections (representative links)

***English Language Arts* –**

Reading: Foundational Skills: Fluency

RF.1.4. Read (grade-level) text with sufficient accuracy and fluency to support comprehension

Writing: Text Types and Purposes

W.1.1. Write opinion pieces in which they introduce the topic or name the book they are writing about, state an opinion, supply a reason for the opinion, and provide some sense of closure.

W.1.2. Write informative/explanatory texts in which they name a topic, supply some facts about the topic, and provide some sense of closure.

Speaking and Listening: Comprehension and Collaboration

SL.1.1. Participate in collaborative conversations with diverse partners about grade 1 topics and texts with peers and adults in small and larger groups.

Mathematics—*This mini-unit does not* include any first-grade mathematics content standards, but it does align with the mathematical practices:

1. Make sense of problems and persevere in solving them.

3. Construct viable arguments and critique the reasoning of others.

Engage Phase

Students will observe several discrepant event demonstrations that will intrigue and fascinate them. They will use science notebooks to record their observations, questions, and ideas. These entries will act as a diagnostic assessment of students' prior knowledge and skills and will likely include some misconceptions that can be addressed later as the mini-unit unfolds.

Materials

- CD player, radio, or other portable speaker

- Large coffee can

- Piece of thin, black, plastic garbage bag (or cut off and use the end of a large dark colored balloon)

- 2 g salt

- Rubber band large enough to fit around the can

- One (or more) of the following demonstrations:

    ◆ Thunder drum (available from Educational Innovations: *www.teachersource. com*, catalog number TD-150 for $14.95)

    ◆ Singing wine glass: Rub the rim of a cheap wine glass half-filled with tap water. For more detailed descriptions of how to make a wine glass sing, the scientific explanation, a simple song, and an invention by Ben Franklin see:

        • *http://recipes.howstuffworks.com/ food-facts/question603.htm www. ccmr.cornell.edu/education/ask/index. html?quid=1143*

        • *www.youtube.com/ watch?v=7mKsV4fROtU* (*Twinkle, Twinkle, Little Star*)

        • *www.glassarmonica.com* (Franklin's Magical Musical Invention)

    ◆ Bullroarer: For instructions see:

        • *www.youtube.com/ watch?v=b9Z-zEXEb6o*

        • *www.youtube.com/watch?v=b9Z-zEXEb6o* (string, rubber band, and plastic spoon version)

Preparation

1. If you need background information about this topic, it is suggested you read Bill Robertson's *Sound: Stop Faking It—Finally Understand Science So You Can Teach It* (see Resource). You may also wish to consult online resources before beginning the unit.

2. Place the piece of black plastic garbage bag, or balloon over the open end of the coffee can. **Safety note:** Take care to avoid being cut by the sharp inside edge. Secure with the rubber band. Adjust the membrane so it is tightly stretched across the top. Select a station (talk radio works the best) or an audio book on CD. Try the activity yourself.

3. Practice using the thunder drum or rubbing a clean damp finger (avoid hand lotion) around the rim of the wineglass to make it sing, and/ or construct the bullroarer.

Activity 1

1. You may wish to begin the unit with students contributing to a KWL (Know-Want to know-Learned) chart. If so, complete the Know column.

2. Tell students to observe your two (or three) demonstrations very carefully, looking for any similarities or patterns or common causes that connect the various sound effects.

3. Sprinkle a small pinch of salt crystals onto the plastic bag or balloon membrane and have the students gather around you (or use a document camera so all students can simultaneously have a close-up view). As a challenge, ask students to brainstorm ways that they can make the salt crystals move without directly touching the salt. Encourage discussion of a wide variety of possibilities. Someone will probably suggest tapping the stretched plastic or rubber membrane. Do this, so the students can see the salt dance. Then ask them to suggest ways they can make the salt move without directly touching the salt or the membrane. Provide time for discussion of their ideas. Now sprinkle more salt onto the membrane, so individual grains are spread across the surface. Switch on the radio, CD player, or other sound source. Move the speaker close to the top of the can without touching it. Adjust the volume until the salt jumps, and then turn it up louder. The salt should jump higher and may bounce off the membrane. (**Teacher note:**This shows how invisible sound waves can vibrate the membrane that in turn causes the salt crystals to move; do not prematurely give this answer to students but rather elicit their ideas.)

4. Now show students a second demonstration. If using the thunder drum, hold it while shaking it back and forth so the spring wiggles. It will produce a loud, rolling sound, like thunder. Alternatively, you can demonstrate the singing wine glass and/or spin the bullroarer. Any of these demonstrations will activate students' attention and catalyze their questions about sound. **Safety note:** Ensure that students are sitting several arm-lengths away from the spinning end of the bullroarer and that the wine glass does not contain any cracks or a rough rim.

FIGURE 5A.1 THUNDER DRUM

5. Pose the question, "What did you see and hear in each case?" Answers will vary. Ask students, "What are some questions you would like to ask about the demonstrations?" If you are using the KWL chart, complete the Want to know column. Answers will vary but may include *How are the sounds made? Why did the salt move? How did the salt move if the radio wasn't touching it? Why did it move more when the sound was louder?* Have students write in their science notebooks to respond to the following prompt.

> _____ was absent today. Wow, they really missed something interesting. Draw or write to tell them all you observed. Can you suggest some reasons why this happened?

Teacher note: Consider challenging students to design and draw another invention that could make salt crystals jump on the membrane on the tin can that we used in class. This optional challenge will use the process of design engineering to embellish the lesson.

6. Teachers may use a word bank generated by class brainstorming to scaffold support for those students who need it. Remind students to write some questions that they would like to ask and to explain what they think happened.

7. Invite students to pair and share what they wrote or invented. Students should then add three things that they learned below a line of learning in their notebooks. This is a colored line drawn on a page to differentiate the original work of the student and ideas that they may learn from a partner, the teacher, books, or the internet. In this case, students should start their sentences with [Student's name] said … .

8. Collect the notebooks and use them as a formative assessment for the next lesson. Pay particular attention to references to sound, movement of the salt, spring, water in the glass, or the string and spoon/paint stirrer of the bullroarer, vibration, and shaking. You should make a note of these and refer to them in the class discussion at the start of the next lesson.

Explore Phase

Students will review the questions they wish to answer and then visit a series of stations to explore the connections between sound, matter, and vibration. The goal is that students will come to see the commonalities (or cause-effect patterns) that connect all the different examples of sound generation.

Materials

- Labels for stations 1–8
- Station-specific procedure guides inserted in page protectors

Station 1: Tuning Forks

- Two tuning forks with long tines (These can be borrowed from the music department, or purchased from either a music or science supply store. Ideally, they should be different sizes or pitches. **Note:** the larger, more massive tuning fork will have a lower pitch.)
- Two aluminum pie plates

Station 2: Ruler Rattling

- Two 30 cm solid wooden rulers

Station 3: Rubber Band Bass

- Two empty, rigid, plastic salad containers approximately 20 cm × 15 cm × 10 cm
- A selection of rubber bands of different thicknesses stretched around the containers

Station 4: Bottle Band Basics

- Plastic water bottle (500 ml) filled with play sand with the lid taped on
- Plastic water bottle (500 ml) filled with tap water with the lid taped on
- Plastic water bottle (500 ml) empty (actually filled with air) with the lid taped on

Station 5: Reading Research

- Four copies of Wendy Pfeffer and Holly Keller's *Sounds All Around* (see Resources). If available and appropriate, the classroom science textbook may be used as a supplement to or substitute for this trade book.

Station 6: Sound Simulations

- Two to four computers with internet access, showing the following website

◆ Sound Interactive: *Changing Sounds Simulation www.bbc.co.uk/schools/science-clips/ages/9_10/changing_sounds.shtml*

This simulation allows students to explore how to change loudness and pitch on a guitar, drum, water- or air-filled bottle, and recorders and includes an interactive 10-item quiz. Even though this website is listed as being for 9- to 10-year-olds (grades 4–5), there is a read-aloud feature that makes it suitable for first graders. Students should be reminded to click on the speaker on the top left of the screen. All subsequent written instructions and choices (on the quiz) will be read to them anytime they click on one of the speakers.

Station 7: Talkie Tapes

• Four talking cups: Available from *www.teachersource.com* TC-150 $16.95 for 12 tapes; *www.arborsci.com/talkie-tapes-class-set-of-30-tapes* PT-7320 $16 for 30 tapes; or *www.talkietapes.com* $10 for 25 tapes in a variety of spoken messages

If possible, purchase talkie tapes with two different recorded messages. If you do not have the money to purchase official talkie tapes, for a cheap alternative use standard hardware store plastic tie strips with uniformly spaced, equal height ridges. The latter will generate sounds (but not spoken words) that will be amplified by the cups.

Station 8: Music Making

• A selection of elementary musical instruments such as maracas, tambourines, shakers, and so on or toys that make sounds

Preparation

1. Gather the materials needed, and copy the student instructions (i.e., the procedure guides) for each station. Each procedure guide directs the students in their discoveries and consists of the procedures to be followed and guiding questions and should be placed in page protectors and taped to the table at each station. Assign students to groups of three to four.

Activity 2

1. Bring the class together to share their observations from the previous Engage phase lesson. Consider using a three-column table to record the discussion with headings:

   ◆ What did you observe (feel, see, or hear)?

   ◆ How might you explain this (i.e., constructing explanations)?

   ◆ Why do you think your explanation is a good one (i.e., engaging in argument from evidence)?

2. Students should refer to the notations in their notebooks.

3. Summarize the explanations that the students have given. For example, "Some of you thought that the salt was 'jumping' because the garbage bag (or balloon) is like a trampoline." Model how to turn this into a question, "How could we find out what was making it bounce or vibrate?"

4. Explain that they will be visiting eight stations for six minutes each. At each one, they will be using hands-on activities to explore sound, vibrations, and how they affect objects. As they visit the stations, they will start to find

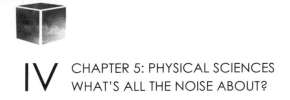
the answers to some of their questions. They will have a procedure guide at each station to direct their discoveries, but teacher modeling may be necessary as well.

5. Remind students to collect and record information in order to answer the following key guiding questions:

- ◆ What do you have to do to materials to create sound (i.e., what common causes lead to the effect of sound)?

- ◆ Can sound go through matter (solids, liquids, and gases)?

- ◆ What happens to matter when it interacts with sound?

6. Not all the stations involve manipulating materials. This is a good opportunity to emphasize the relationship between science, reading, and research. Stations 5 and 6 have reading and interactive web-based activities. During the time that students are investigating, it is important to facilitate their learning by circulating between stations with appropriate questioning. Examples might be, "What happened there? What did you have to do to create the sound? What is vibrating? How is sound being produced? Is the sound loud or soft? Is it high or low pitched? Can you find some ways to change the sound?" As you are talking to student groups, ask probing questions to access developing understanding. Pay particular attention to and make a note of misconceptions that students may have (e.g., students may see each case of sound production as unique and context-specific without a common, underlying pattern of vibrations of matter that can be seen, felt and/or heard depending on their magnitude). Misconceptions and conceptual holes will be addressed in the following session (Explain phase). During the Explore phase, it is important to avoid giving students premature answers but instead to let them play with questions the activities evoke.

Station Procedure Guides

Station 1: Tuning Forks

- Hold the handle of a tuning fork. Hit the tuning fork *gently* against the side of the table.

- Pick up a pie plate. Touch the two ends of the tuning fork *gently* against the edge of the pie plate.

- Let everyone else try it, too.

- Write down what you hear and feel. (**Teacher note:** Students should feel the vibration of the pie plate and hear a distinct buzzing sound.)

- Do the two different-size tuning forks sound the same or different?

- What are the tuning forks doing that causes a sound to be produced?

Station 2: Ruler Rattling

- You need two people to try this activity.

- One person should hold the ruler down on the table. Let some of the ruler stick out over the edge of the table. The other person should pluck the ruler with a fingertip. **Safety note:** The ruler should not be bent or struck with whole hand as it will not vibrate as well and will likely break.

- Repeat this activity, but trade places with your partner.

- Find out how you can change the sound the ruler makes. Record your observations.

(**Teacher note:** Students can change the length of ruler hanging over the edge of the table and see how much is vibrating. The more matter that is vibrating, the lower the pitch of the sound produced.)

- Make sure you draw a diagram to show what you did. Explain how you changed the sound.

Station 3: Rubber Band Bass

- **Safety note:** Some students want to remove the rubber bands and use them as projectiles; supervision is always necessary with hands-on science.

- Pluck the different rubber bands that are stretched across the container.

- Observe the rubber bands carefully. Listen to the sounds they make.

- Write or draw what you see happening to the bands when you pluck them. (**Teacher note:** When students pluck the bands they move back and forth, they vibrate. When the vibration stops so does the sound.)

- What are some things you notice about the sounds the rubber bands make? (**Teacher note:** Thinner, lower-mass bands and bands that are stretched more tightly have a higher pitch.)

Station 4: Bottle Band Basics

- Hold a bottle up to your ear. Tap on the side gently with your fingernail or a pencil. (See Figure 5A.2.)

- Write down the number of the bottle and what you hear. (**Teacher note:** Students should hear a tapping sound with all three bottles.)

FIGURE 5A.2. BOTTLE BAND BASICS

- Try the other two bottles.

- What were some differences you noticed in the sounds? (**Teacher note:** Assuming that students were tapping the same way each time, the bottle containing the sand should sound loudest in your ear, the bottle with the water in it next loudest, and the bottle containing air should be the least loud.)

Station 5: Reading Research

- Read pages 8–10 in *Sounds All Around* (and/or the classroom science textbook).

- Answer these questions in your notebook.

- What does the word *vibrating* mean? (**Teacher note:** Answers may be *moving back and forth* or *shaking very fast*)

- Where are your vocal cords? (**Teacher note:** Answer will be *in your throat*)

- Explain how you can hear your friend singing. (**Teacher note:** Answer may be *Your* *friend's vocal cords vibrate when they sing and make the air vibrate, too. The vibrations in the air travel to your ears and make the eardrum and small bones in your ears vibrate. Your brain interprets this as singing.*)

Station 6: Sound Simulations

- Write down the name of the interactive you are doing first: loudness or pitch.

- What are two things you learned from this interactive? (**Teacher note:** Answers may include *Loudness—big vibrations make loud sounds; sounds are louder when you are close to what is making them; amplitude tells you how big or loud a sound wave is; blowing hard into a recorder makes a loud sound; loud sounds can hurt your ears; you can protect your ears with earplugs. Pitch—frequency tells us how fast something is vibrating; fast vibrations make high pitched sounds; you can show frequency on a graph; the holes in a recorder help you change the pitch; a long air column gives a low note; a short air column a high note; guitar strings vibrate to make sound; long strings make a low sound; short strings make a high sound.*)

Station 7: Talkie Tapes

- Pick up a cup. Hold it in one hand.

- With the other hand, hold the tape between your thumb and finger next to the cup. Squeeze your thumb and finger together, and pull them along the tape.

- Draw a diagram to show what you did. In your notebook, record what you observed and what you heard. (**Teacher note:** The tape is specially made to have carefully spaced grooves along its sides. Vibrations are produced when students pull the tape

between their thumbnails and index fingers, which will reproduce a recorded message that is amplified by the cup.)

Station 8: Music Making

- Choose an instrument.

- Use it to make a sound.

- Optional: Explore how you can change the pitch of the sound.

- Record answers to the following questions for each instrument you used.

  - What do you have to do to make the sound? (**Teacher note:** Answers may be *Make something vibrate by plucking, shaking, hitting the instrument, and so on.*)

  - What evidence (feeling, seeing, or hearing) do you have that something is moving back and forth (or vibrating)?

  - What is moving back and forth (or vibrating) to make the sound? (**Teacher note:** Answers will depend on instrument; students will probably not recognize that in some wind instruments, it maybe the air itself that is directly vibrating.)

  - What can you do with the instrument to make a higher (or lower) pitch sound?

Once students have completed each station, you may let them pair and share with a few others. They should compare what they discovered at each station, adding any information they wish to their notebooks, with attribution, under a line of learning.

Explain Phase

Students will have the opportunity to refine their understanding of the disciplinary core ideas and crosscutting concepts in this mini-unit via interactive, scaffolded classroom conversation, a video clip (that allows student to see sound waves) and teacher-led, model-based demonstrations.

Materials

- Slinky toy

- Two sets of dominoes

- Tennis ball

- Internet or video clip: *Magic School Bus: In the Haunted House* (Session 1, Episode 8): *http://vimeo.com/38388572 or*

- Scholastic's *Complete Magic School Bus* series (8DVD/52 episodes/26 hrs/$79.95): *www.scholastic.com/magicschoolbus/tv/index.htm*

Preparation

1. Gather the materials needed. Set up the dominoes on a table away from students prior to lesson as follows.

2. Line up dominoes in a series of straight lines radiating out from a central open circle area like the spokes of a wheel.

FIGURE 5A.3. DOMINO MODEL OF SOUND TRANSMISSION

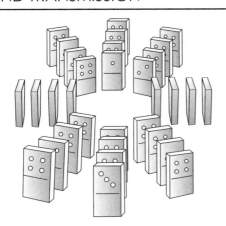

Activity 3

1. Review each station the students visited in the previous lesson. Ask them in what ways all the stations were the same. (**Teacher note:** They all were about sound, vibration, and how matter interacts with sound.) Collect their thoughts as to how sounds are created. What evidence do they have that all sounds are created by vibrations of matter? Encourage students to refer to their science notebooks and to question one another directly. Come to a consensus that sounds make vibrations and vibrations make sounds (a reciprocal cause and effect pattern). Sound waves can travel through solids, liquids, and gases. As sound travels through the air, we receive (hear) the sounds in our ears; sometimes (but not always) we can feel or see vibrations in solids that result in sound. Your students may need to provide evidence that air is real by capturing it in plastic bags and pressing their hands against it, demonstrating that air takes up space.

2. Explain that you will be using two different models that will help them understand how vibrations (sound waves) travel as compression waves through solids, liquids, or gases as they spread out from a source.

   a. Slinky Model: Create a compression (or longitudinal) wave in a Slinky stretched out along the floor (with one student holding one end and the teacher the other) by pushing rapidly in on one end of the Slinky to create a pulse that can be seen to travel down the length of the stretched spring. Alternatively, suspend a Slinky in air by tying pieces of string about every 18 inches of the stretched Slinky and have a student posted at each string to hold the

Slinky in a straight line. Once again, a compression wave can be created by pushing rapidly on one end of the Slinky. **Teacher note:** A compression wave is different than the more familiar transverse wave (see the Slinky Home Page at *http://wiki.cs.messiah. edu/~bbarrett/index.html*).

FIGURE 5A.4. A SLINKY MODEL OF SOUND TRANSMISSION

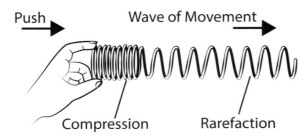

Push → Wave of Movement →

Compression   Rarefaction

b. Dominoes Model: Tell the students that in this model, they will see how sound waves can spread out from a source of sound in all directions whether it is through a solid, liquid, or gas. Show them the dominos set up on the table. Tell them that this is a model of how sound waves spread out from the source of the sound. Drop a tennis ball in the middle of the open area. The dominoes should fall and create a radial wave pattern like ripples in a pond. (This rippling effect can also be demonstrated in a shallow, transparent bowl of water placed on an overhead projector or under a document camera.) Have students add three more things that they learned about sound from the demonstrations in their notebooks.

Teacher note: In using these two models, emphasize the macroscopic, visual analogy of sound as a compression wave; do

not attempt to lead students to consider molecular level explanations.

3. Finally, show students a very short animation of how sound waves travel through the air in *The Magic School Bus: In the Haunted House* episode: *http://vimeo.com/38388572*. The time of the section that you want to show is from 13:35 minutes to 16:54 minutes.

a. Assist students in coming up with working definitions for the key vocabulary words (*sound, vibration, pitch, volume,* and *wave*), and add them to their glossary at the end of their science notebooks.

b. Ask students to tag three places in their notebooks, using colored page turners, where they have used scientific and engineering practices (see the list provided on the *NGSS* Correlation Chart). It is assumed that teachers will have these posted in their classroom and that students' attention will be directed to them throughout the yearlong science curriculum.

As they write the appropriate numbers on the page turners, students should discover that they have used seven of the eight practices. (**Teacher note:** all except for using mathematics and computational thinking). Also point out that scientists (and observant first graders) look for patterns in nature that help explain causes and effects. In the case of their experiences in this unit, it is important to note that "sound can make matter vibrate and vibrating matter can make sound" [*NGSS* PS4.A].

Elaborate Phase

The goals of this lesson are to reinforce the concept that sound can travel through a solid medium

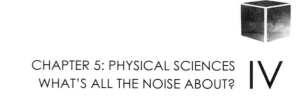

(as well as through air) and to allow students to develop solutions to one of two engineering design problems. The first engineering design problem demonstrates one example of how "people use a variety of devices to communicate (send and receive information) over long distances" [*NGSS*, PS4.C]. The following websites offer additional ideas for designing, tin can–type telephones:

- HowStuffWorks *http://science.howstuffworks.com/question410.htm* and

- Dallas Symphony Orchestra *www.dsokids.com/athome/instruments/telephone.aspx*.

Teacher note: After Activity 4A is completed, be sure to address the possible misconception that students might develop that equate their tin can telephones and how sound waves are converted into electricity and transmitted over wires in conventional telephones. The second engineering design problem (4B) challenges students to figure out how to muffle sound. In introducing and debriefing these two activities, briefly introduce students to the idea of engineers as applied scientists who design technologies (i.e., products or processes) to meet human needs or solve human problems.

Materials (for Activity 4A Tin Can Telephones)

For the class:

- Soup cans, frozen juice cans, plastic yogurt or sour cream containers, Styrofoam cups, and plastic and paper cups of various sizes. **Safety note:** Make sure that containers are clean and edges are not sharp. Tape the edges, if necessary (i.e., if metal cans are used). Alternatively, you may wish to use plastic containers in lieu of the classic tin can telephone.

- Hammer and nail to make holes in the containers as needed.

- Fishing line, dental floss, nylon twine, kite string, yarn, and so on.

For pairs of students:

- Two waxed paper cups

- One piece of string (approximately 1 m long)

- Two paper clips, toothpicks, or small steel washers (No. 10, 12 mm diameter)

Activity 4A Tin Can Telephones

1. Tell the students that in this unit we have found out that sound is vibration, and sound can travel through solid objects. They explored an example of this at Station 7. Challenge students to think of a way in which they could use the materials provided to communicate a spoken message across the classroom without shouting. How could they use the cups? What could they do with the string? Tell students that engineers solve problems like this. They design something to solve a problem, experiment, and then refine their design to make it better. You may need to brainstorm with the students how to set up the first prototype. They should be able to explain how it works. As you talk, sound waves cause the bottom of the first cup to vibrate. These vibrations spread to the string and along it. The string causes the bottom of the second cup to vibrate together with the air inside the cup. This transmits the sound to your partner's ear.

2. Have students make a basic telephone and try it out. The string will probably come through the hole in the bottom of the cup very easily,

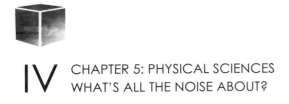

so an early modification would be to tie the string to a paper clip or washer. A single taut string stretched between two such cups is the simplest model for a two-way conversation between two students at a distance.

3. Have students record their findings in their science notebooks (see assessment below) as they go along. Remind students that scientists always record their design plans, tests, and results so that they remember exactly what they did and what changes they made. That way when they write up a paper, patent an invention, or when someone else wants to repeat the experiment, he or she knows how it was done.

4. Next have students select their own materials from those available to the class. Remember they have to get the message across the classroom so they will need to use a longer string or filament. How could they test to see if the new telephone was better? They would have to compare it to the original. What happens when you whisper? What happens if you touch the string when talking? Why? Can you add another telephone to the system to create a conference call? You might test the best telephone by giving one member of each pair a simple message to read on the phone. They should whisper. Their partner then repeats the message that they heard. How accurately they do it is a measure of the phone's effectiveness.

5. Bring the students together to share what they found out. How did the type of string or thread affect how well the telephone worked? Did the type of container affect the sound quality? What combination of type of cup and string seemed to transmit sound most efficiently?

6. Summarize the core idea that sounds can be transmitted over a distance [PS4.C].

FIGURE 5A.5. TIN CAN/PAPER CUP TELEPHONE

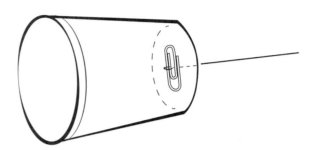

7. Formative Assessment: Have students draw a picture of their final telephone and label the materials they used. They should then answer the following questions in their science journal:

   ◆ How did the type of string affect the transmission of sound?

   ◆ Which materials worked best to make a telephone?

   ◆ What were the most difficult parts of the project?

   ◆ If you could do this activity again, what would you do differently?

   ◆ Why is it so important for engineers to write or record clearly what they do as they work?

8. Complete the Learned column of the class's original KWL chart. (**Teacher note:** Use what the students record to assess what the students feel they have learned during the unit.)

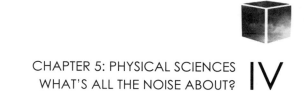

Materials (for Activity 4B Sound Insulation)

Internet (for Chinese Spouting Bowl *www.youtube.com/watch?v=65lpXIQ2cIY* and *www.youtube.com/watch?v=8Q-QinVdDA4*)

- Kitchen timer that rings or pings

- Shoe boxes

- Foam rubber

- Bubble wrap

Activity 4B Sound Insulation

1. Show students the Chinese spouting bowl You-Tube video demonstration and ask them how it relates to other activities they've completed (e.g., singing wine glass). Note student use of words like *sound waves*, and *vibrations of solids*, *liquids*, and *gases* to explain what they hear and see in this video clip. The spouting water is easy to see as a result of the vibration of the bowl that is not so easily observed. This can be used to reinforce that "sound can make matter vibrate and vibrating matter can make sound." [PS4.C].

2. Discuss how sound or audio engineers and building architects sometimes want to dampen, deaden, or insulate a sound source or location so that other people nearby are not disturbed. Have students brainstorm how they could use different materials to soundproof a source of noise such as a windup kitchen timer. After they generate ideas, share bubble wrap, soft foam, empty shoe boxes and other materials that groups of three to four students can use to design and construct their soundproof box. After product testing, have students answer the following questions:

- When did the timer sound loudest—inside or outside of the box? Why was there a difference?

- What materials and design seemed to work to dampen, deaden, or absorb the sound?

- If you were trying to improve the design of your team's box, list two changes that you would make and explain why these changes would be an improvement.

Evaluate Phase

This phase serves as a summative evaluation of students' understanding of the scientific and engineering practices, crosscutting concepts, and disciplinary core ideas developed in this unit.

Activity 5A: Invent-A-Sound Authentic Assessment

Materials for each group:

- Four paper cups

- String

- Four craft sticks

- Two toothpicks

- Two soda straws

- One plastic comb

- One sheet waxed paper

- One balloon

- Water (as much as you wish)

- Several rubber bands

1. Challenge: Using any of these materials, design several interesting ways to generate sounds.

TABLE 5A.2. STUDENT SCIENTISTS' SURVEY FORM

Check off how well each of these activities helped you learn during the sound unit	My favorite	I liked this (but not my favorite)	I did not like this
Watching the demonstrations			
Trying the hands-on stations			
Reading about sound			
Working in pairs			
Working in small groups			
Class discussions			
Writing in my notebook			
Trying the interactive websites			
Asking questions in class			
Listening to others			
Word wall			

- For each sound you create, explain how the sound is made. What is vibrating?

- For each sound you make, suggest a way you might make the sound louder.

- How might the pitch of each sound your group has made be changed?

2. Prepare a Sound Show for your class to demonstrate your most unique or interesting sound. Note that this optional engineering design activity parallels the Concerto for Invented Instrument challenge that Ms. Frizzle's class faced in *The Magic School Bus: In the Haunted House* episode that was used in the Explain phase of this unit.

Activity 5B Student Sound Science Preferences

1. Project and read the above optional survey form (Table 5A.2.) to your students. Tally the students' answers and if desired, make a simple bar graph of the results.

Resources

Robertson, W. C. 2002. *Sound: Stop faking it! Finally understanding science so you can teach it*. Arlington, VA: NSTA Press.

Pfeffer, W., and H. Keller.1999. *Sounds all around*. New York: Harper Collins.

PHYSICAL SCIENCES

B. Where's My Sugar?
EXPERIMENTING WITH DISSOLVING

Jenay Sharp Leach
Woodley Hills Math and Science Focus School (Alexandria, Virginia)

Recommended Level
Grade 2

Topic Focus
Physical Sciences

Disciplinary Core Idea
PS1: Matter and its interactions

Time Frame

Engage Phase
15 minutes (Activity 1)

Explore Phase
120 minutes* (Activities 2A, 2B, and 2C)
*If instructional time is restricted for this unit, different teams of students can complete the three different activities and share their results with the whole class.

Explain Phase
45 minutes (Activity 3)

Elaborate Phase
45 minutes (Activity 4)

Evaluate Phase
45 minutes (Activity 5A or 5B)

Objectives
As a result of these experiences, students will be able to

- use the terms *solids* and *liquids* to describe *mixtures* and the process of *dissolving*,

- design and execute experiments to (a) determine whether or not all solids and liquids can dissolve in water and (b) how temperature affects dissolving of materials in water,

- name common substances that dissolve in water and others that do not,

- explain the relationship between temperature and dissolving, and

- (optional) explain the evidence for conservation of matter during dissolution.

- **Teacher note:** Experiences with mixtures and the process of dissolving serve as conceptual precursors for the idea of atoms and molecules that will be introduced later in the middle grades.

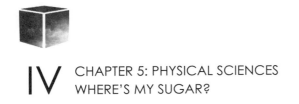

TABLE 5B.1. CORRELATION TO THE *NEXT GENERATION SCIENCE STANDARDS*

2. Structure and properties of matter		
2-PS1-1. Plan and conduct an investigation to describe and classify different kinds of materials by their observable properties.		

Scientific and Engineering Practices (Dimension 1)	Disciplinary Core Ideas (Dimension 3)	Crosscutting Concepts (Dimension 2)
1. Asking questions (for science) and defining problems (for engineering)[1]	PS1: Matter and its interactions	
	PS1.A: Structure and properties of matter * Different kinds of matter exist. ... Matter can be described and classified by observable properties. * Different properties are suited to different purposes.	2. Cause and effect: Mechanism and explanation
3. Planning and carrying out investigations		
4. Analyzing and interpreting data		
5. Using mathematics and computational thinking		5. Energy and matter: Flows, cycles, and conservation[1] (*Optional teacher demonstration in Elaborate phase touches on this idea.*)
6. Constructing explanations (for science) and designing solutions (for engineering)		
7. Engaging in argument from evidence		7. Stability and change
8. Obtaining, evaluating, and communicating information		

---

[1] This mini-unit does not address all portions of the standard as written; the relevant elements are underlined.

Note: PS = Physical sciences

Continued

Table 5B.1. (continued)

Scientific and Engineering Practices (Dimension 1)	Disciplinary Core Ideas (Dimension 3)	Crosscutting Concepts (Dimension 2)
Common Core State Standards Connections ***English Language Arts –*** <u>Reading Informational Text</u> **RI.2.10.** By the end of the year, read and comprehend informational texts, including history/social studies, science, and technical texts, in the grades 2–3 text complexity band proficiently, with scaffolding as needed at the high end of the range. <u>Writing</u> **W.1.8.** With guidance and support from adults, recall information from experiences or gather information from provided sources to answer a question. **W.2.2.** Write informative/explanatory texts in which they introduce a topic, use facts and definitions to develop points, and provide a concluding statement or section. <u>Speaking and Listening</u>: Comprehension and Collaboration **SL.1.5.** Add drawings or other visual displays to descriptions when appropriate to clarify ideas, thoughts, and feelings. **SL.2.1.** Participate in collaborative conversations with diverse partners about grade 2 topics and texts with peers and adults in small and larger groups. ***Mathematics*** Measurement and data: Represent and interpret data: **2.MD.10:** Draw a picture graph and a bar graph (with a single unit scale) to represent a data set with up to four categories.		

Engage Phase

This phase allows students to explore matter and its interactions by observing how various solids and liquids behave when placed in water. The teacher will engage the learners by performing a discrepant event: dissolving sugar in water (i.e., a process that is considered a physical change). Students will wonder, *Where did the sugar go?* This event is used to spark students' curiosity about dissolving. Using the students' questions surrounding this phenomenon, the teacher will guide the students to design experiments to answer their questions about dissolving.

Materials

- One clear cup
- 1 lb bag of table sugar (sucrose)
- One spoon
- Chart paper or similar method for recording and displaying student ideas

Materials for Optional Teacher Demonstration

- Petri dishes
- Kosher or pickling salt
- Water

Activity 1: The Disappearing Sugar Act: Where Did It Go?

1. Display a clear cup of warm water. Tell the students that you will add a spoonful of sugar to the water. Do not disclose that the water is warm. Use the Think-Write-Pair-Share strategy to ask students to **P**redict (in writing and then discuss) what will happen when the sugar is added to the water.

2. Add a spoonful of sugar to the water and stir. Ask the students to make **O**bservations. After the sugar sinks to the bottom and dissolves, the students will observe that the sugar can no longer be seen.

3. Probe the students' thoughts, asking them to offer plausible **E**xplanations as to what happened to the sugar and recording the students' ideas on chart paper. Students may use a variety of phrases to describe what they think happens to the sugar (or solute) during the dissolution process, including that it just disappeared, went away, melted, or turned into water. A few might correctly infer that it breaks down into smaller particles too small to be seen. Do not prematurely introduce this correct response.

Engaging students with a **P**redict-**O**bserve-**E**xplain (POE) sequence helps students learn how to interpret physical phenomena in terms of cause and effect: mechanism and explanations (crosscutting concept 2). When linked in a 5E teaching cycle, a series of POE activities help students learn how to account for phenomena that would otherwise be mysterious (i.e., consider the short stories of Edgar Allen Poe).

4. Next, ask the students what questions they have about this scenario. The students will most likely ask if anything else disappears in water and if the temperature of the water matters; however, if they do not ask these questions, guide them to these questions. Students of this age may make a statement and need help developing their statement into question form. Record the questions on another piece of chart paper, as they will be used to develop a series of student-designed experiments to determine the answers.

5. Optional Teacher Demonstration: Repeat the above demonstration, except use several teaspoons of kosher or pickling salt to form a fairly saturated saltwater solution. Ask the students to predict what will happen when you pour the clear solution into a series of petri dishes (or any clear plastic containers with a large surface area) that are placed on a windowsill in bright sunlight and left out for the duration of this unit. The students can quickly make daily observations of the setup and begin to formulate possible explanations as the unit unfolds. **Teacher note:** Unlike sugar water, a saltwater solution will not attract insects.

Explore Phase

The purpose of this phase is to allow students to design and execute their own experiments to explore dissolving. Over a period of three classes (or as three specialty teams within one class), students will investigate scenarios in which solids and liquids are combined with water. **Safety note:** Although all the chemicals used in this experiment are found in homes, proper safety precautions must be taken to avoid injury. Make sure students wear indirectly vented chemical-splash goggles, and warn students about the importance of keeping materials away from their eyes. Instruct students to never taste anything while experimenting, to use care when handling the equipment, and to avoid contact with hot water (i.e., sometimes tap water can become hot enough to burn children's more sensitive hands; the teacher should pretest). As previously noted, if instructional time is restricted for this unit, different teams of students can complete the three different Explore phase activities (2A, 2B, and 2C) and share their results with the whole class.

Materials

- Chart paper with questions created during Engage phase

- Student data sheets (pp. 91–93)

- Three beakers for each group (if plastic beakers are unavailable, use clear plastic cups and mark fill lines on them)

- One spoon for each group

- Three plastic medicine cups (30 ml) for each group

- Timer or clock

- Crayons

- Solids to test (e.g., kosher or pickling salt, table salt, table sugar, sugar cubes, baking powder, flour, sand, marbles, and rocks—all known materials provided by the teacher)

- **Teacher note:** In addition to sodium chloride (and small amounts of potassium iodide), table salt contains a small amount of an anticaking agent that causes a saltwater solution to appear a little cloudy unless it is filtered or allowed to settle over an extended time period. Kosher salt and pickling salt do not contain this additive and will form a clear, noncloudy solution.

- Liquids to test (rubbing alcohol, liquid soap, vegetable oil, and corn syrup)

- Two thermometers (nonmercury) for each group

- Warm water (teacher should pretest to ensure students can't get burned) and cold water

In the first activity, students will determine if all solids can dissolve by adding various solids to samples of water (salt, sand, dirt, and so on). In the second activity, students will test the effect of temperature on dissolving by dissolving sugar in warm or hot and cold water and comparing the dissolving times for each. Finally, students will determine if liquids can dissolve in water by adding various liquids to water (oil, liquid soap, etc.).

Activity 2A: Can All Solids Dissolve in Water?

1. Refer to the class questions recorded on the chart paper and ask students how we could find the answers to these questions. The students will most likely suggest that we try combining solids and liquids with water to see what happens. Explain to students that by doing so, they will be doing an experiment. Experiments are scientific tests that we can do to find answers to our questions.

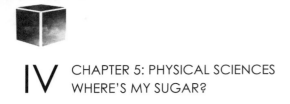

2. Highlight a question on the chart paper that asks if other substances can seem to disappear in water. Ask students how we could design an experiment to find the answer. Today we will focus on combining solids with water.

3. Review the definitions of the terms *matter*, *solid*, and *liquid*. Solids have a definite shape, while liquids take the shape of their container (*NGSS* Kindergarten: Structure and properties of matter). Ask students to describe solids and liquids and name examples around the room. Ask students, "When I added sugar to water, which type of matter was the solid and which was the liquid?"

4. While the students themselves will design the investigation, the teacher will need to guide the experimental design by focusing the students' questions and ensuring a fair test (by only manipulating one variable at a time). Describe how they will change the type of solid (independent variable) and observe to see if it is visible after mixing with water (dependent variable). Ask the students how they will know when the solid disappears. Write each step of the experiment on the board. A sample plan for the investigations follows:

   a. Fill three plastic beakers (or cups) with 100 ml of water.

   b. Fill three medicine cups with 10 ml of each solid being tested.

   c. Predict what will happen when each solid is mixed with water, and record the prediction on your data sheet.

   d. Add each solid to the water and stir for one minute.

   e. Record results on data sheet (i.e., does the solid completely dissolve or does some or all settle on the bottom after you are done stirring the mixture?).

5. Divide students into groups and distribute data sheets (Activity 2A: Can All Solids Dissolve?) and materials. It may be helpful to assign roles to each student (i.e., one student stirs, another times, and so on).

6. Display the solid materials and allow each group to choose three solids to test. Examples include table sugar, sugar cubes, sand, soil, kosher or pickling salt, table salt, rocks, blocks, flour, baking soda, or marbles.

7. Students must first predict (based on their prior experiences outside of school) what will happen when each of their solids is mixed with water before they may begin experimenting. **Teacher note:** Students are likely to have the misconception that anything that seems to be made up of a powder or small crystals (e.g., baking powder, flour, table sugar or salt, and sand) will necessarily dissolve, and bigger solids (sugar cubes, marbles, and rocks) will not. The nonsolubility of sand and the solubility of sugar cubes are likely to run counter to their prior conceptions and predictions (i.e., be discrepant events).

8. Students will collect qualitative evidence by observing their containers and drawing their results using crayons. Their drawings will show if solids or liquids remain undissolved in the water. They will leave the space blank to show that the water is clear.

Activity 2B: A Dissolving Race: How Does Temperature Affect Dissolving?

1. Highlight a question on the chart paper that asks if the water temperature affects dissolving. Ask students how they could design an experiment to find the answer. Use a similar process as in Activity 1 to ensure a fair test. A sample experiment is as follows.

   a. Fill one plastic beaker or cup with 100 ml of warm or hot tap water.

   b. Fill another beaker with 100 ml of cold tap water.

   c. Measure and record the temperature of the water for each beaker.

   d. Add one sugar cube to each beaker.

   e. Observe each beaker until the sugar cube is completely dissolved, keeping track of the time.

   f. Record results on the data sheet (Activity 2B).

2. Follow the same process as above to guide lab work.

Activity 2C: Can Liquids Dissolve in Water?

1. Begin by reviewing the definition of the terms *solid* and *liquid*. So far, the students have tested solids, but today, they will test liquids to see if liquids can dissolve in water (also a liquid). Ask students to describe a liquid. They may say that it feels wet, flows, or takes the shape of its container.

2. Repeat the steps in a manner analogous to Activity 2A, but this time measure 15 ml of individual test liquids in separate plastic

30 ml cups. Examples include rubbing alcohol, liquid soap, vegetable oil, corn syrup, or other choices. Pour 15 ml of each test liquid into separate plastic beakers (or clear plastic cups) that contain 100 ml of water. Use data sheet (Activity 2C) to record whether the test liquids dissolve in water or are insoluble in it (i.e., form an immiscible layer at the bottom or top of the water, depending on whether the test liquid is more or less dense than water.). Once students have finished experimenting, move on to the Explain phase.

Explain Phase

The purpose of this phase is for students to explain their observations and for teacher-facilitated development of students' understanding of concepts. Teacher guidance is needed to scaffold students' understanding and to avoid misconceptions.

Materials

- Student data sheets (pp. 91–93)

- Chart paper or similar to record class results

Activity 3

1. This phase builds the students' understanding of matter and how it interacts (disciplinary core idea PS1). Students will explain their observations through their writings, drawings, and class discussions, further developing their understanding of the crosscutting concepts of cause and effect, energy and matter, and stability and change. The teacher can make the students aware of the scientific and engineering principles that they employed by asking the students to reflect and describe how they asked questions and designed their experiments. As the students explain how

they answered their questions about dissolving through experimentation, the teacher will record these practices on an anchor chart. This scientific and engineering practices anchor chart should remain hanging in the room and be referred to in subsequent lessons so that the students can review and add practices as they use them. This anchor chart becomes a permanent fixture in the classroom for making students aware of the practices that they employ. Teachers can also ask students questions about their experimental design, such as why it was important to predict (hypothesize) or use the same volume of liquid each time.

2. Students will observe the introductory discrepant event and assume that the sugar disappeared. After completing the first experiment (Activity 2A), students should reach the conclusion that not all solids seem to disappear in water. It will be the teacher's role to facilitate the discussion and scientific argumentation that will follow. Have the students sit in a circle for a whole-class discussion. Direct the students to share their results and offer explanations for why some solids seemed to disappear while others did not. The teacher must lead the students away from their misconceptions and get them to understand that some solids actually dissolve in water. The teacher can do this by asking the students if they have ever added solids to water at home. Students will have experience making and drinking hot chocolate, tea, and Kool-Aid. Ask them to describe how they make hot chocolate at home. Does the cocoa disappear? Does the sugar disappear? How do they know? If necessary, guide students to this conclusion by asking them to think about the observations they have made with their senses. Students

will come to the conclusion that the solids do not in fact really go away or disappear because they can still taste and smell them in their beverages. Thus, the solids must be present: They are just unable to be seen. Students will infer that some solids become too small to be seen when they dissolve in water.

3. Create a class data chart to record the results of each test (see, for example, Table 5B.2). Since each group did not experiment with each type of solid and liquid, it will be important for students to share results. After completion of Activity 2A, students should be able to use the word *dissolve* to describe their experimental results. Use whole-class discussion to encourage students to share the results of their experiments and draw conclusions. Students should conclude from Activity 2B that a higher water temperature increases dissolving and from Activity 2C that some liquids can dissolve in water (e.g., rubbing alcohol), while others do not (e.g., vegetable oil).

TABLE 5B.2. SAMPLE EXPLAIN PHASE DATA

Create a class chart to compile the results of each test.

Material	Solid or Liquid?	Did It Dissolve in Water?
Gravel	Solid	No
Salt	Solid	Yes
Sand	Solid	No
Vegetable Oil	Liquid	No
Rubbing Alcohol	Liquid	Yes

Elaborate Phase

The purpose of this phase is to enable students to extend their learning and solidify their understanding of the process of asking and answering questions through scientific experimentation. Students will revisit key vocabulary and use it to make connections, read about matter (English language arts skills), and use their math skills to create a graph to extend their understanding of the data from Activities 2A, 2B, and 2C. The optional teacher demonstration challenges students to revisit the Engage phase (Activity 1), but consider it through the lens of conservation of matter.

Materials

- Table salt

- Table sugar (optional)

- Hand magnifying lenses

- One piece of dark construction paper for each group

- Chart paper or similar for making a graph

Materials for Optional Teacher Demonstration

- A double-pan (or bucket) balance:

  - EAI Education: Elementary Balance with Mass, #53119, $24.50, *www.eaieducation. com/Product/531139/Elementary_School_ Balance_with_Mass.aspx*

  - Homemade *www.ehow.com/ how_12134503_make-double-pan-balance-scale.html*

  - Mpm School Supplies: *www.mpmschool-supplies.com*: Pan Balance SKU# SS-6873,

$22.99; Bucket Balance, SKU# SS-6702, $19.99

- Ohaus Student Balance with Double Pan, #WW60349M05, $40: *http://sciencekit.com/ ohaus-student-balance-with-double-pan/p/ IG0025703*

Activity 4: A Closer Look at Matter: ELA and Mathematics Connections

1. Substances like table salt and sugar are solids, though they appear to behave somewhat like liquids as they can be poured and will assume the shape of their containers. Explain to the students that this is because each salt particle is so small. Pour a small amount of salt onto dark construction paper and invite students to view the grains of salt under a magnifying lens to see their definite, cube shapes. If students look at table sugar in the same way, they will notice that the crystals do not appear as uniform-size cubes.

2. Ask students to use the data from Activity 2C to create a bar graph that displays the results of their experiment. Create a model bar graph on chart paper using sample data. Students can also be asked to compare how much more time it took the cold water to dissolve the sugar cube than the warm or hot water.

3. Ask students to brainstorm other real-world applications in which warm or hot water is better than cold: dissolving Jell-O, making tea or hot cocoa, and so on. More generally, invite students to brainstorm as many examples of water solutions in and around their home as they can list (e.g., soft drinks, fruit drinks, tea, coffee, milk, wines, vinegar, window cleaners, liquid laundry soap, dishwashing liquids, rubbing alcohol, automo-

bile antifreeze, windshield wiper fluid, and so on.). Although a common chemical on Earth (known as the water planet), water is remarkable in that it can dissolve a broader range of solids and liquids than most any other liquid in the universe! Consider displaying a number of these household products to emphasize how scientists and engineers use the dissolving ability of water to make a large number of consumer products with particular properties and uses.

4. Read one or more of the following books as a class (see Resources).

  ◆ Linda Beech's *The Magic School Bus Gets Baked in a Cake: A Book About Kitchen Chemistry*

  ◆ Rebecca Matos's *Measuring Matter: Solids, Liquids, and Gases*

  ◆ Angela Royston's *Water*

  ◆ Lola Schaefer's *What Is Matter?*

  ◆ Rozanne L. Williams's *What Happened?*

Then make them available for students to read at other times during the day, perhaps as they finish experiments or during language arts time.

5. Optional Teacher Demonstrations: Return to the optional teacher demonstration completed in the Engage phase and challenge the students to account for the "disappearance" of water (due to evaporation of the water into the air) and the "reappearance" of the salt (since it never really was gone). If time permits, repeat Activity 1, except this time, place several teaspoons of sugar (or kosher or pickling salt) plus the cup of water on one side of a simple double pan balance. Add weights to the other

side of the balance until the balance is even. Now, add the sugar (or salt) to the water, stir until it dissolves, place it back on the balance and note that the balance returns to its original state of equilibrium. Lead students to connect (a) their observations that the total amount of matter does not change and (b) their prior experiences outside of school with tasting sugar water or salt water. Together these observations suggest that the sugar (or salt) did not really go away (i.e., in fact if the optional demonstration with salt water in petri dishes was set up, students should be able to see that the salt reappeared as the water evaporated into the air). That is, even though the process of dissolving involves change (i.e., the white crystals are no longer visible), when one substance is dissolved in another, it is still there even if it can no longer be seen (stability and change). Experiences in the home such as dissolving flavored, colored gelatin in hot water when making Jell-O provides additional evidence of this claim.

Teacher note: The *NGSS* recommend that while weighing (with a spring scale) or massing objects (with a balance) is appropriate in the second grade, the two concepts should not be distinguished at this grade level. Also, formal introduction to the conservation of matter and chemical reactions in which new types of matter are formed (versus physical changes such as dissolution) are reserved until the fifth grade in the *NGSS* (5.SPM: Structures, properties, and interactions of matter).

Evaluate Phase

In the Evaluate phase, students and teachers evaluate how well students have met the original objectives and *NGSS* standards. These early experiences with dissolving lay a foundation for understanding other physical and chemical changes and further developing the crosscutting concepts of stability and change and energy and matter conservation in the fifth grade.

Materials

- Student data sheets (pp. 91–93)

- Summative assessment

Activity 5A: Written Summative Assessment

1. The students' data sheets will provide a formative assessment of their skill in data gathering and analysis. Their written conclusions will integrate ELA skills and also provide documentation to both the teacher and the student of their understanding of dissolving.

   Students should be able to define the key scientific terms and explain their results using these terms. The scaffolded nature of the lesson sequence will allow for increasingly complex understandings of matter and its interactions. As the students' understanding improves, so too will their explanations of the phenomenon observed. Students should move away from explaining results as solids and liquids *disappearing* in Activity 1 to *dissolving* in subsequent activities. The act of constructing, defending, and communicating these explanations places emphasis on scientific and engineering practices.

2. A simple, written summative assessment might take the form of asking students to answer the following five questions:

1. How did you know when a solid or liquid dissolved in water?

2. What happens to sugar when it dissolves?

3. Name one solid that dissolves in water.

4. Draw a picture of what a transparent container looks like when a liquid that does *not* dissolve in water is added to water.

5. I want to make tea. Should I use hot water or cold water to dissolve the sugar faster? Why?

3. Alternatively, if time permits, a more authentic, hands-on summative assessment follows.

Activity 5B: Gumball Science

To the Student: We invite you to try an exciting experiment. As usual, we would like you to predict *before* you do the experiment what you expect to happen as you observe the results of the experiment.

Materials

- Two petri dishes

- 25 ml hot water in one dish

- 25 ml cold water in another dish

- Four gumballs (two each of the same color, for example two red and two blue)

What To Do

Pour cold water in one dish and hot water in another.

Predict: What will you observe in each dish when you place a red gumball on one side and a blue gumball on the opposite side, as shown:

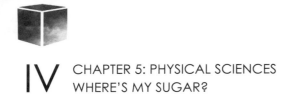
FIGURE 5B.1. GUMBALL SETUP

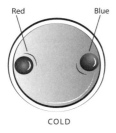

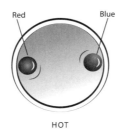

COLD   HOT

1. What did you observe over a five-minute period?

2. Explain what is happening.

3. If this same experimental setup is used a second time with a different color gumball (e.g., red and blue are replaced with either yellow and blue or red and yellow), how will the results be the same or different?

ACTIVITY 2A

Can All Solids Dissolve in Water?

Where did my sugar go?

Predict: Which solids will be invisible after mixing with water? Write or draw:

Data: Draw the results of your experiment below. Label each drawing with the solid used.

How can you tell when a solid has dissolved?

_____

Which solids dissolved in water?

_____

Which solids did not dissolve in water?

_____

ACTIVITY 2B

A Dissolving Race: How Does Temperature Affect Dissolving?

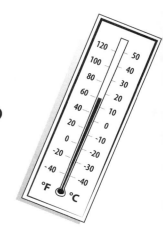

Predict: Will warm water or cold water make a sugar cube dissolve faster? Why?

_____

Data:

Warm Water:	Cold Water:
Temperature = _____ degrees C	Temperature = _____ degrees C
The hot water dissolved the sugar in _____ minutes.	The cold water dissolved the sugar in _____ minutes.

_____ water dissolves sugar faster than _____ water.

If you are going to make hot cocoa, should you use hot water or cold water? Why?

_____

_____

Draw a bar graph to show the time for the sugar to dissolve in hot and cold water.

Graph: _The Effect of Temperature on Time to Dissolve Sugar_

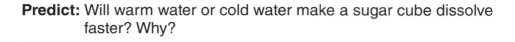

5
4
3
2
1

Cold Water (_____ °C)   Hot Water (_____ °C)

ACTIVITY 2C
Can Liquids Dissolve in Water?

Predict: Which liquids will dissolve in water? Write or Draw:

Data: Draw the results of your experiment below. Label each drawing with the liquid used.

Which liquids dissolved in water? _____

_____

Which liquids did not dissolve in water? _____

_____

How can you tell when a liquid has dissolved? _____

_____

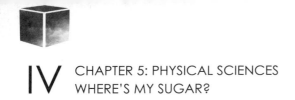

Supplemental Reference

Agler, L. 2002. *Involving dissolving.* Great Explorations in Math and Science series. Berkeley, CA: UC-Berkeley, Lawrence Hall of Science.

Note: This grade K–3 Teachers' Guide activity book contains additional optional explorations. 0-924886-63-3, $15 *http://lhsgems.org/GEM145.html*

Resources

Beech, L. 1995. *The magic school bus gets baked in a cake: A book about kitchen chemistry.* New York: Scholastic.

Matos, R. 2005. *Measuring matter: Solids, liquids, and gases.* Pelham, NY: Benchmark Education.

Royston, A. 2008. *Water.* Chicago, IL: Heinemann-Raintree.

Schaefer, L. 2011. *What is matter?* Pelham, NY: Benchmark Education.

Williams, R. L. 1994. *What happened?* Huntington Beach, CA: Creative Teaching Press.

CHAPTER 6

Life Sciences

INTRODUCTION

THE IMPORTANCE OF TEACHING SCIENCE IN ELEMENTARY SCHOOL

Eric R. Kandel, MD
Columbia University Professor and Kavli Professor of Brain Science
Nobel Prize in Physiology 2000
National Medal of Science 1988

Science is the best means that we have to learn about the world around us. From the very small to the very large, from single atoms to expanding universes, from single nerve cells to the functioning of the brain and mind, science has taught us what we know about life on our planet. From a biological perspective, science has taught us what makes us human, why our mental processes are so special, and how we relate to our animal ancestors.

In addition, I find science to be one of life's most exciting activities. I enjoy coming to the laboratory every day—every new discovery, no matter how small, is infinitely more enjoyable than winning a tennis game or a round of bridge. More importantly, science is essential in our technologically sophisticated world. For citizens to make informed decisions, they need to have an understanding of science.

It is therefore essential that we teach science at the first opportunity—in elementary school. Science has so many functions for society. Science is the engine that drives the economy, how we learn about important and exciting new developments in the world, and the means whereby we can advance the treatment of major physical and mental illnesses that confront our world. Without doubt, science is one of the most inspiring, exciting, and rewarding activities young people can engage in.

To have an electorate that is informed, knowledgeable, and prepared to deal with the future, we need to start early and teach science at the very beginning of a child's education—to encourage scientific research and the development of industries that require a scientific background. But even more importantly, science needs to be made part of the intellectual fabric of responsible citizenship. It is increasingly clear from the public media—the major newspapers, and the major television reporters such as Charlie Rose—that science is now included together with sports, movies, theater, national and international politics, and economics as part of the basic intellectual fabric of society. For science to become central to modern life the teaching of science needs to be central from the very beginning.

LIFE SCIENCES

C. Zoogle Zoology

Jennifer Baxter
Palmyra-Macedon Primary School
(Palmyra-Macedon Central School District, New York)

Recommended Level
Grade 2

Topic Focus
Life Sciences

Disciplinary Core Idea
LS2: Ecosystems: Interactions, energy, and dynamics

Time Frame
As an integrated science-art-English language arts (ELA) mini-unit, actual time spent on individual lessons may vary, depending on the teacher's assessment of student needs in each of the three individual subject domains.

Engage Phase
40–60 minutes (Activity 1)

Explore Phase
40–90 minutes (Activity 2; variable use of web games)

Explain Phase
30–60 minutes (Activity 3; break into two sessions of one hour)

Elaborate Phase
Two to three 30–45 minute sessions (Activities 4A and 4B)

Evaluate Phase
Two 30–40 minute sessions (Activities 5A and 5B)

Objectives
As a result of these experiences, students will be able to

- understand that animals depend on their own specific habitat to meet their basic needs for survival (food, water, shelter, and acceptable body temperature) and are interdependent with plants, other animals, and nonliving parts of their habitat (water, soil, rocks);

- demonstrate understanding of characteristics of various habitats previously studied: desert, grassland (savannah), temperate forest, rain forest, tundra, freshwater and saltwater habitats, including plants, animals, and nonliving parts (water, soil, rocks);

- demonstrate understanding of basic needs of an organism using a planning checklist for an imaginary animal's habitat (Zoogle Observation Checklist);

- construct a model (or diorama) of a Zoogle and its complementary habitat;

- explain, defend, or communicate how the form of their Zoogle fits or is adapted to the habitat where it lives;

- given a picture of any actual animal, be able to identify adaptations of the animal that help it survive in its native environment (or habitat); and

- demonstrate understanding of predator/prey relationships.

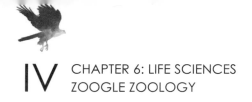
TABLE 6C.1. CORRELATION TO THE *NEXT GENERATION SCIENCE STANDARDS*

2. Interdependent relationships in ecosystems

2-LS4-1. Make observations of plants and animals to compare the diversity of life in different habitats. (Assessment boundary: Assessment does not include specific animal and plant names in specific habitats.)

Scientific and Engineering Practices (Dimension 1)	Disciplinary Core Ideas (Dimension 3)	Crosscutting Concepts (Dimension 2)
1. Asking questions (for science) and defining problems (for engineering)	LS2: Ecosystems: Interactions, energy, and dynamics	1. Patterns
2. Developing and using models	LS2.A: Interdependent relationships in ecosystems "Animals depend on their surroundings to get what they need, including food, water, shelter, and a favorable temperature. Animals depend on plants or other animals for food." (*Framework*, p. 151)	
3. Planning and carrying out investigations	LS4: Biological evolution: Unity and diversity *Note: Focus only on LS4.C and LS4.D (below), NOT the broader concept of evolution.*	
4. Analyzing and interpreting data	LS4.C: Adaptation "Living things can survive only when their needs are met. If some places are too hot or too cold or have too little water or food, plants and animals may not be able to live there." (*Framework*, p. 165)	4. Systems and system models
	LS4.D: Biodvisersity and humans * There are many different kinds of living things in any area, and they exist in different places on land and in water.	

Note: LS = Life sciences

Continued

Table 6C.1. (continued)

Scientific and Engineering Practices (Dimension 1)	Disciplinary Core Ideas (Dimension 3)	Crosscutting Concepts (Dimension 2)
6. Constructing explanations (for science) and designing solutions (for engineering)	ETS1.B: Developing possible solutions * Designs can be conveyed through sketches, drawings, or physical models.	6. Structure and function
7. Engaging in argument from evidence		
8. Obtaining, evaluating, and communicating information		

Common Core State Standards Connections

English Language Arts –

Reading Standards for Informational Text

RI.2.1. Ask and answer such questions as who, what, where, when, why, and how to demonstrate understanding of key details in a text.

RI.2.7. Explain how specific images contribute to and clarify a text.

RI.2.10. By the end of the year, read and comprehend informational texts, including history/social studies, science, and technical texts, in the grades 2–3 text complexity band proficiently, with scaffolding as needed at the high end of the range.

Writing Standards

W.2.2. Write informative/explanatory texts in which they introduce a topic, use facts and definitions to develop points, and provide a concluding statement or section.

W.3.7. Participate in shared research and writing projects (e.g., read a number of books on a single topic to produce a report; record science observations).

W.3.8. Recall information from experiences or gather information from provided sources to answer a question.

Speaking and Listening

SL.2.1. Participate in collaborative conversations with diverse partners about grade 2 topics and texts with peers and adults in small and larger groups.

SL.2.2. Recount or describe key ideas or details from a text read aloud or information presented orally or through other media.

SL.2.4. Tell a story or recount an experience with appropriate facts and relevant, descriptive details, speaking audibly in coherent sentences.

Mathematics—*No mathematical connections are developed in this mini-unit.*

Engage Phase

The purpose of this phase is to introduce Zoogle Zoology, an integrated science-art-ELA project-based unit that follows a prior science unit on habitats (e.g., desert, grassland or savannah, temperate forest, rain forest, tundra, freshwater and saltwater habitats). At this point in their study of habitats, students have already become familiar with vocabulary and concepts relevant to living and nonliving parts of habitats. (See Appendix: Habitats Vocabulary List, p. 106). A fictional story is used to engage students' interest in a Zoogle, a newly discovered animal. The student zoologists will ultimately be challenged to design a realistic model (or diorama) that demonstrates their understanding of the fit between their Zoogle's form (or structural adaptations) and how it functions and survives in its particular natural system (or habitat).

Teacher note: Students may have had ongoing experience with a classroom pet or an aquarium. If not, setting up a small terrarium or aquarium habitat at this time will encourage engagement and further motivation for the project. A variety of internet sites provide directions as to how to do this (see Resources).

Materials

- Activity Sheet 1: Zoogle Zoology! (p. 108)

- Computer(s) and projector for small-group or whole-class use of web simulation games (see Resources)

- Two-pocket folders or 12 in. × 18 in. piece of construction paper for Zoologist's Portfolio (one per student)

- Model of a sample Zoogle, completed by the teacher prior to the lesson

- Michael Dahl's *Do Ducks Live in the Desert?*

Activity 1: The Zoogle Zoology Story and Introduction to the Science-Art-ELA Project

1. Optional stage setting and review activity: Remind students of their previous science unit (on habitats) by playing a song (e.g., Bill Oliver's *Habitat*), displaying the lyrics and encouraging a sing-along. Alternatively, use one or more tracks from a nature sampler or environmental and ecological sounds type CD as background music to set a sonic stage for an exploration of an intriguing habitat. See Resources for music that can be used during one or more of Steps 2–6. You may ask students to analyze and interpret the particular sound tracks to infer what particular habitats are being depicted. For additional fun context setting, consider dressing up as a zoologist or explorer when reading the introductory story.

2. Inform students that they will be role-playing famous zoologists who have just returned from an expedition to observe organisms in their natural environments. During their expedition they encountered a brand new type of (imaginary) animal called a Zoogle. They took notes and made sketches of the Zoogle in its natural habitat, recorded its physical appearance, where it takes shelter in its habitat, what the Zoogle eats, what eats the Zoogle, and how the Zoogle protects itself from predators—all without actually removing the Zoogle from its natural habitat.

3. Present Activity Sheet 1: Zoogle Zoology! to generate interest with students. Inform them that they have been called upon to create a museum exhibit to display a model Zoogle in its habitat.

4. To review the various habitats previously studied and to get students thinking about which previously studied habitat they would like to learn more about, read *Do Ducks Live in the Desert?* Alternatively, you may view selected clips from one or more of *The Magic School Bus* episodes and/or read portions of the related books to focus student attention on the fit between an animal's form (or structural adaptations) and its particular home or habitat. See Resources.

5. From a list of habitats, have each student (or working pair of students) select one habitat they would like to learn more about by designing a Zoogle that would live there. The habitat list might include desert, grassland or savannah, temperate forest, rain forest, tundra, or freshwater and saltwater habitats. If you allow students to make individual dioramas, you may want to encourage them to find a parallel partner (i.e., a partner who is designing his or her own individual Zoogle for the same type of habitat) to encourage and help each other with their research and design ideas.

6. Show the sample Zoogle created by the teacher. This sample Zoogle may resemble a real animal, such as a bird, fish, or other four-legged creature, or a completely fictional one. In any case, it should be designed for a specific habitat so that students can be challenged to make observations of the Zoogle's characteristics and make logical inferences about its most likely habitat. If desired, this discussion could take place in a game of 20 (yes or no) Questions. The intent is to model the kind of thinking students will be asked to do in creating a well-matched Zoogle habitat system.

7. Distribute pocket folders or 12 in. × 18 in. construction paper to fold into a Zoologist's Portfolio. The young zoologists must keep all important research notes and papers in the portfolio as they work and must submit the complete portfolio at the end of the project.

8. Close the lesson by informing students that in the next session they will begin to research their chosen habitat.

Explore Phase

During this phase students will research the habitat they have selected and fill out a graphic organizer to list and organize details pertaining to that habitat. They will use details from the graphic organizer when creating their diorama projects. While Explore-phase activities typically include hands-on investigations, it is important for students to learn that scientists also do literature searches to review the published research using books, articles, and internet sources to help them ask and answer questions and design realistic models.

Materials

- Activity Sheet 2: Habitat Graphic Organizer (p. 109)

- Books, DVDs and/or website resources to be used as student references (see Resources)

Activity 2: Reading and Writing Researchers

1. Inform students that in keeping with their roles as zoologists, they must gather more specific information about the habitat in which their particular Zoogle was discovered in order to create the museum exhibit. Informal groups (scientific communities) may

be formed based on choice of habitat. Tell students that in real life scientists often work in groups to share data and ideas about what they are studying.

2. Using books, notes, and/or internet sources, students complete Activity Sheet 2: Habitat Graphic Organizer to list specific details about the animals, plants, and nonliving parts of their chosen habitat. **Teacher note:** (optional) You may choose to work with the whole class or small groups on web-based simulation games on habitats. (See Resources.)

3. At the end of the lesson, remind students to keep all their notes in their Zoologist's Portfolio for the next session.

Explain Phase

During this phase students will complete the Activity Sheet 3: Zoogle Observation Checklist, which serves as a planning page to list information prior to the actual construction of the Zoogle. Here students demonstrate their understanding of vocabulary and concepts pertaining to living and nonliving aspects of the chosen habitat as they describe how their Zoogle's traits are appropriate to the chosen habitat. Since this unit follows a previous unit on habitats, it is the students, rather than the teacher, who do most of the explaining during this phase.

Materials

- Activity Sheet 3: Zoogle Observation Checklist (p. 110)

- See Resources in the Classroom: Books and Websites as a source of animal photographs.

Activity 3: Animal Adaptations and Zoogle Lifestyles

1. Show (or project) a small sampling of pictures of actual individual animals in their natural habitats. Invite students to point out parts of the animal's body that help it survive in its particular home environment (or habitat). Point out that structural features (or forms) that aid an animal's survival are called adaptations.

2. Briefly review the Zoogle Zoology! from the first day and the museum exhibit task presented to the young zoologists. Orient students to Activity Sheet 3: Zoogle Observation Checklist, which includes sections to write their notes on the Zoogle's specific habitat and lifestyle. Depending on the students' capabilities, the teacher may model his or her own Zoogle Observation Checklist, using details that match up with the previously displayed sample Zoogle.

3. The remainder of the lesson will be used to complete the checklist. Remind students to use their best spelling and refer to Activity Sheet 2: Habitat Graphic Organizer as well as other information that has been gathered from lessons earlier in the unit. Encourage students to verbalize their ideas and discuss them with other students as they work.

Elaborate Phase

The purpose of this phase is to encourage students to extend and apply their prior understanding of the relationship between animal adaptations and habitats by constructing physical models of a matched set of an animal (Zoogle) to a habitat system. It also serves as a form of curriculum-embedded (or formative) assessment in which the teacher can informally assess students' understanding by observing and listening to them as they work on their science-art construction projects.

Students use their Activity Sheet 3: Zoogle Observation Checklist to create their own original Zoogles. It would be advisable to have an adult volunteer or other teacher to help during this lesson. Students alternate between Zoogle creation and making a sketch of its complementary habitat using Activity Sheet 4: Zoogle Habitat Planning Sketch, based on information in the checklist. They then move on to actually construct their dioramas (Activity 4B). The actual building of the diorama may extend to two periods.

Materials for Activity 4A

- Previously completed Activity Sheet 3: Zoogle Observation Checklist

- Activity Sheet 4: Zoogle Habitat Planning Sketch

- Small, smooth river-type rock, available at garden centers or local dollar stores (Or if you want to reduce the need for glue and allow for more variation in the shape of the Zoogles' torsos, modeling clay can be used instead of rocks.)

- Craft supplies such as chenille stems or pipe cleaners (for arms, legs, tails, or antennae), large sequins or spangles (for scales for snakes or fish), feathers or colored construction paper (for wings or fins), fake fur, rickrack or ribbons (body stripes), craft puffs or pompoms (body decorations), wiggle or googly eyes (preferably the peel and stick variety)

- Craft glue (fast drying) or glue gun (but only if there is another adult to help with it)

- **Teacher note:** Craft paint is optional.

Materials for Activity 4B

- Activity Sheet 4: Zoogle Habitat Planning Sketch

- Shoe box or other similar size box

- Construction paper in green, brown, blue, and black

- Craft supplies: Clear and colored plastic wrap (sky or water), craft moss, green or brown Easter basket grass, raffia (grass or vines), craft sticks, sandpaper (desert sand or trees), wallpaper, waxed paper, and so forth

- Scissors, glue sticks, and craft glue

- Clothespins, wiggle eyes, feathers, chenille stems, and other craft materials from Zoogle lesson to create Zoogle predators and prey

Activity 4A: Creature Construction and Diorama Design

1. Using simple craft and art supplies and the Activity Sheet 3: Zoogle Observation Checklist, students create their own Zoogle. Remind students that the Zoogle's physical traits (or adaptations) must be suited to match their chosen habitat and lifestyle. It might be a good idea to give examples and nonexamples. For instance, a Zoogle living in the ocean would need body parts with which to swim, and a bird Zoogle would need some kind of feathers to fly. The color of the Zoogle must also match or fit its survival need; if the

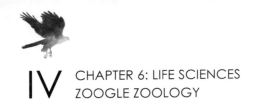
Zoogle uses camouflage as a means of protection, it must be a color that will blend in with its habitat. Alternatively, a Zoogle might use bright coloration to alert predators that it is poisonous (or to help it attract a mate). A Zoogle that lives on the tundra would probably not be brightly colored, and a Zoogle that lives in a hot rain forest would probably not have a thick fur coat.

2. A good way to manage Zoogle creation is to have a table set with craft materials. While some students take turns constructing their Zoogle, other students use Activity Sheet 4: Zoogle Habitat Planning Sketch to plan the physical environment for their dioramas, including water, soil, rocks, sand. They may also add in trees or other plants and possible predators and/or prey.

3. As they plan the physical diorama habitat, encourage students to refer to their notes, sketch lightly with pencil, keep an eraser handy to make changes, think carefully about what will be included, and know when to stop with their ideas. Young students sometimes get carried away with ideas and end up adding elements that are not important. In this situation, simple is better. Teacher modeling of a sketch with examples and nonexamples is a good way to illustrate the concept of not overdoing an idea. Similarly, as a prelude to Activity 4B, the teacher may choose to construct a sample diorama along with students. Watching the teacher work through the process can be highly motivating. The shared diorama may be worked on briefly at the beginning of each lesson or as time allows during the lesson while the teacher also facilitates and monitors the work of the students.

4. Use judgment about how long to let students work to keep time productive. About five minutes before ending the lesson, encourage students to find a stopping place where they feel comfortable finishing for the day and can easily find their place the next day. Keep the Zoogles in a safe place to dry and have students return all notes and sketches to their portfolios.

Activity 4B: Homemade Habitats: Constructing Dioramas

1. Establish expected behavior guidelines for working with craft materials. Remind students again that simple is better, and that they stick to their sketches and checklist notes and know when to stop. If a teacher or shared diorama is being built, briefly model how some of the materials may be used, but stress to students to use materials creatively. Students may then begin to build the diorama. Encourage them to be creative with the box orientation; a bird's-eye top view can be as interesting as the traditional side view.

2. After physical elements and plants of the habitat have been created, other animals representing Zoogle predators and prey may be added using craft materials or drawings.

3. Monitor and facilitate as needed. Young students usually work productively for up to 30 minutes, but if they are fully engaged, they may work up to 45 minutes. As with the prior lesson, inform students when there are approximately 5 to 10 minutes left to work and to come to a stopping place to allow closure for the day and sufficient time to clean up.

Evaluate Phase

As a summative assessment, students prepare and present a verbal presentation to explain the elements of their dioramas. They are assessed using a rubric that considers the completeness and accuracy of the diorama and the thoroughness with which the student explains the project. Students are not assessed on their artistic abilities or the elaborateness of the diorama. The expectation is that all elements are represented clearly and accurately.

Materials

- Completed dioramas

- Activity Sheet 3: Zoogle Observation Checklist (for reference)

- **Teacher note:** A digital camera to photograph dioramas is optional.

Activity 5A: Zoologists' Reports to the Museum's Board of Directors

1. As dioramas are completed, students prepare oral presentations (show and tell) to explain how the elements of their Zoogle habitat dioramas fit together with their Zoogle's particular adaptations to provide the Zoogle with its basic needs for survival in a particular type of environment (or habitat). Have a brief group brainstorming time to discuss and outline a logical sequence for the information in the presentation, which can be framed as if the student zoologists were reporting on their work to a museum's board of directors or making a presentation for visitors to the exhibit. This activity is an ideal setting to explicitly teach and assess students' development of speaking and listening skills (*CCSS ELA*).

2. Encourage students to refer to the checklist for specific details to include in their presentations. It is desirable for student zoologists who worked together on their dioramas to practice and present together.

3. Depending on the level of student engagement, the remainder of this lesson may be devoted to collaboration and practice or may move directly into presentations.

4. Before the presentations, the teacher should model examples and nonexamples of presentation behavior: voice volume and eye contact, references to parts of the diorama, proper listening, and how to ask appropriate questions.

5. Dioramas may be displayed in an area where they can be enjoyed by as many members of the school community as possible.

6. **Teacher note:** As an optional step, invite parents, other teachers, and the principal to attend presentations.

Activity 5B: Self-Assessment

In this final session, students use the Zoogles rubric to rate themselves on their own presentation and experience with the project. This is an opportunity to further develop students' writing skills and consolidate the lessons learned from their work. The teacher can use the feedback both to help inform the design of subsequent science, art, or ELA units and to further diagnose students' writing skills.

Materials

- Zoogle diorama

- Activity Sheet 5: My Zoogle Learning Experience (p. 112)

- Zoogle Portfolio

- Pencils

- **Teacher note:** Zoogle Teacher Rubrics (pp. 113 and 114) are optional.

1. Distribute Activity Sheet 5: My Zoogle Learning Experience and read it together. Although most second-grade students should be able to read it independently, shared reading is encouraged to check for understanding and clarify any questions that may arise. Students may complete the rubric independently, or the teacher may read each question before they respond.

2. Students complete the last portion independently to tell what parts of the project they liked the best and parts they did not like as much. Finally, ask students to answer the question to describe one thing they learned throughout the process.

3. Share the last part to tell about favorite and least favorite parts and one thing learned.

4. **Teacher note:** As an optional step, teachers may use Zoogle Teacher Rubrics to evaluate student dioramas and presentations.

Appendix: Habitats Vocabulary List

Basic Needs: what a living thing needs in order to live and grow; food and water; air; shelter (for animals); suitable temperature range; and adequate space

Carnivore: an animal that eats meat only

Habitat: a place where a living thing (plant or animal) can meet its basic needs for survival; a natural system that includes a combination of living and nonliving things

Herbivore: an animal that eats plants only

Living Parts of Habitat: plants and animals

Nonliving Parts of Habitat: rocks, soil, water, overall temperature, and rainfall

Omnivore: animal that eats both plants and meat

Organism: a living thing; second-grade *NGSS* focus on macroscopic plants and animals

Predator: an animal that hunts another animal

Prey: an animal that is hunted

Shelter: a safe place for protection from predators, raising young, or from harsh weather

Resources for the Classroom

Books

Dahl, M. 2004. *Do ducks live in the desert?* Minneapolis, MN: Picture Window Books/ Heinemann.

Lindeen, C. 2004. *Pebble plus living in a biome series: Life in a desert, life in a forest, life in an ocean, life in a polar region, life in a pond, life in a rain forest, life in a stream, life in a wetland.* Minneapolis, MN: Heinemann-Raintree Classroom.

Moore, J. E. 1998. *Habitats: Grades 1–3 science works for kids series.* Monterey, CA: Evan-Moor Educational Publishers.

Press, J. 2005. *Animal habitats: Learning about North American animals and plants thru art, science, and creative play.* Nashville, TN: Williamson Books.

Scholastic's *The Magic School Bus* series made-for-TV books appropriate for this unit:
  Hops home: A book about animal habitats (1995)
  Gets all dried up: A book about deserts (1996)
  Takes a dive: A book about coral reefs (1998)

*Butterfly and the bog beast: A book about
butterfly camouflage* (1996)
Gets eaten: A book about food chains (1996)
*Gets cold feet: A book about warm and
cold-blooded animals* (1997)

DVDs

Scholastic's *The Magic School Bus* series DVDs (and
accompanying books): *www.scholastic.com/
magicschoolbus/tv/index.htm*. Episodes may be
available for free viewing at *www.qubo.com*. TV
Tie-Ins: *www.scholastic.com/resources/booklist/
the-magic-school-bus-tv-tie-ins and www.
goodreads.com/series/69611-magic-school-bus-
tv-tie-ins* (27 titles). If the clips are not available,
select pages from the books could be shared via
a document camera.

The Library Video Company: *www.libraryvideo.com*.
Ecosystem DVDs:

All About (series): *Forest Ecosystems, Deserts and
Grasslands, Ecosystems*

Habitats: *Homes for Living Things*

Music for Science Teaching

Mr. Habitat (Bill Oliver) Music: Albums (see *Have to
Have a Habitat*): *www.mrhabitat.net/recordings.
php*

Song lyrics (e.g., *Habitat*): *www.mrhabitat.net/
songbook.php*

Songs for Teaching: Using Music to Promote Learning
(*e.g., short clip of the Habitat song;* search for
other adaptation and habitat-related songs under
Science/Life Sciences*): www.songsforteaching.
com/jeffschroeder/habitat.htm*

Sounds of Nature (series): *Nature Sampler* and
Environmental and Ecological Sounds

Terrarium and Aquarium Design Instructions

Carolina Biological (3:24 mins): search company
site (*www.carolina.com*) for "How to Set up
a Terrarium" or go to *www.youtube.com/
watch?v=YLkUNXG8vqE*

Fourth Grade Science Activities With an Aquarium
and Terrarium: *www.vrml.k12.la.us/4th/
science/Science_by_Unit08/4th_SC_Unit5/
UN5Act3_SC.htm*

Terrarium Man (variety of plans): *www.stormthecastle.
com/terrarium*

Websites About Animal Habitats and Ecosystems

ARKive: Free wildlife photos and videos: *www.arkive.
org*

BBC Science Simulations: *www.bbc.co.uk/schools/
scienceclips/index_flash.shtml*

Habitats: *www.bbc.co.uk/schools/scienceclips/
ages/8_9/habitats.shtml*

Plants and Animals in the Local Environment Game:
*www.bbc.co.uk/schools/scienceclips/ages/6_7/
plants_animals_env.shtml*

Elementary Science—Animals: 69 links to pictures,
videoclips, games, webcams, etc.: *www.
internet4classrooms.com/science_elem_animals.
htm*

iKnowthat.com: Animal Universe Game (Match
animals to habitats): *www.iknowthat.com/com/
L3?Area=Habitats*

Sheppard Software: Free online educational
games and activities (e.g., *Producers
Consumers Decomposers, Food Chain*): *www.
sheppardsoftware.com*

Switch Zoo: Build an Online Habitat: *http://switchzoo.
com/games/habitatgame.htm*

ACTIVITY SHEET 1
Zoogle Zoology!

Name _____

You are a world-famous zoologist. You and your team of zoologists have traveled to every ecosystem in every continent to observe and write about animals. You thought you had seen them all. But during your last expedition you discovered a new animal. Your team named it a Zoogle.

You are the very first scientists to discover and observe the Zoogle in its natural habitat. You have taken notes on how the Zoogle meets its basic needs, what its habitat is like, and how it is interdependent with plants and other animals in its habitat.

The American Museum of Unusual Creatures (AMUC) has asked you to create an exhibit to show the Zoogle in its natural surroundings. Now of course you would <u>never</u> take a Zoogle from its habitat, but you would create a model of a Zoogle in a model habitat.

Are you ready to begin? First, make sure all your notes about basic needs and habitat are complete (see Activity Sheet 2). Then decide how you will represent the Zoogle's habitat in the form of a diorama. Make a detailed and labeled sketch first to show all the plants and other animals in the Zoogle's habitat. You may work alone or with a team. Are you ready? Let's begin!

ACTIVITY SHEET 2
Habitat Graphic Organizer

Name _____

Habitat Name: _____

Nonliving things (soil, sand, rocks, relative amount of water, wind, sunlight, and so on) _____ _____ _____ _____ _____ _____	Plants that can be eaten by the Zoogle (unless the Zoogle is a carnivore) _____ _____ _____ _____ _____ _____
Prey (other animals) that can be eaten (unless the Zoogle is an herbivore) _____ _____ _____ _____ _____ _____	Predators that may eat the Zoogle _____ _____ _____ _____ _____ _____

ACTIVITY SHEET 3

Zoogle Observation Checklist

Name _____

Directions: Use this checklist to tell about your Zoogle and plan the museum display.

1. Habitat: _____
   (ocean, desert, forest, prairie, rain forest, wetland)

2. Where in its habitat does the Zoogle make its shelter?

   _____

   _____

3. How does the Zoogle move about? (crawl, fly, hop or jump, run, slither, swim)

   _____

4. Diet: _____
   (herbivore, carnivore, or omnivore?)

5. Predators of Zoogles: _____

6. How does a Zoogle protect itself from predators?

   _____

   _____

7. Is your Zoogle an   adult   <u>or</u>   young   Zoogle? (circle one)

   Is your Zoogle a   male   <u>or</u>   female? (circle one)

8. Other information about the Zoogle: _____

   _____

   _____

NATIONAL SCIENCE TEACHERS ASSOCIATION

ACTIVITY SHEET 4

Zoogle Habitat Planning Sketch

Name _____

On this page make a labeled sketch of the Zoogle in its natural habitat.

Be sure to include the following:

• The Zoogle and its physical structures (adaptations) to match the habitat

• Plants

• Zoogle prey and Zoogle predators

• Shelter

• Water and other nonliving parts of the habitat (rocks, and so on)

ACTIVITY SHEET 5

My Zoogle Learning Experience

Name _____

Directions: Read the Zoogle Habitat Rubric. Put a check mark or × in the box to tell how you think you did. Answer the questions at the bottom of the page.

	I did my best work.	I did not do my best work.
My diorama shows a Zoogle that looks like it lives there.		
My diorama shows water and soil for the habitat.		
My diorama shows a Zoogle predator.		
My diorama shows a Zoogle's prey.		
My diorama shows plants and other animals in the habitat.		

1. What part of the Zoogles project did you like best? _____

_____

_____

2. What part of Zoogles did you like the least? _____

_____

_____

3. What is the most important thing you learned during Zoogles?_____

_____

_____

Zoogle Diorama Design Rubric

(FOR THE TEACHER)

Name: _____

Category	3	2	1
Physical elements of habitat: Water Soil/sand/rock	Accurately depicts elements of physical habitat; type of habitat is easily identifiable.	Includes many elements of physical habitat; type of habitat is identifiable with explanation.	Includes few elements of physical habitat; type of habitat is not clearly identifiable.
Zoogle's physical structures and overall appearance match habitat.	Physical structures and overall appearance accurate and clearly identifiable.	Physical structures and overall appearance identifiable with explanation.	Physical structures and appearance do not match habitat or are unclear.
Plants and other animals accurately represented in habitat.	More than two additional plants or animals represented.	Two additional plants or animals represented.	One additional plant and one additional animal represented.
Predator/prey relationships shown.	Zoogle predator and Zoogle prey are represented.	Either Zoogle predator or Zoogle prey is represented.	Neither Zoogle predator nor prey is represented.

Zoogle Diorama Presentation Rubric

(FOR THE TEACHER)

Name: _____

Category	3	2	1
Volume of voice during presentation.	Uses appropriate volume of voice consistently and independently.	Uses appropriate volume with minimal teacher prompting.	Requires multiple teacher prompting to use or maintain appropriate volume.
Uses vocabulary appropriate for habitat.	Describes diorama with appropriate vocabulary independently.	Requires minimal teacher prompting to describe diorama with appropriate vocabulary.	Requires considerable teacher prompting to describe diorama with appropriate vocabulary.
Refers to diorama during presentation.	Refers to diorama consistently to support explanation.	Refers to diorama to support explanation with minimal prompting.	Refers to diorama to support explanation with considerable prompting or not at all.
Able to answer appropriate questions from audience.	Answers most or all questions independently and confidently.	Answers questions with some prompting.	Has difficulty answering questions even with prompting.

LIFE SCIENCES

D. Animal Behavior in Groups

Helen Pashley, PhD
Consultant
Putnam/Northern Westchester Board of Cooperative Educational Services (BOCES)

Recommended Level
Grade 3

Topic Focus
Life Sciences

Disciplinary Core Idea
LS2: Ecosystems: Interactions, energy, and dynamics
LS2.D: Social interactions and group behavior

Time Frame

Engage Phase
60–70 minutes (Activity 1A and 1B)

Explore Phase
120 minutes (Activity 2A and 2B)

Explain Phase
60 minutes (Activity 3)

Elaborate Phase
90 minutes and half or full-day field trip
(Activity 4)

Evaluate Phase
60 minutes plus extension into English language
arts (ELA) lesson (Activity 5)

Objectives
As a result of these experiences, students will be able to

- use science practices to observe physical characteristics and individual and group behavior of humpback whales and gorillas in field-based video clips, and pill bugs and termites in hands-on explorations;

- identify and categorize behavioral interactions within groups of like animals;

- provide evidence-based arguments on the advantages of belonging to a group; and

- research, obtain, and communicate information about social interactions and group behavior in an animal species of their choosing using various print and electronic media.

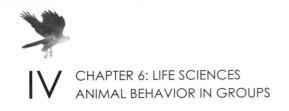

TABLE 6D.1. CORRELATION TO THE *NEXT GENERATION SCIENCE STANDARDS*

3. Interdependent relationships in ecosystems
3-LS2-1. Construct an argument that some animals form groups that help members survive.

Scientific and Engineering Practices (Dimension 1)	Disciplinary Core Ideas (Dimension 3)	Crosscutting Concepts (Dimension 2)
1. <u>Asking questions (for science)</u> and defining problems (for engineering)[1]	LS2: Ecosystems: Interactions, energy, and dynamics	1. Patterns
2. Developing and using models (***Note:*** This is a minor focus of this 5E mini-unit. Pillbugs and termites can be viewed as small-scale, manipulable models for related group behaviors in larger mammals that are studied indirectly through video clips).	LS2.D: Social interactions and group behavior * Being part of a group helps animals obtain food, defend themselves, and cope with changes. Groups may serve different functions and vary dramatically in size.	2. Cause and effect: Mechanism and explanation (***Note:*** Although animal behaviors can be viewed through this lens, cause and effect is not explicitly discussed in this 5E mini-unit)
3. Planning and carrying out investigations		3. Scale, proportion, and quantity (***Note:*** This is a minor focus of this 5E mini-unit)
4. Analyzing and interpreting data		4. Systems and system models (not explicitly discussed, though animal groups are systems)
6. Constructing explanations (for science) and designing solutions (for engineering)		6. Structure and function
7. Engaging in argument from evidence		7. Stability and change
8. Obtaining, evaluating, and communicating information		

[1] This mini-unit does not address all portions of the standard as written; the relevant elements are underlined.

Note: LS = Life sciences

Continued

Table 6D.1. (continued)

Scientific and Engineering Practices (Dimension 1)	Disciplinary Core Ideas (Dimension 3)	Crosscutting Concepts (Dimension 2)
Common Core State Standards Connections ***English Language Arts –*** <u>Reading Informational Text</u> **RI.3.10.** By the end of the year, read and comprehend informational texts, including history/social studies, science, and technical texts, at the high end of the grades 2–3 text complexity band independently and proficiently. <u>Writing</u> **W.3.2.** Write informative/explanatory texts to examine a topic and convey ideas and information clearly. <u>Speaking and Listening</u> **SL.3.1.** Engage effectively in a range of collaborative discussions (one-on-one, in groups, and teacher-led) with diverse partners on *grade 3 topics and texts*, building on others' ideas and expressing their own clearly. **SL.3.4.** Report on a topic or text, tell a story, or recount an experience with appropriate facts and relevant, descriptive details, speaking clearly at an understandable pace. ***Mathematics—****No mathematical connections are developed in this mini-unit.*		

Note: Since the pill bugs, sow bugs, and termites that are used in the Explore phase are involved in the decomposition and recycling of dead or dying plant life (which is not a major focus of this unit), this third-grade unit is best taught before the other third-grade unit in this book (Demystifying Decomposers). That is, this unit (whose primary focus is on Animal Behavior in Groups) can raise questions that will later be explored in more detail.

Engage Phase

Although social interactions between animals and group behavior have rarely been included as a formal unit of study at the elementary level, it is a specified component of the third-grade *Next Generation Science Standards* (*NGSS*). In this introductory phase of this unit, students will watch two dramatic video clips (i.e., collaborative hunting behavior in humpback whales and interactions in four gorilla families) that will engage them and raise their interest in animal behaviors in groups. After listening to a read-aloud passage about Jane Goodall, and recalling the zoologist in the gorilla video, they will begin to understand the science practices that are used

to study animal behavior. Finally, they will brainstorm how the human groups that they belong to might be related in structure and function to groups formed by other animals.

Materials

- Internet access and projector to display the two YouTube video clips cited below; additional background information on these two mammalian species can be found at the following.

  - Enchanted Learning

    - *www.enchantedlearning.com/subjects/ whales/species/Humpbackwhale.shtml*

- www.enchantedlearning.com/subjects/apes/gorilla/Mtgorillaprintout.shtml

  ◆ National Geographic

    - http://animals.nationalgeographic.com/animals/mammals/humpback-whale

    - http://animals.nationalgeographic.com/animals/mammals/mountain-gorilla

  ◆ Wikipedia

    - http://en.wikipedia.org/wiki/Humpback_whale

    - http://en.wikipedia.org/wiki/Mountain_gorilla

- Passage from the book by Jeannine Atkins *Girls Who Looked Under Rocks: The Lives of Six Pioneering Naturalists.* Use pages 50–57 as a read-aloud.

- Students' science notebooks

- Sticky notes for each student

Activity 1A: Humpback Whales Help Each Other Hunt Herring and Gorillas Gather in Groups

Teacher note: Students' prior knowledge related to animal behavior may include caring for individual pet animals in their homes, watching natural history PBS and cable TV programs, and visiting aquariums, nature centers, or zoos with their families. Less privileged students typically lack many of these experiences. The following activities will create a common experiential foundation to help all students develop an enlarged conceptual framework for understanding the behaviors of animals in groups.

1. Prepare students to view the first video clip by using the following focus questions.

   ◆ What kind of organisms do these large (12–16 m or 39–52 ft; you can show this length using the diagonal of your classroom), water-dwelling mammals eat? [Answer: 1–2 cm krill and small schooling fish such as herring]

   ◆ Are humpback whales good at hunting fish? Be prepared to share your evidence.

   ◆ How is being part of a group important for a humpback whale?

2. Show the YouTube video clip (2:10 minutes) Apexpredator11. 2007. Humpback whale: Hunting Technique at *www.youtube.com/watch?v=vJvfjiCTvq4.*

3. Many other fascinating segments can be found on the original source for this video clip: Nature (PBS series): Ocean Giants, a three-part, three-hour series (Giant Lives, Deep Thinkers, and Voices of the Sea): *www.pbs.org/wnet/nature/episodes/ocean-giants/introduction/7563.* This website contains whale fact sheets, size comparisons, sample video clips (e.g., killer whales using an alternative approach to group hunting of herring) and other resources.

4. Tell students to spend five minutes in a quick write, summarizing what they observed and making inferences on how belonging to a group might help a humpback whale survive.

5. Form student pairs to discuss the content of their quick writes. Students should then add three things that they learned from their partners below a line of learning, a colored line drawn on a page that differentiates the original work of the student from ideas that

they may learn from a partner, the teacher, books, or the internet; in each case students should cite where they got the information by naming the students with whom they worked. Encouraging cooperative group interactions between students can serve as an example of the focus of this unit.

6. Prepare students to view the second video about gorilla groups by posing the following questions.

   ◆ Which different individuals make up a gorilla group?

   ◆ How is being part of a group important for a gorilla?

7. Show the Explore.org video: Explore Team (2009): Gorillas 98.6% Human: *www.youtube. com/watch?v=co8NneR8ilc&feature=related*. The whole clip is 22 minutes and 10 seconds. Show only the first 10 minutes and 33 seconds. As with all internet clips, check for possible unsuitable comments below the frame before showing to students.

8. Share student comments as a whole class, reminding them to provide evidence for their statements.

9. Ask students the following questions to get them to see the connections between the two videos with respect to the common science practices that underlie the videos.

   ◆ What challenges or difficulties would you face if you were studying these animals (i.e., humpback whales and mountain gorillas) in their natural habitats?

   ◆ What equipment did you see being used?

   ◆ In what ways were the studies done by the scientists the same? How were they different?

   ◆ Which skills did the scientists use?

   ◆ Which of these science practices are the same as you might use in a science class?

Teacher note: You may want to refer to a class wall chart where you have posted the eight science and engineering practices from the *NGSS* for use throughout the school year.

10. Read aloud to the class the informational text passage (pages 5–57) from *Girls Who Looked Under Rocks*. Have them follow on their copy. Give students the following writing prompt to answer in their notebooks.

   Louis Leakey thought that Jane would be successful in studying chimpanzees. What characteristics did Jane have that helped her be successful? Cite specific evidence from the text in your answer.

Activity 1B: Third Graders Group Together, Too

1. Have students think about the groups to which they personally belong. These will include their family, their class, their grade, activity groups such as sports teams, music or dance groups, Boy/Girl Scouts, afterschool clubs, and so on. Ask them the following questions.

   ◆ What is the name of the group? (Sport teams may have animal names.)

   ◆ What is the purpose of the group? What can the "team" accomplish together through cooperation that they could not achieve as well (or at all) as individuals?

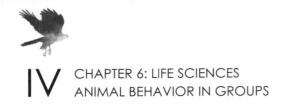
◆ Who is in the group? Are all the members the same gender and/or about the same age or is the group more diverse in composition?

◆ How is the group organized? Is there one leader or several leaders?

◆ Do all the members of the group have the same role, or do some members have different, specialized roles?

◆ How long lasting is the group (stability)? Does it last for a few weeks, a season, a school year, or multiple years?

2. Now give each person a small booklet of sticky notes. Tell students to take two minutes to silently brainstorm anything that comes to mind with the phrase *group of animals*. Students should write one concept on each sticky note and place all completed sticky notes on their desks. After the initial two minutes, they should work in groups of four to sort the items written on the sticky notes, classifying or grouping them by an unspoken relationship. You may ask the groups to remain silent (to model nonverbal means of animal communication).

3. Next ask the groups to share how they sorted the sticky notes and to state what commonalities they see in their ideas. What items stand out? If possible, have students recall what different groups of animals they might have seen on television, such as Animal Planet, Discovery Channel, National Geographic, PBS Nature, or in movie theater films or DVDs such as the *March of the Penguins*. Ask students the following.

◆ Do animals belong to groups with similar and/or different purposes than humans do? Cite some evidence or examples to support your answer.

◆ How does belonging to a group offer advantages that help an animal survive?

◆ Why might it be important to study animal groups and behavior?

Teacher note: All organisms exist within natural ecosystems where a combination of intra- and inter-group interactions is critical to both individual and group survival. Both cooperative and competitive interactions within and between species are important to the ecological balance of nature. Preserving endangered species requires that we know how many animals need to be in a group to find suitable mates and how much land to allow groups of animals for their health and well-being. Scientists also study nature's animal engineers to look for ways to mimic some of the successful features of natural systems (e.g., the movement of schools of fish or flocks of birds may help us design better transportation or tele-communication systems. For more information, search the internet for resources on biomimicry).

Although the intent of the Engage phase is more to raise questions than answer them, at this point students should be developing a sense that (1) human and other animal groups may differ in composition, organization, specialization, and stability; and (2) belonging to a group provides advantages for the survival and well-being of the individuals. Synergy between individuals working together enables the group to accomplish things that isolated individuals could not accomplish as well (if at all).

Explore Phase

In this phase, students will share, compare, and contrast the interactions and group behavior of two different species of animals in direct hands-on explorations. Pill bugs (or sow bugs) and termites serve as easily manipulated, low-cost, safe, small-scale models of relatively nonsocial and highly social (respectively) group-oriented animals.

Teacher note: Direct hands-on exploration with both organisms is optimal. But if time is limited, half of the students might investigate one of the animals and half the other (a common set of procedures), followed by a group sharing of results. Alternatively, if resources only allow the study of one animal, the termites are the better choice since they are a social species with clearly observable group interactions. In this case, the teacher may still want to demonstrate the dissimilar behavior of the pill bugs using a document camera to project images to the whole class. In either case, anyone working with the small animals should wash their hands with soap and water upon completing the activities.

The term *bug* is somewhat ambiguous. In everyday life, people refer to any relatively small (but visible) creepy, crawly, or flying nonamphibian, nonavian, nonmammalian, or nonreptilian animal as a bug (e.g., spiders, millipedes and centipedes, snails, and so on). Scientifically speaking, true bugs are any animal that is a member of the insect order Hemiptera. Thus, neither pill bugs, sow bugs, (terrestrial crustaceans that are *not* classified as insects) nor termites (a member of the insect order Hymenoptera) are true bugs. As with many other cases, scientific terminology is more restrictive (and descriptive) than everyday language.

Materials

- Pill bugs or sow bugs, enough for five in each petri dish or for each pair of students (See Carolina Biological, Terrestrial Isopods, catalog 143062. See also Carolina's "Critters" in the Classroom: Pill bugs at *www.youtube.com/watch?v=s90Eknn9NVg*. These organisms are also available from Ward's Natural Science)

- One petri dish for each pair of students (e.g. Polystyrene Square Integrid Petri Dish available from Carolina Biological, catalog 41470 for pill bugs or sow bugs)

- White paper cut to fit into the petri dishes

- Paper towels cut into approximately 4–5 cm squares (at least one square for each dish) that will later be dampened with water

- Metric rulers (12 in./30 cm size)

- One pack of 100 sterile worker termites (Available from Carolina Biological, catalog 143736 or two packs of 25 termites and Wards' Scientific, catalog 87 V 6460)

- Thick black construction paper cut into semicircles stapled together to cover half of the petri dishes completely

- Sticky tape

- Magnifying glasses and/or bug boxes with magnifiers

- Paintbrushes

- Bic brand pens

- Photographs of soldier and reproductive termites (queen and king) (see Resources)

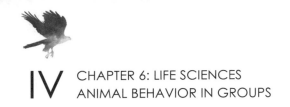

- Digital microscope, digital camera, or video camera (optional)

Order the living materials from a science supply company. If desired, pill bugs or sow bugs (but *not* termites!) may be collected from outdoors and released back into their natural habitats at the end of the mini-unit. Animals ordered from supply companies will come with care and feeding instructions. In either case, do not leave the animal in dry dishes for longer than 15 minutes since their small size results in a high surface-area-to-volume ratio that makes death by dehydration a potential problem. As always, respect for life is demonstrated by proper care and treatment of any living organism. The teacher may want to precut paper circles to fit inside the petri dishes and the small, paper towel squares (approximately 4–5 cm squared before being wetted and formed into a squeezed out ball).

Teacher note: Pill bugs and sow bugs are small, oval crustaceans (*not* true bugs or even insects) with seven pairs of legs and two pairs of antennae. They are commonly found in damp leaf litter and under stones or logs where they mostly feed on (and help recycle) dead plant matter.

They are typically nocturnal. Unusually for land living animals, they breathe through gills as well as through the thin cuticle on their underside. Some species (known as pill bugs) roll up into a ball if disturbed (as a form of protection from predation and to limit water loss). They are hydrophilic (they prefer dampness), photophobic (they avoid light), and thigmophilic (they like contact with surfaces). Although *not* social animals, they tend to congregate where the optimal environmental conditions are met. They also respond positively to the presence of other pill bugs, so if one animal finds a suitable

FIGURE 6D.1. PILL BUG

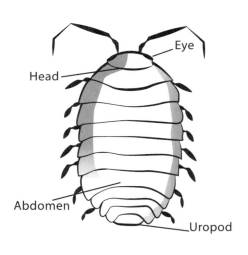

PILL BUG

FIGURE 6D.2. SOW BUG

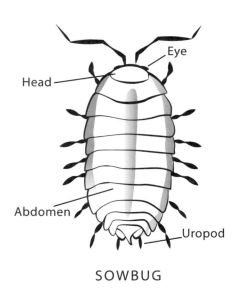

SOWBUG

FIGURE 6D.3. TERMITES

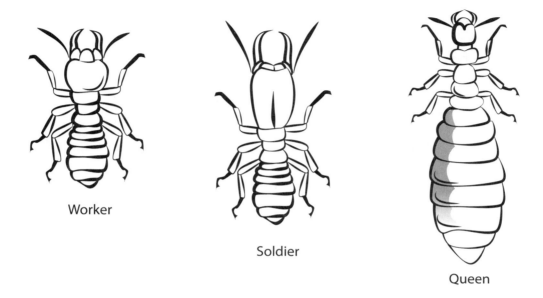

Worker

Soldier

Queen

location, others will tend to stay in the same place. Animals interact with the environment by constantly sensing conditions with their antennae. When they meet, they will touch the other animal, but there is no exchange of materials and unlike termites they do not follow a scent trail left by another pill bug (or a Bic pen). Interactions are random and animals do not have different roles within a group. Students may observe different sizes (i.e., ages) and possibly different species of pill bugs or sow bugs clustering together in their natural habitat. Animals will leave the group to find food or if conditions are not suitable. Brief family groups may also occur. Females carry their eggs and eventually the young in a brood pouch. For more information, see Resources.

In contrast, termites are highly social insects. They have the typical body plan of an insect with head, thorax, abdomen, and six legs. The blind, pale workers live underground in a colony and feed on dead plant material such as rotting wood. The number of animals may number up to 60,000 or more, with different specialized roles (castes) filled by members of the group.

Soldier termites have large jaws to defend the nest from predators such as ants, and one or more queens (fertilized by one male termite) lay the eggs. Worker termites feed the other members of the group. The queen may live for up to 45 years, and colonies are long lasting even though individual workers only have a life span of one to two years. Members constantly communicate with each other by chemical signals known as pheromones and follow scent trails to find their way to and from food sources discovered by their team mates. In this experiment, termites will follow an ink trail that contains chemicals similar to termite pheromones. They also tap their heads to produce vibrations when alarmed. At this grade level, do not go into details of the caste system.

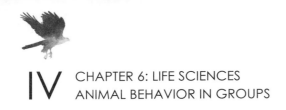

Activity 2: Activity 2A: Pill Bug or Sow Bug Explorations + Activity 2B: Termite Explorations

The following experimental designs and procedures refer to the generic phrase "small animal(s)" to refer to either pill bugs or sow bugs or termites as an identical set of tests should be run with both types of animals—either concurrently with different student teams specializing on different animals or with every student team working with both animals in two different sessions). The two types of animals should *not* be mixed or placed together in the same petri dish. Each pair of students will need to pick up a petri dish, magnifying glasses or bug boxes, a piece of black construction paper, and a damp paper towel square. To begin their explorations, they should add one small animal to their dry petri dish using a paint brush and tape the lid shut.

1. Observing Behavior of an Individual Small Animal

    ◆ Observations of the Animal's Structure

    ◆ How many body segments does it have?

    ◆ How many legs?

    ◆ What is its approximate size?

    ◆ List all of the other features of the animal's body that you can observe.

    Teacher note: It might help to use a magnifying glass. To observe the underside of an insect, place it in a clear, empty petri dish and look up from the underside.

2. How Does the Animal Explore the Petri Dish?

    Draw a circle in your notebook the same size as the petri dish. On your circle, map where the animal is during a five-minute observation period (by making a dot or an X at each location at regular 30–60 second intervals and then connecting the dots to draw the approximate path it followed). Where does the animal spend most of its time?

3. *Intra*species Interactions (using two or more of the *same kind* of small animal)

    Predict what you may observe when a second small animal is added to the dish. Then, use a paintbrush to add a second individual (of the same species) to the environment. If desired, make a second circle-map in your notebook with the two animal's five-minute trails in different colors (i.e., each student should pick a different animal to track with a different color pen or pencil and place a dot or X on the paper for each 30–60 second interval). Do the two same kind of small animals interact with each other? Do they stay close together or mainly stay farther apart?

4. Experimenting With Different Environmental Conditions

    Teacher note: Test only one variable at a time.

    Do the Animals Prefer Light or Dark Habitats? Place two or more of the small animals inside a dry petri dish. Use tape and a stapled piece of black construction paper to cover ½ of the petri dish. This will set up a habitat in which the animals have a choice between a light and a dark place. Do they spend more of their time in light or in darkness (i.e., check their location once every 30–60 seconds for five minutes and keep a simple tally of their location)?

FIGURE 6D.4. PETRI DISH AND PAPER TOWEL SETUP

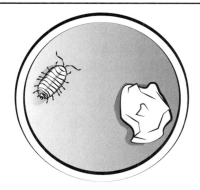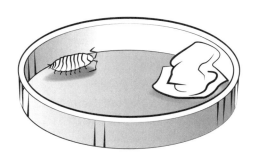

Teacher note: Do not use any water or moisture in this setup.

Can the Animals Follow a Trail Left by a Bic Pen? Cut a circular piece of white, unmarked paper (or paper towel) to fit inside a clean, dry petri dish. Use a Bic pen to draw a straight or wavy line, triangle, or circle on the paper, keeping at least 1 cm away from the circumference of the paper or petri dish. Place the marked paper inside the petri dish, add an individual animal, and observe if it seems to sense and respond to the trail. Add a second individual and see if it behaves similarly.

Do the Animals Respond to Dampness? Place the damp paper towel square inside your petri dish near one side. Place two or more small animals near the inside of the dish opposite to the dampened towel. Observe—do the animals seem to move toward the dampened towel? Do they spend more time near to, or away from, the towel?

How Do Small Animals Behave in Large Groups? Teacher-directed, whole-class demonstration: If available, a digital docu-ment camera would be useful to project the termite's group behaviors to the entire class at one time. Cover the bottom of an empty aquarium or large plastic dish pan with slightly dampened paper towels, making a flat, damp surface. Place all the small animals (of one kind at a time) used by the entire class inside the container. How do the animals behave? Do they tend to aggregate together or stay apart? In the case of the termites, you may also want to repeat the ink-following trail tests using a dry paper towel–lined aquarium and larger scale trails as follows.

Can Termites Find Damp Wood? Place a small piece of damp, rotting wood at one end of the aquarium and draw a wavy line with a Bic pen from the other end of the aquarium to the damp, rotting wood on a dry piece of paper. Next, place a worker termite on the end of the aquarium opposite the damp, rotting wood with a paintbrush. Ask students to watch the termite closely.

◆ How quickly does the termite find the wood? Does it seem to follow the path of

IV

the Bic pen or does the termite seem to wander aimlessly all over the aquarium? **Teacher note:** The ink has chemicals similar to a termite scent trail.

- Now add more termites to the end of the aquarium opposite the damp wood.

- Do the other termites take the same path as the first termite, or go a different way to get to the damp piece of wood?

- How might leaving a scent trail help other members of the colony?

- Alternatively, the class can brainstorm and test other ways to use the Bic pen ink lines to change the path the termites follow (e.g., put the termites between two concentric circles). They might also be able to observe other behaviors such as the grooming or the exchange of food.

Ask students the following questions:

- What other kinds of additional observations or tests can we make to find out if these animals live in groups?

- What behaviors suggest that they do (or do not) form organized groups?

Answers might include might include observing animals moving together, staying in the same place, interacting with another animal, and so on. If desired, the class can devise a suitable data recording sheet (tally sheet). Other options might include taking turns observing and describing what they see for their partner to write down, taking photos or recording with a video camera.

Teacher note: Individual pill bugs or sow bugs do not belong to any special social organization. The groups that they form are random, based on the habitat they prefer. Small groups may gather under rocks and logs for a few hours or days depending on the weather and food supply. Individuals may be different ages, but they do not have specialized roles within the group, nor do they leave or follow trails left by other members of their same species. Termites (as students will learn in more detail during the Explain phase) are members of a highly social species with specialized roles for different types of individuals.

5. Have students share their data and compare and summarize the behavior of the two kinds of animals. As a transition to the next Explain phase of the mini-unit, ask students the following.

- Why might scientists want to study these animals and their behavior? Possible answers include home destruction caused by termites or the beneficial role pill bugs play in decomposition and recycling of decaying matter.

- What did you do today that was like the scientists we saw in the first session studying gorillas and humpback whales (i.e., common science practices)?

- Since termites are clearly a social, group-oriented species, what evidence do you have that a termite colony might be made up of different kinds of individuals with different roles (like the different body builds for football players who have different roles or functions—quarterbacks, running backs, linemen, and so on)?

Explain Phase

The purpose of this session is to focus students' attention on classifying animal groups into the following categories: size, composition, organization, member roles (specialization), and stability. This is also the time to formally clarify any relevant terminology and concepts.

Materials

- Photographs of and information on a wide variety of animal groups (see Resources and Appendix for suggestions)

Preparation for Activity 3

1. Use digital projection or a document camera to remind students of the last question about termites from the Explore phase. After reviewing their answers to this question, project sketches or actual photographs of other members of a termite colony: the soldiers and the queen. Ask the following:

    - Are all the members of the termite colony the same?

    - If not, how might their different body shapes, sizes, and structures allow the different individuals to serve different functions and play different roles within the group? Answer: Different members of the colony have different roles. Soldier termites have large brown heads with large black jaws for attacking creatures, such as ants, that might threaten the colony. The queen is huge with a large abdomen. Her role is to lay eggs that hatch into new members.

2. Read the background information and select pictures that students will use as resources for Activity 3. It is important to preview the pictures yourself to ensure that they are suitable for your classroom situation.

Activity 3: Picture Perfect Animal Groups

1. Give each group of four students a selection of photographs of different animal groups. Have them discuss these questions:

    - Why might it be an advantage to an animal to live in a group?

    - How might being in a group help an animal to survive?

    Remind students they can also use evidence from their notebooks, prior knowledge, and the ideas they learned from the Engage and Explore activities.

2. Have students summarize and communicate the information they have already learned about the characteristics of animal groups. They differ according to composition and organization (i.e., the group may contain equal individuals, hierarchies, families, small groups containing animals of a single gender, mixed genders and animals of the same age). In some groups members may have special tasks, or roles. Groups may have different functions (e.g., protection, breeding, finding food, migration). Groups may be stable over a long time, or only come together for a short time (see background information in the Appendix).

3. Allocate a different characteristic (e.g., stability) to each student group. Students sort the photographs on their desks and choose labels for their categories (e.g., long-lasting and short-lived). Each group shares its examples

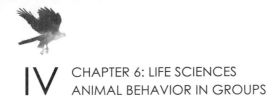
with the rest of the class in a gallery walk around the classroom.

4. Next have students brainstorm how or when these groups might change.

♦ What might happen if new individuals move into the group?

♦ How do individuals leave the group?

♦ What is the purpose of the group?

♦ How is the group different from a collection of individuals of that species?

♦ How do members of the group interact?

♦ Are all the members of the group equal, or do they have different roles?

♦ How long does the group last?

Elaborate Phase

In this session student pairs or triads choose from a teacher-approved list an animal species that they would like to investigate. They may use a combination of direct observations (in the classroom, at their homes or from a fieldtrip), internet, video, and print resources to determine the characteristics of the group their animal lives in. This formative assessment is designed to strengthen and extend their understanding of animal behavior in groups to other species not previously investigated. Additionally, it should help ensure that they are ready for the individual summative assessment in the next Evaluate phase.

Materials

• Laptops and internet access to video clips (see Resources for suggestions)

• Books, magazines, databases (see Resources for suggestions)

• Notebook, pencil, and—if available and depending on the particular animal and location to be observed—magnifying lenses, binoculars, and/or digital cameras for use in direct, field-based observations

Preparation

1. If the teacher is able to arrange a school-sanctioned and -supported field trip to a local zoo, aquarium, or nature center, a teacher pretrip visit and discussion with the facility's staff will help maximize learning outcomes. Most such facilities maintain active websites that can be used as teacher and student resources for pre- and postvisit lessons.

2. Depending on the school's location, it may be possible for students to collect information on different animal groups without the need for transportation or an admissions fee. These might include the schoolyard or a nearby field or park to observe flocks of Canadian geese and waterfowl, pigeons, house sparrows, and ants or bees. Another possible site is bird feeders, either at home or on the school grounds, as a site for observing squirrels and regional birds. In any case, it is important to identify potential safety issues (e.g., avoid poison ivy, be aware of any student allergies, and limit closeness to bees). It is also important to have additional adult supervision (classroom aides, parent volunteers, and so on).

3. Alternatively, if these team-based investigations are going to rely on internet clips, be sure to preview and select a short list of appropriate video clips (see the examples provided in the Evaluate phase and the Resources section that follow).

Activity 4: Team-Based Project Presentations on Animal Behaviors in Groups

1. Tell students they are now going to apply what they have learned by investigating and reporting back on another animal that can be found in groups. Remind students that they should try to avoid anthropomorphizing (i.e., inferring human emotions or motivations in their animals), while still considering how their animal's group behaviors might relate to similar behaviors in humans.

2. Allocate an animal species to student pairs or triads, have students pick an animal from a list, or choose an animal with teacher approval. Students can use electronic or print media to research the following questions about their animal:

   ◆ Describe the animal group of your species in detail. Be specific about the typical number of individuals per group and state whether individuals in the group are related, and if so, how this is known.

   ◆ Do different individuals within the group seem to have different structures, sizes, or shapes?

   ◆ What tasks (or functions) do members of the group perform? Are they the same or different?

   ◆ What behaviors do you see the animals showing? What does this tell you about how members of the group communicate?

   ◆ Can you see any patterns or repeated behaviors in the group?

   ◆ Can you find out how long the group lasts?

   ◆ What are some advantages for an individual to be a member of this group?

   ◆ What are some questions you would like to answer if you could go and study this animal group in more detail in their natural habitat?

3. Have students present the results of their research as a poster, podcast, web 2.0 page, or a PowerPoint presentation to share with the rest of the class, other classes, parents, or the community. Having a larger purpose and audience for the presentations on the investigations is critical.

Evaluate Phase

The purpose of this session is to provide summative assessment (i.e., typically for individual grading purposes). Students are challenged to individually transfer and apply the lessons learned in the previous activities to video clips of different animal species that live in groups.

Materials

- Computer linked to projector and internet access

- Student notebooks

Activity 5: Video Verification of Student Knowledge of Animal Behaviors in Groups

1. Select one or more of the following video clips to show to your students and ask them to individually write responses to the following questions.

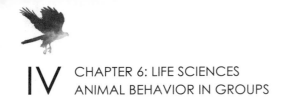
◆ What evidence-based arguments can you make to support the idea that this animal lives in a social group?

◆ What survival benefits do the individual organisms gain from living in this group? What, if any, risks or costs might individuals experience as a direct result of living in this group?

◆ How is this animal's social behavior like one of the other animals you studied in this unit? Select and discuss a specific example.

◆ What additional experimental tests would you like to be able to do (or see done) on the social behavior of this animal species?

◆ If any of the mammal video clips are used, ask: How important do you think is it for zoos to house social mammals in groups (versus isolation)?

Teacher note: This activity should be integrated with ELA instruction where students have an opportunity to work on refining their ability to articulate their understanding of science in a written, expository form over a more extended period of time. It is also possible to challenge students to use poetry or other creative forms of writing.

Sample Video Clips of Animal Behavior in Groups

Ant Antics

• Ant Colony Raids a Rival Nest (3 mins, 44 secs; BBC video clip with graphic visuals and narration): *www.youtube.com/watch?v=X5YaihAtnC4*

• Ants: Nature's Secret Power (54 mins; first 6 mins, 30 secs include graphic close-up views of the ants collectively overcoming larger insects, protecting their nest from a human and a bear, and attacking a bee hive): *www.youtube.com/watch?v=Z-gIx7LXcQM*

• Anty Social Behavior (2-mins, funny video clip without narration; ants remove pasta letters that spell out this title): *www.youtube.com/watch?v=q7tNnKvZi3A*

• Mass of Ants Behave as a Fluid (2 mins, 25 secs with subtitles but without narration; engineers draw multiple analogies): *www.youtube.com/watch?v=uZSqx0PJ8XU*

Elephants Are Extraordinary

• Elephants show cooperation on (human-designed) test (1 min, 28 secs): *www.youtube.com/watch?v=CXcRw6Piaj8*

• Female Elephants Rescue a Drowning Baby (in the wild) (3 mins, 10 secs without narration): *www.youtube.com/watch?v=Cd-LtWtNvDw*

Honey Bees Huddle

• Honeybee Waggle Dance Experiment (1 min, 38 secs): *www.youtube.com/watch?v=ywdTfEBVcSY*

• Interpreting the Language of Bees (2 mins, 41 secs): *www.youtube.com/watch?v=Vaszh2bY3mc*

• Why Do Honeybees Dance? (1 min, 58 secs): *www.youtube.com/watch?v=7UukNSmcUa8*

Meerkats

• Meerkats United (9 mins, 52 secs; 4:30–7:40 mins features meerkats taking turns as lookouts): *www.youtube.com/ watch?v=zGR0bAeP350*

- The Meerkats. (full BBC episode): *www.imdb. com/title/tt0892391* Natural World: Meerkats, Part of the Team (48 mins, 59 secs): *www. youtube.com/watch?v=F5zym-xuhJ4*

Prairie Dogs

- Prairie Dog Snake Alarm (3 mins, 48 secs): *www.youtube.com/watch?v=icaGIeOY9gc*

- Prairie Dog Coyote Alarm: *http://animal. discovery.com/tv-shows/wild-kingdom/videos/ prairie-dogs-sound-the-alarm.htm*

- Prairie Dog Language (full episode sequenced in short clips): *http://animal. discovery.com/tv-shows/wild-kingdom/videos/ prairie-dog-language.htm*

Primate Pairings

- Chimpanzee Problem Solving by Coopera-tion (with humans; 2 mins, 13 secs): *www. youtube.com/watch?v=xOrgOW9LnT4*

- (Capuchin) Monkey Cooperation and Fairness (intraspecies): *www.youtube.com/ watch?v=aAFQ5kUHPkY*

Resources

Books

Atkins, J.. 2000. *Girls who looked under rocks: The lives of six pioneering naturalists.* Nevada City, Nevada: Dawn Publications.

For Background on Pill Bugs and Termites

Himmelman, J. 1999. *A pillbug's life.* (Nature up close) Danbury, CT: Children's Press.

Hartley, K. 2006 *Termite (Bug books).* Chicago, IL: Heinemann Raintree.

Markle, S. 2007. *Termites: Hardworking insect families.* Minneapolis, MN: Lerner Publishing Group.

St. Pierre, S. 2008. *Pill bug.* Chicago, IL: Heinemann/ Raintree.

For Student Research on Animal Groups

Carney, E. 2010. *Great migrations: Whales, wildebeests, butterflies, elephants, and other amazing animals on the move.* Washington, DC: National Geographic Children's Books.

Markle, S. 2006. *Army ants.* Minneapolis, MN: Lerner Publishing Group.

True Books: Animals series (e.g., Cheetahs, Zebras, Grey Wolves). Chicago: Children's Press.

Weaver, R. 1999. *Meerkats.* Mankato, MN: Bridgestone Books.

See also NGS books in the Face to Face series (e.g., Lion, Gorilla, Wolves).

Videos and Online Picture Resources for Student Research

ARKive: *www.arkive.org* Free multimedia guide to animals; includes photos and videos.

BBC's Nature Wildlife: *www.bbc.co.uk/nature/wildlife* Search by animal or by behavior and adaptations. Make sure you click on the Show All link to pull up all the species. The animals are arranged by classification *not* alphabetically.

Discovery Education Streaming Video (subscription): *http://streaming.discoveryeducation.com*

Explore.org: *http://explore.org/search/?q=animals* Explore is a multimedia organization that champions the selfless acts of others, documenting leaders around the world who have devoted their lives to extraordinary causes. It offers free both educational and inspirational films on a range of topics including animal conservation and preservation of endangered species. It also offers free photos and live-cam views. See also: *www.youtube.com/user/exploreTeam*

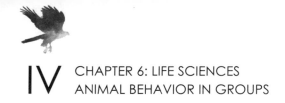

Marty Stouffer's *Wild America* TV series (over 120 programs): *www.wildamerica.com*

Mutual of Omaha's *Wild Kingdom* (154 clips and/or full-length videos): *http://animal.discovery.com/tv-shows/wild-kingdom*

National Geographic Society: Animal facts, photos and videos: *http://animal.discovery.com/tv-shows/wild-kingdom*

PBS *Nature* episodes sorted by animal. Short online clips free; DVDs for purchase: *http://www.pbs.org/wnet/nature/category/episodes/by-animal*

Appendix

Animal Groups: A Quick Guide for Teachers

Pairs

- Male and female only come together briefly for mating (e.g., bears, tigers)

- Male and female pairs, once formed, last for life. (e.g., swans, geese). Offspring each year for a short time.

Family Groups

- Mother and offspring relatively short term only until offspring can fend for themselves (e.g., pill bug, crayfish)

- Father and offspring for a short period (e.g., ostrich, seahorse)

- Extended family, long-lasting stable group; individuals mostly equal except for leader: matriarch (led by old female) (e.g., elephants, whales); patriarch (led by old male) (e.g., gorillas, chimpanzees, wild horses)

- Mixed-groups, long lasting, male/female, and offspring; may have hierarchy and only top pair reproduce (e.g., wolves, cape hunting dogs, Florida scrub jays, marmosets, meerkats)

- Mixed-group, long lasting, different roles in group; all females in group reproduce (e.g., lions, baboons)

- One male and a group of females; only last during mating season; different roles: males fight to defend females (e.g., elephant seals, sea lions, seals)

- Group of same gender and age (e.g., young male dolphins and orcas)

Social Animals

- Long-lasting colonies or nests lead by dominant female; individuals have specific roles: worker, guard, reproduction (e.g., bees, ants, wasps, bumblebees, termites, naked mole rats)

- Animal groups for a purpose

- Group forms as a response to local supply of food or aggregation in the short term. Animals are not related (e.g., water fleas, grackles, jellyfish).

- Group forms for reproduction; short term; males and females of reproductive age; not related to one another (e.g., horseshoe crabs, grunion fish, hammerhead sharks, penguins, terns, dragonflies, puffins, free-tailed bats, fireflies including leks, grouse, ruffs, red deer)

- Crèche: large group of offspring looked after by nonbreeding adults (known as aunties); relatively short term during breeding season; older individuals have protective role; not closely related to young (e.g., eider ducks, Patagonia cavy)

- Group forms for safety or to avoid predators; short term; nonrelated individuals; dominant

individuals may be on the inside of the group where they are less likely to be attacked as in schools of fish or flocks of birds (e.g., dark-headed juncos, sparrows, pigeons, herons)

- Group forms to move between habitats or to migrate; relatively long term; individuals are

not closely related (e.g., wildebeest, spiny lobsters, monarch butterflies)

- Group forms for hunting; nonrelated animals; short term or while food lasts; individuals are not related (e.g., pelicans, tuna, marlin, barracuda)

L I F E   S C I E N C E S

E. Demystifying Decomposers

Lori Farkash

Moses Y. Beach Elementary School (Wallingford, Connecticut)

Recommended Level
Grades 3–5*

Topic Focus
Life Sciences

Disciplinary Core Ideas
LS2: Ecosystems: Interactions, energy, and dynamics. See the multi–grade level standards in the chart below*

Time Frame*
*If done as a multi–grade level unit, a unique mix of activities and time frames will be needed for each grade level. Ongoing daily observations (i.e., quick check to assure adequate moisture and take a digital photo) will be made on the composting system over an extended period of time overlapping with other science units. Also, several activities naturally integrate with ELA and could be continued and completed in time devoted to addressing ELA standards. Thus, these time estimates underestimate the time that could optimally be devoted to completing the individual activities and unit as whole.

Engage Phase
60–120 minutes (Activity 1; time depends on the mix of strategies selected for grades 3–5)

Explore Phase
Three sessions, 60 minutes each (Activities 2A, 2B, and 2C)

Explain Phase
60–120 minutes (Activity 3)

Elaborate Phase
60 minutes (Activity 4A) and 1–2 weeks for plant growth experiment (Activity 4B)

Evaluate Phase
Two sessions, 60 minutes each (Activity 5)

Objectives
As a result of these experiences, students will be able to

- closely examine red wiggler earthworms to understand the physical characteristics (or structures) and behavioral adaptations that help them function and survive in natural and artificial (compost bin) habitats;

- determine how earthworms use dead organisms (and by extension, the waste products of living ones) for matter (and energy) in order to grow and survive, but also return useful materials to soil. That is, earthworms serve as part of nature's garbage collection and cleanup and recycling crew;

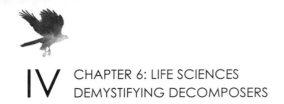
- understand the complementary roles of producers, consumers, and decomposers (e.g., earthworms) and their interrelationships in matter recycling within food chains or webs (the latter, for grade 5);

- understand how organisms are both impacted by and have an impact on their environments and how humans can use part of nature's recycling systems (i.e., earthworms) to turn some of our organic waste into a natural fertilizer (i.e., worm castings); and

- use metric measurement skills and mathematics to collect and present quantitative data about earthworms and/or compost systems. **Teacher note:** This objective is optional.

*Teacher note: Unlike this book's other mini-units (that focus on a single grade), this one incorporates *NGSS* that cut across grades 3–5. Given that the earthworm explorations and the vermicomposting system should optimally continue over multiple months (if not years) and could evolve into a schoolwide project, a cross-grade level focus is appropriate. It is recommended that third- to fifth-grade teachers use this unit's activities and internet references to collaboratively develop a multi–grade level sequence of lessons where the activities completed at each grade level lay the foundation for those developed in the next.

TABLE 6E.1. CORRELATION TO THE *NEXT GENERATION SCIENCE STANDARDS*

3. Interdependent relationships in ecosystems
4. Structure, function, and information processing
4-LS1-1. <u>Construct an argument that</u> plants and <u>animals have internal and external structures that function to support survival, growth, behavior and reproduction.</u>[1]
4-LS1-2. Use a model to describe that animals receive different types of information through their senses, process the information in their brains, and respond to the information in different ways.
5. Matter and energy in organisms and ecosystems
5-LS2-1. Develop a model to describe the movement of matter among plants, animals, decomposers, and the environment.

Scientific and Engineering Practices (Dimension 1)	Disciplinary Core Ideas (Dimension 3)	Crosscutting Concepts (Dimension 2)
1. Asking questions (for science) and defining problems (for engineering)	**Grade 3** LS2.C: Ecosystem dynamics, functioning, and resilience LS4.C: Adaptation	

Continued

Table 6E.1. (continued)

Scientific and Engineering Practices (Dimension 1)	Disciplinary Core Ideas (Dimension 3)	Crosscutting Concepts (Dimension 2)
2. Developing and using models	**Grade 4** LS1.A: Structure and function * Plants and animals have both internal and external structures that serve various functions in growth, survival, behavior, and reproduction.	
3. Planning and carrying out investigations	**Grade 5** LS2.A: Interdependent relationships in ecosystems * The food of almost any kind of animal can be traced back to plants. Organisms are related in food webs in which some animals eat plants for food and other animals eat the animals that eat plants. Some organisms, such as fungi and bacteria, break down dead organisms (both plants or plant parts and animals) and therefore operate as "decomposers." Decomposition eventually restores (recycles) some materials back to the soil. Organisms survive only in environments where their particular needs are met. A healthy ecosystem is one in which multiple species of different types are each able to meet their needs in a relatively stable web of life.	3. Scale, proportion, and quantity (*optional in Explore phase*)
4. Analyzing and interpreting data		4. Systems and system models
5. Using mathematics and computational thinking (*optional in Explore phase*)		5. Energy and <u>matter</u>: Flows, <u>cycles and conservation</u>[1]
6. Constructing explanations (for science) and designing solutions (for engineering)	LS2.B: Cycles of matter and energy transfer in ecosystems * Matter cycles between the air and soil and among plants, animals, and microbes as these organisms live and die.	6. Structure and function
7. Engaging in argument from evidence		7. Stability and change

[1] This mini-unit does not address all portions of the standard as written; the relevant elements are underlined.

Note: LS = Life sciences

Continued

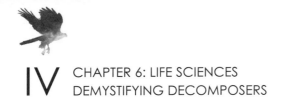
Table 6E.1. (continued)

Scientific and Engineering Practices (Dimension 1)	Disciplinary Core Ideas (Dimension 3)	Crosscutting Concepts (Dimension 2)
8. Obtaining, evaluating, and communicating information		

Common Core State Standards Connections
English Language Arts: Representative for grade 3; see equivalent, yet higher standards for grades 4–5.

Reading Informational Text
RI.3.7. Use information gained from illustrations (e.g., maps, photographs) and the words in a text to demonstrate understanding of the text (e.g., where, when, why, and how key events occur).
RI. 3.10. By the end of the year, read and comprehend informational texts, including history/social studies, science, and technical texts, at the high end of the grades 2–3 text complexity band independently and proficiently.

Writing Standards
W.3.2. Write informative/explanatory texts to examine a topic and convey ideas and information clearly.
W.3.7. Conduct short research projects that build knowledge about a topic.
W.3.8. Recall information from experiences or gather information from print and digital sources and sort evidence into provided categories.

Speaking and Listening
SL.3.1. Engage effectively in a range of collaborative discussions (one-on-one, in groups, and teacher-led) with diverse partners on *grade 3 topics and texts*, building on others' ideas and expressing their own clearly.
SL.3.4. Report on a topic or text, tell a story, or recount an experience with appropriate facts and relevant, descriptive details, speaking clearly at an understandable pace.

Mathematics *(optional)*
Measurement and data: Represent and interpret data (grades 3–5).

Preunit Preparation and Ordering of Supplies

Red Wiggler Earthworms (*Eisenia fetida*) and compost bins can be purchased from any of the following commercial suppliers approximately two weeks before the start of this unit. Alternatively, low-cost compost bins can be easily homemade (see last listing below). Although local fish bait shops are a low-cost source of worms, these will most commonly be night crawlers (*Lumbricus terrestris*), a different species of earthworms. This species is a deep burrowing animal that is unsuitable for use in a closed vermicomposting systems. In contrast, red wigglers are specifically adapted to thrive in surface-level rotting vegetation, compost, and animal manure and are therefore the species of choice for vermicomposting.

Supplies of Red Wiggler Earthworms and Composting Bins

- Frey Scientific: Delta Education Worm-a-Way Compost Kit 110-1770/$89.95. Kit demonstrates the principles of conservation and recycling by allowing students to bury food scraps, harvest compost, and finally grow a plant in the rich compost soil. The kit includes a 2–3 lb garbage capacity, 19 in. × 16 in. × 12 in. bin, the *Worms Eat My Garbage* book, and a mail-in living materials card for 1 pound of red worms. *http://store.schoolspecialty.com/OA_HTML/ibeCCtpItmDspRte.jsp?minisite=10029&item=17789&section=89759*

- Frey Scientific Worm-Vue Wonders Kit, 344024/$34.95. See how earthworms turn waste into soil and dig tunnels to create drainage for plants. Perform experiments to demonstrate how worms live and work underground. Kit includes: Double-sided viewing unit, worm facts and anatomy poster, 4-cell growing tray, tomato seeds, experiment booklet, 2 ft Super Squirmin cutouts, and a mail-in certificate (additional fee) for live worms, soil wafers, and starter food: *http://store.schoolspecialty.com/OA_HTML/ibeCCtpItmDspRte.jsp?minisite=10029&item=24876*

- Uncle Jim's Worm Farm 1,000 Count Red Wiggler Live Composting Worms: $18.95: *http://unclejimswormfarm.com/index.php/Worms.html*. Indoor Composter: Worm friendly Habitat: 14-gallon, 22.5 in. × 17.5 in. × 12.5 in. Worm Bin: $49.95.

- Worm Ladies Rhody Worms: Offer natural science background on red wiggler worms (*Eisenia fetida*) and easy-to-follow steps to make your own low-cost, double bin compost system: *http://wormladies.com/pages/aboutourworms.html*. They also sell red wiggler earthworms and complete composting kits: *http://wormladies.com/pages/shop.html*

- Worm Composting Bins: Directions for easy-to-make, economical, homemade compost bins:

  - Appelhof, M., and M. Fenton. 2006. *Worms eat my garbage: How to set up and maintain a worm composting system, 2nd ed.* Kalamazoo, MI: Flower Press Publishing.

  - Breakdown: Composting with Worms (extensive lesson plans for sixth-grade science): *www.teacherstryscience.org/lp/breakdown-composting-worms*

  - EZ How to Make a Free Worm Factory (view 1:56 –8:50 min): 3 gallon/5 gallon, nested bucket system: *www.youtube.com/watch?v=9r7eEPfGjR8*

  - How Vermicomposting Works: *http://home.howstuffworks.com/vermicomposting2.htm*

  - Raising Earthworms Indoors (7:17 min): Nested, rectangular, 3-gallon Rubbermade bins: *www.youtube.com/watch?v=IaeR7J39ydU*

  - Vermicomposting Classroom Activities (and Student Worksheets): Free download: *www.calrecycle.ca.gov/Education/curriculum/worms/98Activities.pdf*.

Safety note: Although children may have previously encountered and informally explored earthworms in out-of-school settings, several safety-related, good practice precautions should be observed when handling earthworms: (1) anyone with cuts or abrasions on their hands or

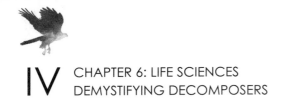
who has a compromised immune system should use nonlatex, vinyl gloves; (2) everyone should be cautioned to keep their hands away from their mouth, nose, ears, and eyes (to avoid spreading germs to/from the earthworms); and (3) everyone should wash their hands with soap and water after working with earthworms. Also, avoid overwatering the compost bins and watch for mold growth, which might trigger allergies. Another thing to watch for is fruit fly infestation that will occur if the lid is left off a bin, and fruit scraps are not covered with sufficient soil or shredded newspaper. Finally, be sure to intentionally teach respect for living organisms by making sure that students handle the earthworms gently and do not leave them away from moisture for too long to avoid their dehydration. When handled to roughly, red wigglers (*Eisenia fetida*) can exude a foul-smelling liquid, presumably as an antipredator adaptation.

Engage Phase

The purpose of the Engage Phase is to activate and informally assess students' prior knowledge related to ecosystems (i.e., roles of producers, consumers, and decomposers), excite curiosity about earthworms as decomposers, and begin a unit- or year-long, multi–grade level project to uncover and discover how earthworms are important organisms in our environment.

Teacher note: Different grade 3–5 teachers can select a subset of the strategies described below that they (and their multi-grade level team) feel is most appropriate.

Materials

- Children's Science Trade Books: One or more of each of the following books can be used throughout this mini-unit:

  - Glaser, L. 1992. *Wonderful worms.* Minneapolis, MN: Millbrook Press.

    - Himmelman, J. 2002. *An earthworm's life.* Danbury, CT: Children's Press.

    - Kalman, B. 2004. *The life cycle of an earthworm.* NY: Crabtree Publishing.

    - Llewellyn, C., and B. Watts. 2002. *Earthworms* (Minibeast). Franklin Watts.

    - Pfeffer, W. 2004. *Wiggling worms at work.* New York: HarperCollins.

- Earthworms and Compost Bins: Pre-ordered and/or prepared (see previous cited suppliers)

- Internet Audio and Video Clips:

  - A Tribute to Earthworms (4 mins, 49 secs) offers an audiovisual overview of form/function facts followed by preschoolers' comments when engaged in guided explorations): *www.youtube.com/watch?v=A0iOx6nSwz0*

  - Banana Slug Band, *Dirt Made My Lunch* album: *http://bananaslugs.bandcamp.com/album/dirt-made-my-lunch* (2 min title track) *http://bananaslugs.bandcamp.com/track/decomposition-3* (3 mins, 38 secs)

  - Circle of Life movie music clip (3 mins, 57 secs; features animals): *www.youtube.com/watch?v=vX07j9SDFcc*

  - Songs for Teaching: *www.songsforteaching.com/index.html*

Activity 1: Introduction to Ecosystems, the Mystery Class Pet and Worm Wonderings

1. Tell students that this science unit focuses on a special type of organism that is an unseen hero that helps communities of different types of living organisms (i.e., ecosystems) live together in an ever-changing (i.e., dynamic) but balanced condition. To loosely model the idea of a natural ecosystem, ask the students to stand in a single large circle around the perimeter of the classroom. Mention that all organisms in an ecosystem are directly or indirectly connected in the Circle of Life. Project the first minute or two of the Circle of Life video clip as a prompt for the following question:

   > Is the role of consumers (e.g., animals featured in the video) more important than that of producers (e.g., plants) in ecosystems (e.g., a local woodlot, field or wetland area, or the African plains highlighted in the video clip)?

2. After giving the class a minute or two to silently think about this question, ask students who think that animals are more important than plants to step into the center to face their peers who hold the opposing view. Ask opposing pairs to take turns discussing and defending their perspectives. After several minutes, ask students if any of them would like to change their answer or position. If so, these students should move to a new position in the inner (or outer) circle as appropriate.

   Teacher note: This format for Agreement Circles is adapted from *http://formativeassessment.barrow.wikispaces.net/Agreement+Circles*. The Agreement Circle strategy (Keeley 2009) is a kinesthetic way to engage students in rich discourse using their schema about a topic. Students are allowed to modify their answers and engage in civil discourse while the teacher gets an overview of students' understanding and uncovers students' preinstructional conceptions. The teacher should not provide a premature answer to the question at this time in the unit. Instead, use this (false) forced choice question to elicit student conversation and assess their prior knowledge. As the unit unfolds, build upon this initial dialogue to help students learn that neither producers nor consumers are more important, and that an often unnoticed, third type of organism (i.e., a decomposer) is equally important to maintaining a balanced ecosystem.

3. Announce: "To help us resolve our differences, let's consider whether our initial question was incorrectly worded because it focused only on the two kinds of living organisms we most commonly notice in the *Circle of Life* (i.e., producers and consumers). Think about what often unnoticed organisms might be involved in cases such as fallen autumn tree leaves (left uncollected by humans), dead trees left in wooded lots, an apple core left on the ground, cake or bread left too long in the cupboard, and a dead animal by the side of the road. What do we call the kind of organisms that are nature's 24/7 garbage collectors, cleanup crew, and recyclers?"

4. After eliciting their ideas, write the word *decomposer* on the black or white board and ask the class if they know what the word means. Complete a simple word dissection by asking them what the word *compose* (to create, arrange, construct or put together) and the prefix *de-* (to do the opposite or reverse). This suggests that decomposers are organisms that

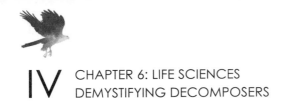
take apart or break down dead or decaying organisms into simpler chemical components (that can later be incorporated into the makeup of new living organisms). Ask students if they can name specific organisms that might help break down, deconstruct, or decompose the previously mentioned fallen leaves, trees, and so on. Students may or may not cite decomposers such as earthworms, pill bugs, millipedes, slugs, fungi (e.g., yeast, mold, and mushrooms), and microscopic bacteria. Do *not* tell them at this time that this unit will focus on a particular species of macroscopic, safe and easy to study earthworm (this will be revealed in the 20 Question Game in Step 7).

5. Ask students to brainstorm (and record on the black or white board) any words or phrases that they associate with the word *decomposer*. Brainstorming and word associations (e.g., descriptive adjectives, examples of specific organisms, where they are found, and so on) can serve as a quick preassessment to activate student thinking about a concept or topic.

6. After this initial posting of ideas, small teams of students or the class as a whole can draft an acrostic poem in which each line starts with a word that uses one of the letters in the word *DECOMPOSER* (written vertically down the black or white board) and the remaining words or phrases reflect some aspect of their prior understanding of the topic. A free, fun, interactive, online tool for making individual or whole-class developed acrostic poems (and samples of student poems) can be found at *www.readwritethink.org/classroom-resources/student-interactives/acrostic-poems-30045.html*. Note there are many possible words or answers to this acrostic (e.g., **D**ecomposers in dirt – **E**at ecosystem's expired – **C**onsumers

– **O**f - **M**any – **P**roducers to – **O**ffer – **S**oil – **E**ssential nutrients – **R**eturned). Their initial acrostic poem(s) can be returned to and refined at multiple points in the unit as part of related ELA lessons.

7. After the first drafts of acrostic poems have been completed, tell the class, "I am happy to say that I've recently obtained a class pet that will help us reconsider our initial question from the Agreement Circle activity about the relative importance of producers and consumers. We will need to take special care of our pet. Our class pet plays a very important role in many ecosystems. I am not going to tell you what our pet is. You will need to ask me questions about this creature's characteristics that can be answered with a YES or NO." This 20 Question game may elicit specific questions about where the unknown creature lives, what it eats, what might eat it, its size, color or shape, and so on. Record student questions on a YES or NO chart. Eventually students should guess the pet (give additional clues if needed).

8. Ask students if they have seen earthworms before and if so (1) where were the worms located (i.e., natural, above or below ground settings, and/or human built structures), (2) how would they describe the worms' characteristics and behaviors, and (3) if students had a hands-on experience, what else they could share about their prior experiences with worms. Student answers may include backyard, compost bins, farm, garden, nature center, worm store (fishing bait), images in books or videos, etc., as locations; segmented body with a slimy texture, they wiggle around a lot and seem to slowly explore their environments for characteristics; and playing with them in the backyard or garden, using

them as fish bait, seeing them eaten by birds or other animals, etc. for hands-on experiences. Almost certainly, one or more students will have a story to tell.

9. After they've shared their past experiences with worms, ask students to draw a life-size picture of a worm in their science notebooks, labeling as much as they can to show what they already know about earthworms (**Teacher note:** This task will probably raise the questions related to head/tail location, gender, typical size, and so on).

10. Explain that there are many different kinds of worms and that the worms they will observe and study are called red wigglers. Walk around the room with a living red wiggler in your hand (i.e., it is good to show students that you are not squeamish about this) and/or use a digital projection image to display one to the whole class at once and let students compare this to their initial drawings. Ask them, "Do you think earthworms are producers, consumers, or decomposers?"

11. Next, guide the class to record their initial collective thinking and wonderings in the first two columns of a KWL chart.

K*	W	L
What I already **K**now about… (or believe to be so)	What I **W**ant to know about… What I am **W**ondering about…	What I have **L**earned about… after completing this lesson

*This column will likely include some misconceptions that will need to be challenged and modified as the unit develops. Do *not* attempt to correct these by telling the students the truth at this time, but do suggest to students that later additions to the *L* column may contradict some of what they initially thought to be true.

12. Worm Wonderings will likely include a broad array of student questions such as

What's it like to be an earthworm? How would the world look, sound, taste, smell, and feel if you lived at ground level (beneath leaf litter or in/on manure) or underground in dark, narrow tunnels? How could you move if you had no arms or legs? Without fur or feathers, could you control your body temperature? How could you find a mate?

13. The answers to many Worm Wondering–type questions can be found through a combination of subsequent hands-on explorations and targeted reading-based research from grade level–appropriate trade books and internet websites. A dozen common question and answers (Q&A) are included in the Appendix section. The level of detail provided is for teachers; students do not need to learn specific terminology or be tested on a set number of these answers. Investigations at the elementary level (i.e., grades 3–5 for this unit) will lay the foundation for later, more extensive explorations in middle school life science and high school biology classes (where earthworms are commonly dissected). Additional Q&A can be found at the sites listed in the Reference section; see especially the Annenberg's Journey North site at *www.learner.org/jnorth/search/Worm.html*. This site categorizes 36 questions as being related to characteristics (12), life cycle (8), ecology (14), and conservation (2).

14. After the first draft of individual and class KWL charts are done, complete one or more of the following mini-activities (see books and URLs in the Materials section on page 140)

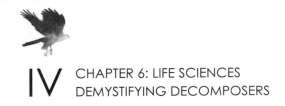
FIGURE 6E.1. EARTHWORM EXTERNAL ANATOMY

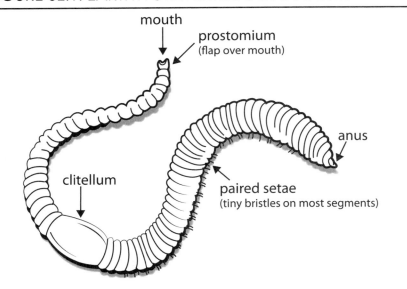

Source: www.enchantedlearning.com/egifs/Earthworm_bw.GIF

to earthworms and the idea of the Circle (or Cycle) of Life. **Teacher note:** Remember the focus during the Engage phase is to (1) raise student curiosity and help them frame questions (that they can explore in subsequent activities), and (2) informally assess their cognitive mix of valid preconceptions, misconceptions, and conceptual holes. The purpose of this phase is not to directly tell them (or explain) the right answers. The following schematic drawing of an earthworm is provided to help orient teachers to the basic external anatomy of an earthworm, and it should *not* be shared with students at this time.

Explore Phase

The purpose of the Explore phase is to allow students to explore earthworms and a worm composting bin (i.e., an artificial habitat that models some aspects of earthworms' natural habitat). The students develop additional wonderings about earthworms and their surroundings and apply their observation, measuring, and data collection skills to dig into and unearth new ideas and concepts.

Materials

- Nonfiction trade books on earthworms (see previous examples in the Engage phase or others found in the Appendix) as student resources

- Rulers (cm), timers (digital), flashlights, plastic trays (or plates), wet and dry paper towels, hand magnifying lenses

followed by a quick round of revisions to their individual and/or class KWL charts.

15. Picture-walk only through one or more of the trade books; a digital projection camera is helpful.

16. Partner-read one of the nonfiction books (in a related ELA lesson).

17. Show the class the YouTube clip: *A Tribute to Earthworms.* **Teacher note:** The first few minutes explain quite a lot. Do not expect students to listen and learn all of this information at this point; rather use the first two minutes to simply excite student curiosity in these underappreciated, often unseen heroes.

18. Listen to and briefly discuss the lyrics to the song *Dirt Made My Lunch* and/or *Decomposition* (URL in Materials section) and elicit questions about how the lyrics might relate

- Previously purchased red wiggler worms in a composting bin

- Digital camera (if available)

- Giant Earthworm video clip (2 mins, 41 secs), from David Attenborough's BBC series, *Life in the Undergrowth*: *www.youtube.com/watch?v=uO4lkv-jLRs_*

Activity 2A: Exploring Earthworms in a Compost Bin

1. Teach students how to design a scientific fair test through a whole-group investigation: How do earthworms act as decomposers that recycle matter from both dead producers and consumers and help complete the circle/cycle of life (i.e., break down previously used matter so it can become available in the soil to be reused as part of the makeup of new living plants that are later eaten by animals)? Set up a long-term, class experiment (i.e., two-week to yearlong investigation) from the ground up by setting up the compost bins with the students so that they can see the component parts and their arrangement in this artificial habitat for earthworms. As a first, simple test, put equal amounts of lettuce and newspaper pieces at the surface of the compost in an experimental worm bin (Bin 1) and in a control test without worms (Bin 2). Ask students to predict what will happen to the organic matter in the two different bins as they observe it daily over a period of two (or more) weeks. **Teacher note:** If the composting experiment is intended to become a yearlong activity, the worms can later be fed bread, tree leaves, vegetable matter, paper napkins, paper towels, coffee grinds, and unbleached coffee filters. Do not use any animal parts or by-products (e.g.,

discarded meat, fat, bone, cheese, and so on) as food for the earthworms as this will create sanitary and odor issues in an internal, classroom environment. Also, avoid juice boxes (i.e., sugar will attract ants and flies), anything waxed, cardboard, plastics, and eggshells. The worms prefer smaller pieces, so large items like bananas peels should be cut up (i.e., this creates a larger surface area to volume ratio so that the earthworms can get to their food more efficiently). For the longer term project, place the garbage just below the top layer of the substrate to avoid attracting fruit flies. As an estimate of how much garbage to feed the worms, consider that 2,000 worms will eat approximately 8 lbs of garbage each week.

2. Ask, "What will the red worms do? Where will they move in the bin? Will the lettuce and/or newspaper change? If so, why and in what way? How will the bin #1 material compare to the material in the bin without worms?" Have students make observations and collect data daily so they can discover the role of worms as decomposers. Students will begin to draw conclusions at quick, daily checkpoints throughout this unit (and into the next science unit). If available, take a digital photo of the two setups each day as a record of the changes over time that can be viewed in a sequential slide show.

Activity 2B: Exploring Earthworms Up Close and Personal

1. Say to students, "Our group experiment is designed to help us learn about the role that worms collectively play as waste recyclers in many ecosystems. We are now going to observe individual worms to learn about their physical characteristics and behavioral adap-

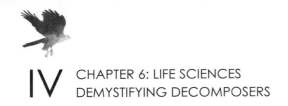
tations that help them survive. When scientists have questions, they design experiments, make careful observations, take notes, and make detailed drawings. Today, we will refer back to our worm wonderings to see which of our questions we might be able to answer by using these same science practices."

2. Lead a class discussion to select questions that are both of high interest and that can be answered through observations and simple tests that do not put the worm's well-being at risk. Distribute one worm with a little of the moist compost bin material on plastic plates to each of the student dyads for an initial round of observations.

3. After the first round of observations are completed, compare students' scientific illustrations, based on their hands-on observations, to their previous sketch of worms (that they made from preinstructional recollections) in their science notebooks. If possible project a few of these pre/post, hands-on drawings. Ask students, "What scientific tools could we use to make more detailed drawings and quantitative observations (or measurements)?"

4. Distribute magnifying lenses, rulers, and stopwatches and have students make another round of observations on the worms in bin material on plastic plates. Circulate and guide students with questions to help them observe the worms more carefully and begin to think about questions to investigate that might involve quantitative measurements with rulers and/or stopwatches. For example, how (and how fast) do they move? How long are they? How many centimeters can they stretch out as they move? Why do you think some are longer, thinner, and so on? Why does the worm sometimes move quickly, slowly, up, down, and so on? How many segments are there? Why do you think it prefers this (lighter/darker) area of the plate? What happens when you … ? Do you notice anything that surprises you? While making observations, students will record other questions they would like to investigate about an earthworm's adaptations in their notebooks.

5. Afterward, gather students for a scientist meeting to discuss observations and wonderings. Create a class T-chart labeled I Notice/I Wonder to facilitate students sharing questions and wonderings they created from worm observations. As a class, sort questions as lab-testable or better for literature-based research. Lab-testable questions may include, How do worms react to changes in their environment (light, dark, temperature, moisture, soil types)? Or, questions may be formed about the life cycle, eating habits, movement of worms, and so on.

6. Optional math connections (completed in math class): Students estimate and measure the length of a sample of worms from the bin. They gather measurements from a worm in a relaxed position, and with care, gather measurements from a gently, stretched-out position. You may even want to bring in several night crawlers for students to measure and compare to the red wigglers. Students may analyze the set of data finding the range, median, and mode. They can create a graph of the different-size worms. Show students the Giant Earthworm video. Discuss the length of the giant worm, and create both a life-size and smaller-scale model of the worm with clay. Measure and discuss its size as compared to red wigglers. After making the

comparison, students can explore nonfiction books that offer reasons for variation in the size of worms (within and across species). Fifth graders might also be asked to measure the area of tree leaves (except oak species, which are very slow to decompose) on graph paper and see how much is consumed.

Activity 2C: Expert Team Earthworm Explorations

1. Say to students, "Scientists often conduct team-based investigations and different teams use the same experimental setup to answer a common question. Scientists make predictions based on prior observations and on what they already know (see optional outdoors Activity 3 below). Well, I was wondering why the directions for our compost bins had us add water initially and periodically check the moisture of the sealed container. Perhaps, earthworms need or prefer water. Therefore, I would like to investigate the question: Do worms prefer a wet (or moist) or dry area?" Through think-aloud modeling and collecting data on prepared charts, guide students through a teacher-led investigation, conducting at least five identical trials in which different teams (of up to four students each) test to see which area the worms prefer. For example, you could place several worms on a plate between a section with moist compost and a section with compost that has been dried out in an oven or with a hair dryer. Together the class will draw conclusions based on their common experimental design.

2. Then say, "Now you, just like adult scientists, will have a chance to conduct investigations of your own about your worm wonderings!" Review student-generated questions from previous observations. Direct students to choose a question of interest to them and to form a small number of expert teams that can split into pairs to replicate one another's investigations. Teams may use nonfiction books or approved internet references to help them set up favorable conditions for investigations. Students develop a plan in science notebooks, collect materials for investigations, create diagrams and tables to collect data, and then conduct investigations. Monitor and encourage discourse among team members to develop thinking about worm adaptations. You can provide plans, frameworks, tables, and charts, and so on to differentiate this experience for various kinds of learners in your class as needed.

3. Optional In-School or At-Home Field Observations: The Expert Team Earthworm Explorations can be informed by observations of earthworms (most likely *Lumbricus terrestris*, rather than the red wigglers used in the compost bins) in their natural habitats during the spring or fall seasons when the temperatures are not too cold and there is adequate moisture so that earthworms can be found near the surface under leaves or near their burrows or castings. In these natural settings, students may also observe robins or other birds preying on the earthworms.

Explain Phase

The purpose of the Explain phase is to further reveal student discoveries and to clarify scientific principles uncovered through previous student investigations. Expert evidence from print and internet sources may be used to inform discussions of the results of student investigations, as can interactive, multimedia presentations from

the students and the teacher. Students should be encouraged to provide evidence and use logical reasoning in interpreting, evaluating, and communicating their findings to each other (i.e., engage in argument from evidence).

Materials

- Nonfiction books on worms and preap-proved internet sites (see also the Additional References)

Activity 3: Explaining the Earthworm Explorations

1. Say to students, "Let's check Bin 1 and Bin 2 from the previous whole-class investigation 'How do worms act as decomposers?' Let's be sure we make careful observations with our eyes as well as our sense of smell. We'll examine our daily photographs of the bin material, and we'll describe what we see and smell with descriptive words." Give the students an opportunity to discuss their observations and share their thinking about worms as decomposers. Note that while some breakdown of the plant material (e.g., lettuce or banana peels) will occur in the control bins (due to dehydration and the presences of fungi and microscopic bacterial decompos-ers), the bin with the earthworms will have significant breakdown of the newspaper as well as the plant material over a period of a week or more. Note that decomposers are the unseen heroes in the Circle of Life—note their total absence from the music video used in the Engage phase! But without decomposers such as earthworms, all life would eventually cease.

2. After the discussion about the compost bins and their own hands-on explorations with

earthworms, say, "Despite your careful, close-up observations, some of your wonderings still have not been answered. For example, using magnifying lenses, you should have noticed little bristlelike hairs on some of the worms, but you may not have necessarily understood the purpose of the hairs as one of a worm's adaptations. Sometimes scientists cannot collect enough data just from observa-tions so they refer to results published by oth-ers. Let's go back to our 'Worm Wonderings' chart. I would like you to research with a partner answers to any wonderings that have not yet been answered through your obser-vations. You may use nonfiction texts and various websites. Be sure to find research that helps explain how the worm's features and behaviors (or adaptations) help it to survive."

3. Tell students to record their answers on chart paper and display charts around the room for all to read, and compare findings. Students may also choose to include scientific illustra-tions with labels.

4. Pass out Justified True and False Statements (Keeley 2009) and have student groups work through rich discourse to answer the ques-tions. The following table is provided for illustrative purposes; the number and types of questions you give to your students should be linked to the particular Worm Wonderings, experiments, and readings you did with your class (which should vary across the grades 3–5 focus of this unit). It is useful to have approximately the same number of true and false statements.

5. Have a full class discussion to confirm the lessons learned (i.e., use the KWL chart) to clarify any misconceptions and help identify

FIGURE 6E.2. JUSTIFIED TRUE-FALSE STATEMENTS (*SAMPLE*)

Group Member Names:

Discuss the following statements in your group, decide whether you think each statement is true or false, and then write a sentence that explains the reasons for your group answer.

1. Earthworms are decomposers that break down and recycle organic matter. **T F** WHY?
2. Earthworms are not able to sense light. **T F** WHY?
3. Earthworms prefer moist areas to those that lack water. **T F** WHY?
4. Earthworms are a kind of insect. **T F** WHY?
5. Earthworms have a head that is visibly different than their tail. **T F** WHY?

the need for further reading or teacher-delivered explanations.

Teacher note: Refer back to the *NGSS* correlations (Table 6E.1) listed at the beginning of this unit to provide grade level–appropriate content instruction as negotiated with your grades 3–5 teacher-colleagues. For example, grade 3 might focus on the notion of habitat, grade 4 on external anatomical structures and how earthworms respond to environmental stimuli, and grade 5 can probe deeper into the broader ecological concept of the flow of matter and energy through food chains and webs (see sample illustrations on pp. 150–151). Related resources for the latter topics can be found at the following.

- Cycling Through the Food Web (National Science Foundation (NSF)-funded site): *www.bigelow.org/bacteria/index.html*.

- Ecology notes and images: *www.biologycorner.com/bio2/index3.html#ecology*

- Food Chains and Webs: Simple information graphics and links to online games: *www.tburg.k12.ny.us/mcdonald/foodch1.htm*

- Food Chain Game (and related ones): *www.sheppardsoftware.com/content/animals/kidscorner/foodchain/foodchain.htm*

FIGURE 6E.3. FOOD WEB, TROPHIC LEVELS PYRAMID

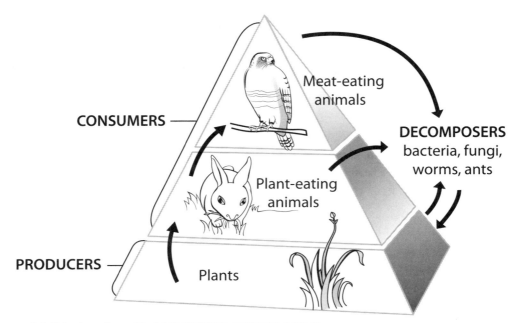

Source: *www.softchalkcloud.com/lesson/files/lcMJtdRUb674Tg/TEKS4SC_LS18.02.png*

Teacher note: Four of the arrows indicate the flow of matter (and energy). All organisms become "food" for decomposers when they die (and in the case of animals, also their eliminated body waste). The sixth arrow (from the decomposers back to plants) indicates only the return of matter (not energy) as plants receive their energy directly from the Sun via photosynthesis.

FIGURE 6E.4. SAMPLE FOOD CHAIN/FOOD WEB FOR MATTER RECYCLING

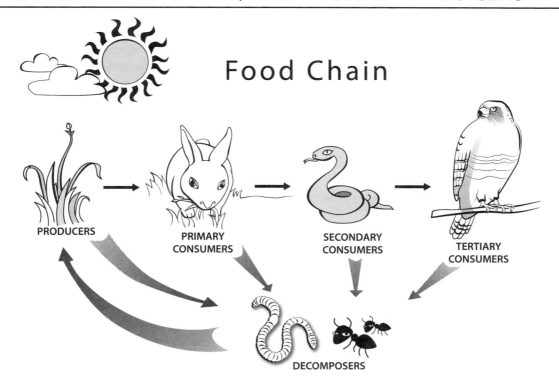

Source: Multiple sites use the same image *www.biologycorner.com/bio2/notes_chap3.html*

http://producersconsumers.wikispaces.com/file/view/salric.jpg2.jpg/37084859/salric.jpg2.jpg

Teacher note: The Circle of Life is a closed cycle in which matter is temporarily borrowed by living organisms and then passed onto another level when they are eaten or die. Decomposers close the loop by breaking down dead and decaying matter and returning matter to the soil to be taken up as part of the noncarbon biomass of living plants (i.e., the plant's carbon mass comes from carbon dioxide in the air).

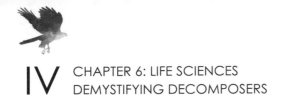
Elaborate Phase

The purpose of the Elaborate phase is for students to continue their exploration of worms' adaptations so they are able to connect previous notions to evidence and data collected to modify and extend their thinking. During this phase, the teacher facilitates and makes observations (formative assessments) to determine how well the students understand the overall objectives and the need for additional direct instruction and targeted reading. This is also the place for emphasizing ELA connections via reading and writing skill development.

Materials

- Worms, worm castings, camera, bin material, soil, plants, cups, 3 seedlings, graduated cylinder, measuring cup, centimeter ruler, worm cocoons, sunny area, newspapers, lettuce, water, 2 identical plastic bins with lids and covered in dark paper (add air holes to lids)

- Rulers, timers, hand magnifying lenses, and other tools necessary to conduct investigations

- Trade books and internet sites previously listed (and/or other listed in the Additional References section) and the following books.

  ◆ Cronin, D. 2003. *Diary of a worm*. New York: HarperCollins. [fictional journal]

  ◆ Larson, G. 1999. *There's a hair in my dirt! A worm's story*. New York: HarperCollins. (This 60-page, teacher read-aloud, "true fiction" book is written by the acclaimed science cartoonist in a children's storybook style. It explains key ecological principles via a story told by a father

earthworm to his son. Its off-kilter humorous text and illustrations and somewhat "dark," discrepant event–type ending are probably not suitable for most third graders, but are more appropriate for fifth graders. This unusual story also serves as wonderful background reading for all science teachers.)

Activity 4A: Earthworms and ELA Reading/Writing Connections

1. Read aloud *Diary of a Worm* by Doreen Cronin and/or, if deemed suitable, the Gary Larson story or other grade-level appropriate texts (during ELA-designated time slots).

2. Ask students to apply what they've learned about worms and think like a worm and take on the perspective of a worm. Ask them to write a diary entry from a worm's point of view (based on worms observed from the worm bin). They should include similes while weaving in facts about worms. Evaluate entries for accurate descriptions and facts about worms. Collect entries and create a class book called *Diaries From a Worm Bin*.

3. Use the online acrostic poem software that was cited in Activity 1 (Engage phase) to assess whether individual student's vocabulary and conceptual understanding about the role of earthworms as decomposers have increased.

4. For grades 3–4 classes, drop down to #2 in Activity 4B.

Activity 4B: An Exploration Into the Extraordinary Excrement of Earthworms (5th grade)

1. Guide students to think about and discuss how worms help the Earth. Then design and lead a whole-class investigation into the following question: Do worm castings return valuable nutrients to the soil for plants? Emphasize and chart which variables are to be kept constant (kind and size of plant, amount of water and sunlight, temperature, and so on). Sample plans you may wish to consult include the following.

   ◆ Growing Plants with Compost, pages numbered 55–57 (actually pages 29–31) in this free, nonsequentially numbered document *Vermicomposting Classroom Activities www.calrecycle.ca.gov/Education/ curriculum/worms/98Activities.pdf*

   ◆ Wife's Biology Experiment (earthworm castings as fertilizer and online commentary): *http://forums2.gardenweb.com/ forums/load/seed/msg0211592032411.html.*

   ◆ *Wiggling Worms at Work,* page 33, "Do Worms Really Help the Soil?" (from the book by Wendy Pfeffer that was cited in the Engage phase)

2. As the investigation takes shape, students should discuss various ways worms help the Earth (aerate the soil; create tunnels so rainwater doesn't run off to better help plants; digest organic matter and expel it as castings that act as a natural fertilizer; and so on). This investigation should last approximately two to four weeks, with data collected and recorded daily. At the conclusion of the investigation, have the class analyze the data and draw conclusions.

3. Next, have students meet in their teams to further reflect on their findings from their small-group investigations previously conducted. Ask them to refine their thinking by checking their explanations against research in books (leveled books).

4. Finally, the teams should consider what they would do differently if they were to repeat their investigation, as well as what new questions they would like to investigate in the future.

5. Help the teams prepare to share their final results with the class (that will take place as part of the Evaluate phase). They need first to decide on a format (e.g., PowerPoint, video clip, and so on). They can use a Rerun (Kelley 2009) strategy to help structure their presentation:

   Recall: summarize investigation

   Explain the purpose

   Results: describe data collected

   Uncertainties: What are they still uncertain about? What needs to be further investigated?

   New: two new things they learned

6. Post a Rerun chart in the classroom so as students reflect, they can complete the strategy in their science notebooks.

Evaluate Phase

The purpose of the Evaluate phase is for the students to evaluate their own and each other's investigations and/or complete additional performance tasks to show their understanding of the concepts studied. Typically teachers assign individual or group summative grades using a set

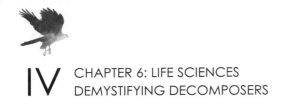

of criteria developed as a class. Afterward, before the start of the next unit, the teacher will review and reteach key concepts as necessary based on student performance.

Materials

- Investigation presentations (class-generated rubric to score)

- Performance tasks (class-generated rubric to score)

Activity 5: Demystifying Decomposers Performance Tasks

1. Students share the results of their worm investigations with the class. Reflecting on their experiences as investigators, students now focus on how scientists use models to answer questions. By comparing the results of their experiments, students also review the importance of using controls and verifying predictions. Students will evaluate their peers' work as well as their own performances, using a class-generated rubric. The teacher will also score each child's performance using the rubric and provide immediate feedback for students. Students may also present their investigations publicly through a science fair (for school, family, or community audience) including PowerPoint presentations, posters, and so on.

2. Students choose and complete an authentic assessment Performance Task. Tasks will be shared and scored using a rubric designed before the Performance Tasks take place and given to students ahead of time.

Performance Task 1

Our principal is interested in reducing waste from the school cafeteria. The best idea will receive an award and will be shown on the Discovery Channel! Using what you know about red worms, come up with a plan and poster to show people your ideas.

Performance Task 2

You and your friend were going fishing. As he was digging for worms, he said the only thing worms were good for was bait. What three things would you tell him so that he would understand the huge impact worms have on our environment? Create a video of you explaining the benefits to this friend.

Performance Task 3

You were listening to a commercial on the radio that advertised, "Worms provide free fertilizer for your yard!" Your family did not think this was possible. How could you prove this ad to be true? Create a poster to demonstrate the truth behind this advertisement.

Performance Task 4

What is the worth of a worm? On a poster, describe at least three disasters that would occur in an ecosystem if worms became extinct. Provide solutions to these potential disasters.

Additional References About Earthworms

Books

Appelhof, M., M. Fenton, and B. L. Harris. 1993. *Worms eat our garbage: Classroom activities for a better environment.* Kalamazoo: Flower Press. (includes teacher curriculum guide with science, mathematics, and ELA activities for grade 4–8 students)

Hand, J. 1995. *The wonderful world of wigglers.* Montpelier, VT: Common Roots Press.

Hess, L. 1979. *The amazing earthworm.* New York: Charles Scribner's Sons.

Kalman, B., and J. Langille. 1998. *What are food chains and webs?* New York: Crabtree Publishing.

Keeley, P. 2009. *Science formative assessment: 75 practical strategies for linking assessment, instruction, and learning.* Thousand Oaks, CA: Corwin Press.

Morgan, S. 1996. *Butterflies, bugs, and worms.* New York: Kingfisher Publications.

Payne, B. 1999. *The worm café.* Kalamazoo, MI: Flower Press.

Rosinsky, N. M. 2003. *Dirt—The scoop on soil.* Bloomington, IN: Picture Window Books.

Silverstein, A., and V. Silverstein. 1972. *Life in a bucket of soil.* New York: William Morrow and Co.

Stone, L. *Creepy crawlers (worms).* 1995. Vero Beach, FL: Rourke Publishing Company.

Internet Resouces: Earthworms Facts, Fictions/Misconceptions and Multimedia

www.enchantedlearning.com/subjects/invertebrates/earthworm/Earthwormcoloring.shtml (basic facts, a quiz and a black-and-white sketch with external body parts identified)

www.arkive.org/earthworm/lumbricus-terrestris (13 close-up photos, and 5 video clips of the common earthworm, *Lumbricus terrestris*)

www.learner.org/jnorth/search/Worm.html (36 Q&As about earthworms and other links)

www.ehow.com/info_8133558_list-misconceptions-earthworms.html

www4.uwm.edu/fieldstation/naturalhistory/bugoftheweek/earthworms.cfm

www.naturenorth.com/Garden/Earthworms.html

http://en.wikipedia.org/wiki/Eisenia_fetida (red wiggler earthworms)

http://en.wikipedia.org/wiki/Nightcrawlers (*Lumbricus terrestris*)

http://en.wikipedia.org/wiki/Vermicompost (earthworm composting)

http://en.wikipedia.org/wiki/Detritivore (a specific type of decomposer such as earthworms)

www.brighthubeducation.com/middle-school-science-lessons/27161-composting-science-projects-with-worms

http://wormladies.com/pages/aboutourworms.html

Appendix: A Dozen Common Questions and Answers About Earthworms

This is a sampling of questions (and answers for teachers) that students *may* want to investigate in this unit. The spirit of the 5E Teaching Cycle is to emphasize student questions and explorations *before* teacher or textbook telling. In fact, even in the Explain phase, the best teachers interact with students in a Socratic style of mutual inquiry more than by a dogmatic lecture approach that tells them the truth. Some of these questions may not be raised by your students. If so, you may choose to use them as prompts (or not), depending on the number of potentially more interesting questions that students may generate on their own.

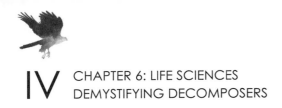
1. Do they have a head and if so, where is it and how can you distinguish it from the tail?

   The head, or first body segment features both the earthworm's mouth and, overhanging the mouth, a fleshy lobe (or prostomium) that seals the entrance when the worm is at rest but is also used to feel and chemically sense the worm's surroundings. Some species of earthworm can even use this prehensile lobe to grab and drag items like grasses and leaves. The worm's head is always located on the end of the worm closest to the clitellum that contains the sex organs and also contains a primitive brain that connects with nerves from their skin and muscles. Their nerves can detect light, vibrations, and even some tastes, and the muscles of their bodies make movements in response. At the other end, the earthworm's tail contains its anus, the end-of-the-line of its linear digestive system from which worm castings ("poop") are eliminated. If an earthworm is placed on a rough piece of paper, it is most likely to extend its head first when crawling.

2. How do they breathe? Why do they come out of the soil when it rains?

   Worms breathe air in (to extract oxygen) and carbon dioxide out, just like humans, but they lack a nose, mouth, or lungs. Instead, they breathe through their skin. Air dissolves on the mucus of their skin, so they must stay moist to breathe. If worms dry out, they suffocate. As fresh air is taken in through the skin, oxygen is drawn into the worm's circulatory system, and the worm's five hearts pump the oxygenated blood to the head area. The movements of the worm's body make the blood flow back to the back end of the body, and the hearts pump the deoxygenated blood forward again. Carbon dioxide dissolves out of the blood back to the skin.

   Earthworms need to stay moist to survive, and they are more exposed to more predators above ground. But they are regularly observed coming out of their underground tunnels in the rain, squirming around on the ground and slithering across sidewalks, driveways, and roads. Various possible theories have been proposed to explain this phenomenon: (1) the water forces the earthworms out of their tunnels by simple displacement; (2) the earthworms leave to avoid drowning in the waterlogged (or saturated) soil, which contains much less oxygen; (3) they come to the surface to take advantage of the atypical above-ground moisture to find and get together with a potential mate in the two-dimensional world on the ground surface (versus the more restrictive tunnels of the three-dimensional underground world); and (4) they use the opportunity of having the damp, above-ground surface to move to new feeding areas or leave overcrowded sites. The jury is still out on this one—scientists aren't sure what sends earthworms to the surface when it rains. Perhaps one of your young scientists will later find a definitive answer! See *www.naturenorth. com/Garden/Earthworms.html*.

3. What do they eat and do they seem to have favorite foods?

   Different species of earthworms have different food preferences depending on their specific physiological adaptations. Some eat dead plant litter while others eat decaying animals. While they do take in and process soil to extract essential nutrients and energy from the organic material from dead plants and animals in the soil, they do not actually eat dirt.

Unlike most other earthworms, the red wigglers that are the species of choice for compost bins are surface feeders with the ability to consume up to half their body weight in decayed matter each day. Household vegetable waste is an ideal food for the red wigglers who turn it into worm castings—a perfect 100% natural organic fertilizer.

4. Are there male and female earthworms, and if so, how can they be identified? How do they have babies and do they take care of them? How long can they live? Do they live in groups or as solitary individuals?

    Earthworms are hermaphrodites; each individual worm has both male and female sex organs (that are contained in their clitellums, or large orangeish bands that become visible only during reproduction). However, most species of earthworms require the sperm of another worm to fertilize their own eggs. To mate, worms line up against each other, facing opposite directions, so that their male sections align against the respective female sections of the other. The two worms exchange sperm. Then, sometime after copulation, long after the worms have separated, the clitellum of each worm secretes the cocoon that forms a ring around the worm. The worm then backs out of the ring, and as it does so,

injects its own eggs and the other worm's sperm into it. As the worm slips out, the ends of the cocoon seal to form a vaguely lemon-shaped, pale yellow, visible-to-the-naked-eye-size incubator in which several fertilized eggs develop into embryonic worms. The baby earthworms (or threads) emerge as small, but fully formed, except for a lack of the sex structures (which develop later in about 60 to 90 days). They attain full size in about one year, sometimes sooner. Each fertilized worm can produce up to two to three cocoons per week that hatch out every three to four weeks producing tiny white baby worms called threads. Scientists predict that the average lifespan under field conditions is four to eight years, but most garden varieties live only one to two years. Under optimal environmental conditions, earthworm populations can grow at a rapid rate. For example, in a well-managed compost bin, 1 lb of red wiggler worms (*Eisenia fetida*) can double in three to four months. Several common earthworm species are mostly *parthenogenetic*; that is, they reproduce asexually, which results in clones. See *www.naturenorth.com/Garden/ Earthworms.html* and *http://wormladies.com/ pages/aboutourworms.html*.

5. How big can they grow?

    The size range depends on the species, but adult earthworms can be anywhere from 10 mm long and 1 mm wide up to 3 m long and over 25 mm wide (an Australian species. See the Giant Earthworm video clips listed in the Explore phase materials). The common night crawler, one of North America's largest species, ranges in size from 9–30 cm with a diameter of 6–10 mm.

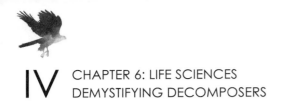
6. How many body segments do they have and do they grow more segments as they age?

The number of segments (or somites) will vary by species, typically numbering about 150.

Individuals are born with the number of segments they will have throughout their lives. Growth to maturity involves segments growing larger.

7. Can they regrow into two earthworms if they are cut in half?

As with many characteristics, the ability to regenerate lost segments varies with species and the extent of the damage. In a number of species, if a large enough number of segments of the front half of the worm (its head) is separated from its rear half by a shovel or a tug-of-war, the front can regenerate a portion of its "tail." For more details, see the references in *http://en.wikipedia.org/wiki/Nightcrawlers.*

8. How do they move and do they usually move head first (or tail first)?

An earthworm's smooth, moist skin contains rows of clawlike bristles (called setae) on each segment that move in and out to grip nearby surfaces. Locomotion through the dirt (or away from potential predators) is achieved by extending their forward-directed end, swelling it so it fills/jams the circumference of the tunnel and its bristles grip, and then using its muscles to contract its rear-directed half. It uses waves of muscular contractions that alternately shorten and lengthen its body. Burrowing is further aided by the secretion of lubricating mucus. Since either the head or tail end can be selected as the forward-directed end, worms can move either forward or backward (relative to its actual head). When students place a worm on a rough piece of paper and observe which direction it travels, it will usually extend its head first.

9. Can they see (sense light), and if so, do they prefer darkness?

Earthworms stay primarily in their dark self-excavated underground tunnels or under plant litter (depending on the species) during the day because sunlight's ultraviolet rays can immobilize them and dry out their moist skin through which they breathe. Although they lack eyes that are able to focus on and form discrete images, they do sense light with their skin. This adaptation allows them to avoid potentially harmful environments. Instead of vision, they rely on their well-developed senses of taste and touch to search for food and to avoid predators in their largely dark, moist habitats.

10. Can they hear when they're above and/or underground?

Earthworms have no ears, but their bodies can sense the vibrations of animals moving nearby underground or on the surface. This adaptation helps them avoid potential predators (e.g., moles, millipedes, large insects, gophers, birds, raccoons, human fishermen, and so on)

11. Are earthworms animals, and if so, are they a kind of bug or insect? Or are they related to snakes?

The term *bug* is somewhat ambiguous. In everyday life, people commonly refer to any relatively small (but visible) creepy, crawly or flying nonamphibian, nonavian, nonmammalian, or nonreptilian animal as a bug (e.g., centipedes and millipedes, earthworms, snails, spiders, and many others that are not even classified as insects). Scientifically speaking, true bugs are any animal that is a member of the insect order Hemiptera. As with many other cases, scientific terminology is more restrictive (and descriptive) than everyday language. Like insects, earthworms are invertebrates (i.e., lack a backbone), but they are neither bugs nor insects. They are even less closely related to snakes since snakes are vertebrates. Earthworms belong to the class of invertebrates known as the Oligochaeta (within the phylum Annelida) that maintain their spineless structure with fluid-filled chambers that function like a hydroskeleton. There are approximately 6,000 different species of earthworms in the world.

12. What role do they play in the circle of life within nature's ecosystems?

   Earthworms are decomposers that have a reputation as highly effective soil builders that honeycomb the soil with their tunnels, letting in air and rain, and building new soil with their copious amount of deposits (i.e., a single worm can produce 50–100% of its weight in worm castings per day). Castings are the worm's manure (or "poop"). They contain a highly active biological mixture of beneficial soil bacteria, enzymes, remnants of plant matter, and animal manure. They are rich in water-soluble plant nutri-

ents and contain 50% more humus than what is normally found in topsoil. They contain a high concentration of nitrates, phosphorous, magnesium, potassium, and minerals such as manganese, copper, zinc, cobalt, borax, iron, carbon, and nitrogen—all in natural proportions. As such, earthworms are highly effective garbage collectors-recyclers (or decomposers) that manufacture new soil and return essential nutrients to the soil that is then available for new plant growth. Thus, earthworms make major contributions to farming and gardening. Fertile soil may contain as many as 30 or more worms under each square meter. Since everything we eat can be traced back to the soil (e.g., cows eat grass), humans depend on decomposers such as earthworms to recycle nutrients and provide some of the building materials for new life. Without these natural recyclers, all life would eventually cease! Earthworms are truly spineless superheroes. In fact as long ago as 1881, Charles Darwin wrote, "It may be doubted whether there are many other animals which have played so important a part in the history of the world, as have these lowly organized creatures." For more information on their beneficial effects, see *http://en.wikipedia.org/wiki/Nightcrawlers.*

But surprisingly, "scientists now believe that non-native, invasive species of earthworms' impact on many forest ecosystems is profound and negative" (e.g., *Lumbricus terrestris*, the common night crawler, was originally brought to North America by European settlers). Before invasive species of earthworms became pervasive, the

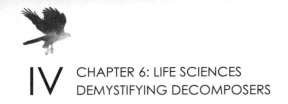

decomposition rate of organic matter on the forest floor was slow, accomplished by bacteria and fungi that made big pieces into little ones, creating below the trees a soft, deep, nutrient-rich duff that sheltered small animals, acted as an insulator, and provided a mulch for seedlings and wildflowers to grow in. In contrast, worms compete with some important fungi, and they mix, rearrange, compact, and eat leaf litter, duff, and topsoil, making conditions hostile for seeds. In the process, worms also eat the seeds, depleting the seed bank and hampering future regeneration. With the character of the forest floor altered, ground-dwelling animals both tiny and large lose both home and food, setting the stage for more alien generalists and lowering biodiversity. Adapted from *www4.uwm.edu/fieldstation/naturalhistory/bugoftheweek/earthworms.cfm*.

Reference

Darwin, C. 1881. *The formation of vegetable mould, through the action of worms.* London: John Murray.

CHAPTER 7

Earth and Space Sciences

INTRODUCTION

UNDERSTANDING OUR PLANET

Brian Vorwald

President 2012–2013, Science Teachers Association of New York State/STANYS
Adjunct Associate Professor of Earth and Space Sciences, Suffolk County Community College,
Ammerman Campus

The *Framework* and the *NGSS* define Earth and space sciences as the study of Earth and its place in the universe (ESS1), Earth's systems (ESS2), and Earth and human activity (ESS3). Traditionally, Earth science has been divided into four separate disciplines: the atmospheric sciences (i.e., weather and climate), astronomy, geology, and oceanography. The study of these disciplines and the related impacts of human activity require applying understandings from chemistry, physics, biology, and ecology.

Earth consists of four major systems, each one shaped by a related set of components and processes. Because these systems are intricately interconnected and interact with one another, a change in one system can result in a change in the other. Each system is referred to as a sphere because it can be thought of as occupying a shell around Earth. These spheres are the atmosphere, which is the part of the system that includes the mixture of gases surrounding Earth and its lower portion where weather occurs; the geosphere, which consists of the crust and Earth's interior; the hydrosphere, which is all of Earth's water, including water vapor, bodies of liquid water, and ice; and the biosphere, which includes all living things.

Understanding the interactions of and feedback mechanisms between the Earth's systems is necessary to understand how our planet works. All of the activities in our everyday lives are in some way connected to Earth, and Earth's processes affect everyone. Weather patterns affect agriculture, transportation, water resources, the safety of many people, and they can significantly impact our economy. Our growing knowledge of Earth processes such as extreme weather, earthquakes, volcanoes, and large-scale erosion can be used to develop plans to protect people from these events. The natural resources necessary for all facets of our daily lives, including the food we eat, the water we drink, the buildings we live in, the energy that fuels our modes of transportation and provides warmth for our homes and power for our lights and electronic devices, all come from our planet. Our increasing demand for natural resources and expanding technologies have affected all Earth's systems and will continue to do so in the future. People must have knowledge about how Earth systems work so that we will have a literate society that can maintain a stewardship of the environment, and make informed decisions about the management of natural resources and the effects of human activities on the land, oceans, atmosphere, plants, and animals.

Earth and space science allows students to understand and value our complex and dynamic planet. It offers an interdisciplinary approach to appreciating the planet Earth and provides young learners with the opportunity to explore the world around them by applying the practices that scientists use in their investigations. Children are very observant and naturally inquisitive. Students can make and record observations, identify problems or discrepancies, and develop possible explanations and consider solutions. Studying the Earth sciences demands inquiry-based education that challenges students to engage in problem-solving, to develop knowledge that explains many day-to-day experiences, and to answer questions that are practical and of great interest.

Many investigations in the Earth sciences can be implemented using activities that don't require expensive equipment and supplies (e.g., the following two 5E mini-units). In fact, many times no equipment is needed and the only supplies necessary are a notebook and a pencil. Students can observe the phases of the Moon, the patterns of the changing length of daylight throughout the year, and examine what comprises beach sand or the soil in their own backyards. Students can do a weather watch, noting changes in weather variables and clouds from day to day and see how they are related to changing weather conditions. Each day it's likely that an event or issue will be reported from somewhere around the world that is Earth science related and can be the source of a lesson. These are only a few samples of activities that can engage students in studying the world around them.

The Earth sciences reveal to students how all of the sciences are interrelated and increases their understanding of critical issues that affect them locally and on a global scale. Through Earth science education, students will be able to appreciate and understand our planet and to develop the 21st-century skills that are necessary to be functional and literate members of our society.

F. Water Use and Mis-Use

Annie Madden
Chappaqua Central School District (Chappaqua, New York)

Recommended Level
Grade 5

Topic Focus
Earth and Space Sciences

Disciplinary Core Idea
ESS3: Earth and human activity

Time Frame

Engage Phase
40–60 minutes (Activities 1A, 1B, and 1C, or the teacher may elect to complete only two of the three suggested activities)

Explore Phase
20 minutes plus 60 minutes (Activities 2A and 2B)

Explain Phase
60–90 minutes (Activities 3A, 3B, and 3C)

Elaborate Phase
40 minutes (Activity 4 plus an additional 40 minutes if the Optional Virtual Tour is used)

Evaluate Phase
40–80 minutes or more (depending on the activity or activities selected)

Objectives
As a result of these experiences, students will be able to

- recognize that organisms need clean fresh water to live and that pollution threatens their health and well-being;

- investigate water quality differences in samples of water and work together to remove pollutants that compromise water quality;

- develop an action plan with partners to solve problems;

- use design engineering practices to develop ways to purify samples of polluted water;

- compare the amounts of salt water and freshwater on Earth and provide examples of ways humans pollute freshwater sources; and

- describe and promote water pollution–preventive actions.

TABLE 7F.1. CORRELATION TO THE *NEXT GENERATION SCIENCE STANDARDS*

5. Earth's systems
5-ESS2-2. Describe and graph the amounts and percentages of water and fresh water in various reservoirs to provide evidence about the distribution of water on Earth.
5-ESS3-1. Obtain and combine information about ways individual communities use science ideas to protect the Earth's resources and environment.

Scientific and Engineering Practices (Dimension 1)	Disciplinary Core Ideas (Dimension 3)	Crosscutting Concepts (Dimension 2)
1. Asking questions (for science) and defining problems (for engineering)	ESS2.C: The roles of water in earth's surface processes * Nearly all of Earth's available water is in the ocean. Most fresh water is in glaciers or underground; only a tiny fraction is in streams, lakes, wetlands, and the atmosphere.	
2. Developing and using models	ESS3.C: Human impacts on earth systems	2. Cause and effect: mechanism and explanation
3. Planning and carrying out investigations		3. Scale, proportion, and quantity
4. Analyzing and interpreting data	LS2A: Interdependent relationships in ecosystems * Organisms can survive only in environments in which their particular needs are met. **Note:** These standards are a minor focus of this mini-unit (see Explain phase)	4. Systems and system models
5. Using mathematics and computational thinking		5. Energy and <u>matter</u>: Flows, cycles, and <u>conservation</u>[1]
6. Constructing explanations (for science) and designing solutions (for engineering)	ETS1: Engineering design ETS1.B: Developing possible solutions	

[1] This mini-unit does not address all portions of the standard as written; the relevant elements are underlined.

Note: ESS = Earth and space sciences; LS = Life sciences; and ETS = Engineering, technology, and applications of science

Continued

Table 7F.1. (continued)

Scientific and Engineering Practices (Dimension 1)	Disciplinary Core Ideas (Dimension 3)	Crosscutting Concepts (Dimension 2)
7. Engaging in argument from evidence	ETS2: Links among engineering, technology, science, and society	
8. Obtaining, evaluating, and communicating information		

Common Core State Standards Connections
English Language Arts –

Reading Informational Text
RI.5.8. Explain how an author uses reasons and evidence to support particular points in a text, identifying which reasons and evidence support which point(s).

Writing: Production and Distribution of Writing
W.5.4. Produce clear and coherent writing in which the development and organization are appropriate to the task, purpose, and audience.

Speaking and Listening: Comprehension and Collaboration
SL.5.1. Engage effectively in a range of collaborative discussions (one-on-one, in groups, and teacher-led) with diverse partners on *grade 5 topics and texts,* building on others' ideas and expressing their own clearly.

Speaking and Listening: Presentation of Knowledge and Ideas
SL.5.4. Report on a topic or text or present an opinion, sequencing ideas logically and using appropriate facts and relevant, descriptive details to support main ideas or themes; speak clearly at an understandable pace.
SL.5.5. Include multimedia components (e.g., graphics, sound) and visual displays in presentations when appropriate to enhance the development of main ideas or themes.

Mathematics
5.MD.2: Measurement and data: Represent and interpret data

Engage Phase

The purpose of the Engage phase is to emotionally connect students to the needs of living things and preassess their prior knowledge of water use and abuse. These three activities invite students to consider both small- (a fishbowl) and large-scale (environmental photos) examples of water pollution and to think about water as an essential resource that we and other organisms can't live without.

Materials

- One or two freshwater aquarium fish in a large glass bowl. **Teacher note:** If tap water is used for aquariums, it should be aired-out in an open container for at least 24 hours. This will remove any chlorine gas (from the water purification plant that may be harmful to the much smaller, more sensitive fish) and allow the water to come to room temperature.

- A second fishbowl (hidden) identical to the first but filled with homemade, simulated polluted water prepared by mixing shredded paper, $1/3$ cup of used coffee grounds, empty cans, a plastic baggie, $1/3$ cup of vegetable oil (i.e., this will float on top due to its lower density and immiscibility), three to five drops of red food coloring, and a volume of water that brings the mixture up to the same level as the other fishbowl.

- An optional display might include a sealed container of unfiltered aquarium water (without its former fish inhabitants) that has been kept after it was swapped out for clean water. **Teacher note:** Such naturally polluted water (i.e., "fouled" by unrecycled fish bodily waste products) can be safely displayed in a sealed container but should

not be directly handled by the students as it may harbor disease-causing microorganisms. Most aquariums make use of filtration systems to greatly reduce the need for whole-tank water exchanges, but even small fishbowls may use an aeration pump to keep the level of dissolved oxygen in an acceptable range. It is likely that some of your students have experience with maintaining a fishbowl or aquarium in their home.

- Chart paper and markers or Smart Board to record students' questions and ideas.

- PowerPoint slide show assembled from internet websites (see Activity 1B)

Activity 1A: Fish Foul Freshwater?

1. Display the fish in the clean bowl and invite the students to observe the newest member(s) of their class! Ask them to observe the fish and their surroundings and describe them in detail, as if they were trying to paint a picture with words for a friend who was blind. Record students' observations on chart paper (or a Smart Board) and invite the class to reread their observations and identify categories among them (i.e., characteristics of the fish versus the nonliving (or abiotic) characteristics of the fish's environment or habitat). Ask, "Which abiotic factors do the fish need to survive?" (Water, food, oxygen, space to swim, and so on). **Teacher note:** Some students are likely to be unaware that fish breathe oxygen that is dissolved in the water through their gills rather than breathing oxygen from the air above the bowl.

2. Refer to the list of observations and ask students to consider which abiotic factors humans need to live. Circle those on the chart

(it will likely be all of them). Point out that our physical needs and those of other animals share many things in common (water, air, space, and food for body-building materials and energy). Remind students that materials we and other living things use from nature are called resources and that all organisms naturally produce waste products as a result of their use of these resources (i.e., in respiration and digestion of food). Ask the students to consider:

- What will happen to our fish bowl over time if we do not either run a water filtration system to periodically cleanse the used water or exchange it with freshwater?

(It will become foul-colored, smelly, and polluted and will eventually become uninhabitable due to the liquid and gaseous waste products that the fish produce. Optional display: A bowl of such used or polluted water can be shown to the students to verify their hunches or prior experiences with a pet fish at home.)

- Does nature have a way of cleansing itself? What happens if humans overwhelm our natural water supply with too many of our waste products or pollutants? After a brief open-ended discussion, shift students' attention to the next activity.

Activity 1B: PowerPoint on Polluted Water and the Wondering About Water Bulletin Board

1. Display pictures of water pollution (e.g., make a PowerPoint slide show or use a short video clip from YouTube or a commercial source)

and invite students to explain why polluted water isn't safe for living things to use (i.e., they contain chemicals or microorganisms that are *not* naturally found in water or concentrations of naturally occurring chemicals or microorganisms that are elevated to unhealthy levels). Sample resources for images and background information about water use and water pollution include the following:

- EPA: Water: Learn the issues: *www2.epa. gov/learn-issues/water*

- Everyday Pollution: *http://everydaypollution.wordpress.com/category/water-pollution/page/9*

- National Geographic's Freshwater Initiative: *http://environment.nationalgeographic.com/environment/freshwater*

- UK Rivers Network (60 copyright-free, public domain images of water pollution from USA agencies): *www.ukrivers.net/pollutionpics.html*

- Water Pollution Photos by David Nunuk: *www.nunukphotos.com* (Type "water pollution" in the search field.)

2. While referencing the specific pictures, ask students questions such as, "Where do you think the water pollution came from? Would you want to drink that water? What would you do if you saw litter like that on the ground or in the water?" and so on. Create a fishbowl-shaped, interactive bulletin board titled Wondering About Water. Students should write their questions down on paper fish and post them inside the fish bowl on the bulletin board. Throughout the five phases of this 5E mini-unit, periodically pro-

vide time for students to process and reflect on the activities and to add to the board when questions are posed and answers are discovered. Possible questions that students might generate for the fishbowl include, *How does pollution like this get into the water? Why do humans pollute resources that living things need to survive? How can we clean up water pollution? How can we prevent pollution in the first place?* Remember, the primary objective of the Engage phase is to raise, not answer questions. Student inquiries may also extend into questions about the water cycle, a topic that the *NGSS* reserves for the middle and/or high school levels. If they have a strong interest in this topic, advanced upper elementary students can be directed to independently research web-based resources during the Elaborate and/or Evaluate phases.

Activity 1C: Personal and Household Water Needs

1. To help students begin to make a connection between the fishes' obvious need for water, water pollution generated by somebody else, and their own daily use of water, ask students to take a mental walk through a typical day from the time they wake up to the time they go to bed and identify all of the different ways they directly use water (e.g., brushing their teeth, washing their hands, drinking, flushing the toilet, making hot chocolate, washing off fruit, bathing or showering, washing dishes or clothes, watering plants, and so on). Have students form pairs and take turns sharing their mental walks.

2. Now ask students to think about ways that water is indirectly used, such as to grow food

(both plants and animals), hidden in their drinks or household cleaners, as part of the manufacturing of paper and other products, or as a source of power (hydroelectric). **Teacher note:** Indirect uses of water far exceed our direct uses in and around our home, but we can more easily personally control the former than the latter.

◆ Background Information and Optional Quantitative Water Use Calculators:

- Grace Communications Foundation (select Water and Water Footprint Calculator): *www.gracelinks.org*

- Water Footprint Network (Water footprint Calculator and Direct and Indirect Water Use): *www. waterfootprint.org/?page=files/home*

- Water Science School: USGS Program (see Water Use Activity Center): *http://ga.water.usgs.gov/edu*. This website contains an interactive questionnaire on personal water use that generates a quantitative estimate (gallons of water/day/person).

- Wikipedia: Water Use: *http:// en.wikipedia.org/wiki/Water_use*

- World Water Council: *www. worldwatercouncil.org*. This website contains comparative information on global water use.

Teacher note: Questions related to where local water comes from and where it goes to be purified should be noted, but answers should be reserved until the Elaborate phase.

Explore Phase

In these two activities, students will (1) explore the relative quality of different sources of water and (2) participate in a simulation to explore how human activities impact water quality by contrasting a desirable fish habitat with an undesirable one. Students will use design engineering processes and tools to try to clean pollutants from the water and recognize that people need to prevent or reduce water pollution because pollutants can cause major health problems.

Materials

- Five small paper cups per student (clean, previously unused), labeled A–E (include 10 ml of each sample at room temperature). Samples include A: water from school water fountain; B: Dasani (municipal source and processing presentation at *www.thecoca-colacompany.com/flash/csr/dasani/index.html*) or Fiji (aquifer-source and comparison to tap/municipal sources at *www.fijiwater.com*); C: distilled or de-ionized water (available at grocery stores; will taste flat); D: water from a different municipality (teacher's home, for example); and E: water from a local pond, lake, stream, or river (*not* for consumption).

- For each group of four students: A sample of freshly prepared homemade, simulated polluted water (from the Engage phase, approximately 1 L) in a large mixing bowl, one spoon, one funnel, three coffee filters, a pair of tongs, one pasta sieve, about ⅓ cup of activated charcoal (available from pet stores), and a large dishwashing basin, 1 one small clear container (optional: nonlatex gloves)

Optional activities:

- Observing a Mixture: Per student: one new, clean small plastic cups; enough clean drinking water to fill each cup halfway; lemonade powdered mix; new, clean spoon to stir; Lucky Charms cereal; clean napkins to distribute cereal to each student

- Cleaning Water With Activated Charcoal: Per student: one small, clean plastic cup; a hole-punch tool; one cotton ball (pulled thin); one wooden skewer; one large, clean plastic cup (the small cup should fit completely into the larger cup); home water pitcher filter (e.g., Brita)

Activity 2A: Sight, Smell, and Taste Tests of Drinking Water

1. Ask, "Do you think all the water humans use has exactly the same properties? How might they be the same? How might they be different?" Explain that they are going to observe and compare five different water samples, one taken from their very own reservoir (water fountain at school), and they will try to figure out if there are any differences between the different water samples. Record the properties they describe on the chart paper. Tell the class where the five kinds of water they will sample come from, but don't tell which is which, except for E (the one from a natural water source nearby). Ask students to predict which type they think will be the most popular with the class. This can be done in a fun, TV soft drink taste test–type manner.

2. Provide each student with the water samples in clean, previously unused plastic cups labeled A–E and a data table (Figure 7F.1, p. 170) to record their results. Review with

students how to record their data in the data table: They will observe how clear the water is, smell the water, and taste the water in each cup and rate each one on a scale of 1–3. Lead the students by demonstrating with cup E (the one that should *not* be tasted). Invite students to observe its clarity by asking, "Can you see the bottom of the cup? Is the water very cloudy (Gross!), sort of cloudy (It's okay.), Is the water clear (I like it!)?" Remind students NOT to taste cup E since it is untreated water from a natural source that may look and smell clean, but may not be safe for humans to drink. Ask students to share some of their ideas of what might make the water unsafe to drink and guide them to recognize that there are some things (like bacteria and chemical pollutants) that we cannot see in the water that might make us sick. Explain that drinking water (i.e., out of our faucets or in bottled water) is regularly tested and treated/cleaned first to ensure that it is safe for us to drink (i.e., municipal water departments send out one or more water quality reports per year to residents).

FIGURE 7F.1. WATER TESTING DATA TABLE

Scale for Smell and Taste Tests			
1 = I like it!			
2 = It's okay			
3 = Gross! (or other describing words)			
Sample	Clarity	Smell	Taste
A			
B			
C			
D			
E			DO NOT TASTE!

3. Connect the activity to mathematics by creating bar graphs to compare students' taste test results. Then reveal the identity of each sample. Draw attention back to the fish bowl and ask students to justify which water sample they would prefer to use in the fish's bowl, based on their results. Remind students that just because they can't see, smell, or taste anything unusual in a water sample does not necessarily mean it is safe to drink. **Teacher note:** Microorganisms and molecules are not introduced in the *NGSS* until the middle school grades, but it might be helpful to briefly mention these factors. But for now, students should learn that uncolored or diluted chemical pollutants or harmful microbes could still be in the water that could make humans sick (i.e., "Just because you can't see (or smell) it, doesn't mean it isn't there.")

4. Pretend that you forgot to give them a sixth sample of water for the taste-testing activity and hurriedly search for it while pretending that you can't remember where you put it. After a moment, pretend to find it by pulling out the previously hidden second fishbowl, filled with polluted water (and sealed with a cover). Ask students if they would consider using this water sample in their fish's bowl instead of the one they selected in the taste test (obviously not!) and then remind them (from the Engage phase slide show or video clips) that some fish in nature are being forced to try to meet their physical needs using water that is heavily polluted by humans. Review the questions posed by the class on the bulletin board during the activity like, *How does pollution like this (hold up the fishbowl) get into the water? How can we clean up water pollution?* Remind students that they will

explore answers to these questions in the next activity.

Activity 2B: Purifying Polluted Water—How Can We Make Foul Water Fresh(er)?

1. Prominently post the inquiry question for the next activity, *What pollutants are in the fishbowl, and how can we get the water clean enough for our fish to use?* Display the clean (#1) and sealed polluted (#2) fishbowls again and review with students their original observations of each. Invite students to record any new questions and answers to previously posed questions in the fishbowl on the bulletin board.

2. Provide each group of three to four students with their sample of freshly prepared, homemade, simulated polluted water. **Safety note:** Do *not* allow students to attempt to clean the actual used, fouled fish water as it could contain pathogens. Invite students to observe and attempt to identify the pollutants in their sample. Create an OWL chart for each group [I Observe/I Wonder/I Learned] (Figure 7F.2) and instruct students to list the pollutants they can identify in their water sample in the left column of their OWL chart.

3. Challenge: Use engineering practices to design a method to purify polluted water: Provide each group with a bucket of materi-

als they can apply to try to remove the pollution from water. Before they begin, explain that during the clean-up simulation their challenge is to use only the materials they are provided to try to get the water as clean as the freshwater in their fish's bowl (no water from the sink is allowed). Explain that using available materials to solve a problem is part of a process known as engineering. Instruct each group to discuss and record an engineering action plan in the second column of their OWL. They should specify which tool(s) they plan to use to remove each pollutant and then rank their plan using sequential numbers in the order that they think will be most effective. Circulate during this planning phase and facilitate group dialogue by asking students to explain why they think a particular tool will work to remove a particular pollutant and why other tools might not be effective.

Optional Demonstrations: This engineering simulation provides an opportunity to show the differences between easily discernible and separable mixtures and true solutions. Guided prelab instruction can be used to introduce students to these two kinds of combinations by comparing and contrasting a sample of Lucky Charms cereal mixed with water to a lemonade solution that students can make in the classroom by dissolving lemonade drink powder into water. Challenge

FIGURE 7F.2. OWL CHART

OBSERVATIONS	WONDERINGS	WHAT WE LEARNED
Pollutant	How can we clean it up?	How successful was our strategy?

students to try to separate each combination or mixture into its parts (only the Lucky Charms is easily separable because it is a heterogeneous mixture). The teacher might also consider demonstrating evaporative separation of the lemonade solution, as well as direct instruction about the use of activated charcoal to remove coloring from the water by setting up the following demonstration: (1) poke two holes in the sides (one across from the other) and one small hole on the bottom in a small, clear plastic cup; (2) line the bottom of the cup around the hole with a thinned cotton ball (pulled apart); (3) insert a wooden skewer into the holes on the side to create handles for the cup to hang on the rim of a larger cup when placed inside the larger cup; (4) insert $1/3$ cup of activated charcoal into the cup; and (5) slowly pour the polluted (colored) sample into the cup with charcoal and allow it to drip into the larger cup. Ask students to observe and compare the filtered results to the original liquid.

4. When each group's OWL chart reflects a thoughtful, sequenced action plan, instruct students to begin executing their plan, recording how effective each strategy was at removing that pollutant from the water in the third column of their OWL. During the water purification activity, encourage students to discuss and adjust their action plan, recording any changes using a different colored marker to allow them to reflect on their adjustments later.

   Procedural suggestions and additional resources: While there is no single effective way to remove these pollutants, some strategies are more effective than others. For example, the plastic baggie and alumi-num cans can be removed by physically picking them out of the water using the tongs. The oil, which will float on top of the water due to density, can be skimmed off of the top of the water with the spoon (or alternatively, the water could be allowed to drain out of a hole in the bottom of a paper cup until just before the oil starts to come through). The shredded paper can be removed by pouring the water from the sampling container through the pasta sieve into the basin and then the coffee grounds can be removed by lining the funnel with one coffee filter (repeatedly, eventually using all three filters) and pouring the water from the basin back into the mixing bowl. The food coloring can be removed using the activated charcoal (see optional teacher demonstration previously described in Step 3).

If a less open-ended, more guided laboratory experience is desired, teachers may download a four-page procedure for designing a simple, but effective sand and activated charcoal water filtration device from the American Chemical Society's Science Activities for Children website: *http://portal. acs.org/portal/fileFetch/C/CSTA_015084/pdf/ CSTA_015084.pdf*. See Figure 7F.3., Sample Water Filtration Setup.

Additionally, after the lab activity is completed, the teacher may want to demonstrate the efficiency of a commercial water filter (e.g., Brita) in removing not only dirt and/or food coloring, but also much of the smell of a fragrant oil (e.g., orange or lemon) that can be added to the water as another pollutant.

FIGURE 7F.3. SAMPLE WATER FILTRATION SETUP

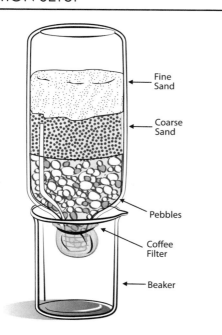

Fine
Sand

Coarse
Sand

Pebbles

Coffee
Filter

Beaker

5. After student groups have finished, pour a sample of each group's cleaned water into a small clear container to observe and compare. Facilitate class discussion in response to questions like, *Which of the pollutants was the easiest to remove? Why do we think that was? How do we think those pollutants are removed from streams, lakes, and other water sources? Which pollutants were challenging to remove? Why do we think that was? How do we think those pollutants are removed from natural water sources? What adjustments did our groups make during their work? Why did we do it differently than we had planned to? Do you think your original plan would have been more successful, why or why not? What questions do we still have about water pollution and how to clean these pollutants out of water? Do you think it is easier to prevent certain kinds of water pollution or remove the pollutants after they're already present?*

Ask students to reflect, based on their experiences so far, on whether or not they would use the cleaned water from the simulation in their fish's bowl and invite students to justify their responses and argue their reasoning in both written and oral forms.

Explain Phase

The purpose of this activity is to provide guided instruction that will develop student understanding of the limited amount of freshwater resources on Earth, despite the fact that water is naturally recyclable, by comparing distribution of freshwater and salt water using a map and a beach ball Earth globe. Students will understand the urgent need to prevent pollution of freshwater sources because the Earth's surface is 97% salt water and 2% frozen freshwater, neither of which is directly available for sustaining life processes for humans or freshwater aquatic life.

Materials

- World map

- Inflatable Earth Globe Beach Ball (Amazon. com distributes a variety of 12 in. to 16 in. models for $2–$15; do not purchase the more realistic Earthballs that use NASA images with cloud cover) Four small clean, clear plastic cups (previously unused) of water per pair of students. Half of the cups will contain salty water and half freshwater. **Teacher note:** Salt water that is made with pure NaCl/sodium chloride (like kosher salt) will *not* be cloudy. The cloudiness of salt water made with regular table salt is due to the anticaking compounds added to make it pour by preventing it from absorbing water from the air (*http://sci-toys.com/ingredients/table_salt.html*). If cloudy salt water (made with table salt) is allowed to settle and slowly decanted or if it is filtered, it will appear clear or noncloudy.

- One resealable plastic bag of 100 white, 2 pink, and 1 green mini-marshmallows per group of three to four students

    Safety note: Remind students that these are not for eating since they will be handled by multiple people. Alternatively, different-color bingo chips or paper clips can be used. In all cases, the items can be counted by weighing since any of these items have a fairly uniform size and mass.

- Chart paper and markers or Smart Board

- A copy of Strauss. R. 2007. *One well: The story of water on Earth.* Toronto: Kids Can Press.

- Consider referencing interesting graphs/ visuals such as those found at *www.water-clean.ca/Facts&Trends.php*.

- The fish and bowls introduced in the previous two activities and a third fishbowl, identical to the others, filled with saltwater solution (visibly cloudy)

Activity 3A: Earth Ball Beach Toss and Catch Game (Simulation)

1. Display both fishbowls (the one with the live fish and the sealed polluted/dirty sample) and begin a review of concepts from the last activity by asking students if they would be willing to move their fish into the second bowl or drink that polluted water with their lunch today. (Warn students not to actually drink the polluted sample.) Encourage them to justify their reasoning by describing their observations of the second fishbowl.

2. Ask students to observe the map and estimate how much of the Earth is covered in water compared to land. Show students an inflatable globe and explain that they are going to play a game where they will toss the globe around the room, recording on chart paper or the Smart Board whether the right thumb of the student who catches the ball falls on land or water. Choose two student volunteers to demonstrate and then invite them to throw the ball to other classmates. Each time, the teacher records the data on the board. Complete at least 25 catches and then look at the data to estimate how much of the Earth's surface is covered by water (about 70% water and 30% land, or about 7 of 10 catches will land on liquid water). **Teacher note:** The continent of Antarctica is actually a land mass whereas much of the frozen water at the North Pole/Arctic Circle does not rest atop land but rather floats in the Arctic Ocean.

Activity 3B: Surrounded by Salty Seas, But Not a Drop to Drink

1. After looking at the class's data from the simulation, ask, "Does all water have the same properties? What did you find out in a previous activity?" Encourage students to use their observations from the taste-test activity to justify their reasoning that not all water on our planet is the same and encourage them to share some differences they have discovered so far (e.g., water may be more or less clean or polluted). Provide each partner pair four small cups (two salty and two not; these can be labeled A and B to ensure that each student tastes both types), then tell students that there is another property that they will discover in this activity and that understanding this prop-

erty is very important to their fish's survival. Instruct students to compare the water samples (sight and smell—no differences should be discernible). Invite them to share their observations with their partners. Then ask the students to taste a small amount of each water sample. Remind students not to exchange cups with each other to avoid potentially spreading germs. **Teacher note:** The sense of taste could detect differences in the two water samples that were not detectable by sight or smell.

2. Produce a third fishbowl that you tell your students is filled with salt water like the sample they tested and ask them if they think it would be safe to move their fish into this bowl. Ask, "Can animals that naturally live in freshwater survive in salty seawater? If you put your freshwater fish into this (fishbowl of) salty water, what do you think will happen to it? Why do you think that? What kinds of animals live in salty sea and ocean water? Do you think they could survive in freshwater?" Check for understanding by inviting students to point to areas of the inflatable Earth globe (and/or class map of the world) where their class's pet fish could *not* live (oceans) and areas of fresh water where their fish could live (most lakes and rivers). **Teacher note:** Biome-specific species and ecosystems are not a major focus here, but encourage students to add their questions to the bulletin board and provide leveled texts like *A Journey Into a Lake* by Rebecca L. Johnson and *A Wetland Habitat* by Bobbie Kalman for independent exploration. If desired, a link can be made to the fifth grade *NGSS* LS2.A standard that states, "Organisms can survive only in environments which meet their particular needs."

3. Ask students, "How much water do we need to drink each day?" To help them visualize various estimates, display a few sample volumes such as a small cup, 12 oz bottle, 2 L container, gallon jug, and so on. Invite them to share their guesses, tally the results, and then reveal that humans require about eight, 8 oz servings of freshwater a day, or about 1.9 L. Point to the 2 L container as a visual reference and tell the students that humans, like other land animals, cannot drink salt water to supply our daily water need. Organisms that live in salt water have biological adaptations that enable them to process and use salt water.

Activity 3C: Saltwater Simulation: Marshmallow Mathematical Model

1. Distribute one bag of 100 white mini-marshmallows (or uniform-color bingo chips or paper clips) to each group of three to four students to spread out on their desks. **Safety note:** If marshmallows are used, stress that they are not for consumption. Invite students to look at the Earth globe and/or world map again and then divide their marshmallows, which together represent all of the water on Earth, into two piles on their desk. One pile should show how much salt water they think there is on Earth, and the other pile will represent the amount of freshwater on Earth. Invite groups to compare piles and explain why they constructed them as they did. What observations were their decisions based on? Assess any misconceptions demonstrated here and adjust the lesson as needed. Additional geographic guidance may be necessary to direct student attention to large inland lakes and rivers and to note that some large inland bodies of water may in fact be salty seas (e.g., the Black, Caspian, Dead, and Red

Seas) and that many smaller lakes and rivers don't show up on the Earth globe or world map (due to scale limitations). In any case, it is likely that most student teams will over-estimate the relative amount of freshwater, so proceed to the next step.

2. Replace three marshmallows (or bingo chips or paper clips) in each group with three different-color ones (i.e., two of a second color and one of a third color) and ask students to create three piles by color. Ask them to infer what each pile might now represent. Invite them to share their ideas by asking, "Does anyone have a different idea? and Does anyone else agree with that idea?"

3. Show students a bar graph like the one in Figure 7F.4 and invite students to explain that their three piles reflect the actual distribution of freshwater and salt water as shown in the graph. Point to the map and show students that 99% of the water on Earth is *not* available for land and freshwater organisms to use because it is salty or frozen and ask them to describe the types of water sources these living organisms *can* use (the 1%) to meet their needs (streams, lakes, etc.) (See *http://ga.water. usgs.gov/edu/watercyclefreshstorage.html*)

Optional: If you wish to introduce the idea of (under) ground water, see the visuals at the USGS website and others such as *http:// en.wikipedia.org/wiki/Groundwater and www. globalchange.umich.edu/globalchange2/current/ lectures/freshwater_supply/freshwater.html*. Most students will be surprised to learn that there is much more freshwater located underground than on the Earth's surface and in fact many individual houses, farms, and communities draw most of their freshwater

FIGURE 7F.4. COMPARING TYPES OF WATER ON EARTH

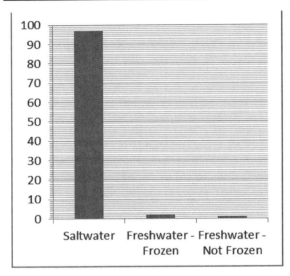

(source: A. Madden)

from underground sources that are *not* visible on the Earth globe or world map. Preventing, detecting, and remediating polluted groundwater is more challenging than with more easily accessible surface waters.

4. After cleanup, share a few short excerpts from *One Well: The Story of Water on Earth* by Rochelle Strauss on pages 13, 14, and 17 using a document camera (if one is available) or by gathering students into a reading circle. The inset on each of these pages provides examples of animal dependence on both freshwater and salt water. Ask each student to share one way humans use water for their daily activities or to grow and create products that we want and need. Show students 'Saving the Water in the Well' (page 24) and challenge each student to reflect on the day's activity by writing an ending to this sentence starter: *Respecting water means understanding that it is … .* (One example

of a thoughtful ending is *a limited resource that all living things need and one that we all share.*)

Elaborate Phase

The purpose of this phase is to encourage students to extend and apply their understanding of water pollution and the limited amount of freshwater to empower personal activism through preservation and conservation strategies. They will learn that because the amount of water on Earth is fixed, conservation involves adopting wise strategies for using and reusing this shared resource. Students will learn about social and environmental activists and recognize that children around the world are affected by these issues and can also be part of the solution.

Materials

- Dominos, at least 25 per group of 4 students

- A copy of Millway, K. S. 2008. *One hen: How one small loan made a big difference.* Toronto: Kids Can Press.

- Websites on global water resources, needs and challenges:

  ◆ *www.youtube.com/watch?feature=player_profilepage&v=vtXHi1lr3H8*

  ◆ *water.org/water-crisis/water-facts/water*

  ◆ *www.youtube.com/watch?v=YvPf_0BGitA*

Activity 4: The Domino Effect Model and Worldwide Wise Water Management

1. Provide each group a set of dominos and invite students to set their dominos up in any shape, as long as one will hit the next when the first is knocked over. Encourage creativ-

ity and sharing of ideas (e.g., straight and curved lines, radial patterns, triangles, and so on). Before the dominoes are set off, explain that each action we choose to take can have a domino effect and invite students to explain what that means before asking each group to demonstrate their setups for the class.

2. If no student group came up with the idea of arranging the dominoes in a shape that causes expanding, accelerating effect, demonstrate the idea of a chain or exponential reaction either by a using a live setup or one or more domino tricks You Tube videos. For example, consider the following.

    Huge Domino Triangle (the segment from 1:50–2:58 minutes shows the post-setup, exponential toppling multiple times): *www.youtube.com/watch?v=GZOghs7eIyM*. An alternative setup for showing how a seemingly small effect can cause increasingly larger outcomes can be found at: Domino Chain Reaction (1 min, 11 secs; small dominoes toppling progressively larger, heavier dominoes): *www.youtube.com/watch?v=5JCm5FY-dEY*.

3. Tell students that they will learn today about the actions of a young boy that had a domino effect throughout his West African village. Read *One Hen* by Katie Smith Millway and remind students that the story is based on true events. Facilitate a discussion about Kojo's accomplishments using the following discussion prompts: Why did Kojo buy the first hen when he was a young boy? If you were friends with Kojo, what do you think he would be like? If you were in his position, what would you have bought with that money and why? Who is helped directly by

Kojo's success? Who is helped indirectly? In what ways did his whole community act like a team?

4. Use a computer and multimedia projector (or Smart Board) to visit one or more of the websites listed above. The site at *http://water.org/water-crisis/water-facts/water* can be used to display the pictographs (each link from the menu on the left side includes topic-based pictographs) for students to spark class dialogue around the water crisis, or lack of access to clean freshwater for more than one billion of the Earth's current, ever-growing population of over seven billion people.

5. Ask students, "Based on the data in the graphs we looked at, do you think people are respecting water resources?" Explain that we can do simple things to reduce the amount of water we use and to keep the water around us in rivers, lakes, inside the ground, and in the sky clean so that all living things can use it safely. Show the YouTube video about what Water.Org is doing to help people get clean water in areas that don't have access. Ask students to think about Kojo's actions in the story and how many people were impacted by those actions. Then think about the people in the video who need clean freshwater. Ask students to think-pair-share with class some actions they can take to help keep water clean. Challenge students to think of ways they can conserve and protect water at home and at school, and then brainstorm ways to implement those ideas. If desired, these ideas can be incorporated into action-oriented projects in the Evaluate phase.

<u>Optional Activity</u>: Live or Virtual Fieldtrip to a Drinking Water Treatment Plant

If time permits and students are interested in exploring the source(s) of their own community's water, how it is purified before and after use, and how the water purification activity (in the Explore phase) is similar to the real processes, students can be taken on a live or virtual field trip (e.g., see animation, games, and more at *http://water.epa.gov/drink/tour*). Also, as mentioned during the Engage phase, some advanced students may be interested in independently exploring how human-engineered purification processes relate to the natural water cycle. The water cycle should be part of the middle school curriculum (according to the *NGSS*), but especially curious students (e.g., those interested in an independent science fair project) can be directed websites such as the following.

- American Water Works: Story of Drinking Water: *www.drinktap.org/kidsdnn/Portals/5/story_of_water/html/hydrocycle.htm*

- Earthguide Animated Diagrams: *http://earthguide.ucsd.edu/earthguide/diagrams/watercycle/*

- EPA: The Water Cycle (animation): *www.epa.gov/ogwdw/kids/flash/flash_watercycle.html*

- Kidzone: *www.kidzone.ws/water*

- The Water Cycle, 2000. Project Learn, University Corporation for Atmospheric Research: *www.ucar.edu/learn/1_1_2_4t.htm.*

- USGS: The Water Cycle: Water Science for Schools: *http://ga.water.usgs.gov/edu/watercycle.html*

Evaluate Phase

Summative assessment of student understanding and mastery of the goals and objectives of this mini-unit should utilize multiple measures and be authentic in design. Some suggested assessment strategies are provided below.

Materials

- Easy Ways Kids Can Conserve Water: *www.youtube.com/watch?v=0Am9JPfuNsw&feature=related*

- 25 Ways to Conserve Water in the Home and Yard: *http://eartheasy.com/live_water_saving.htm*

- 100 Ways to Conserve Water: *www.wateruseitwisely.com/100-ways-to-conserve/index.php*

- Provide students materials specific to the elected assessment strategy

Activity 5: Alternative Summative Assessment Options

1. Show students the YouTube video about what kids can do to conserve and preserve water and encourage students to lobby their parents and siblings to implement those strategies at home (see the previously cited Household Water Footprint Calculator at *www.gracelinks.org/1408/water-footprint-calculator* and the other two water conservation websites listed above). Students can write persuasive letters to their families and/or develop multimedia presentations for their school's PTA that educate them about our need for and use of water resources, the problem of water pollution and engineering techniques of water purification; promote water conservation strategies they wish to implement at home (and school); and provide supporting evidence from their experiences in class during the unit activities (i.e., see the persuasive letter writing graphic organizer provided in the References section).

2. Consider promoting student ideas in discussions with faculty and administrators in your school building to help the school develop action plans that empower students to "think globally, act locally" (See *http://en.wikipedia.org/wiki/Think_globally,_act_locally*) by impacting water conservation measures in their own school. This is a great opportunity to integrate science, mathematics, social studies, ELA, and art.

3. Instruct students on how to create a two-flap foldable to compare properties of salt water and freshwater (Zikes 2004). A map can be incorporated as a second layer and color-coded to visually show salt water and freshwater sources by comparison. Expand the foldable into four-flaps to include animal and plant life that are adapted to live in or examples of specific pollution threats in each environment. Foldables can be glued into students' science notebooks and used as an interactive tool. They also provide an opportunity for students to incorporate artwork into their science study by adding diagrams and drawing pictures of their pollution clean-up action plan or before–after comparisons of their water sample's cleanliness.

4. Students can write and illustrate a children's story using storyboarding techniques. Set the story parameters such that it is written from the perspective of the class's fish, anticipating or reacting to being relocated into the fishbowls that were presented to the class

(polluted/salty) in the unit activities. Specify that the fish character should educate readers about the difference in freshwater and saltwater habitats and the dangers of water pollution to wildlife.

References

Docstoc. 2011. Persuasive letter format. *www.docstoc.com/search/persuasive-business-letter-format*

Earth Policy Institute. *www.earth-policy.org*

Zikes, D. 2004. *Big book of science elementary K–6.* San Antonio, TX: Dinah-Might Adventures.

G. Metric Measurement, Models, and Moon Matters

Thomas O'Brien, PhD
Professor of Science Education
Binghamton University (SUNY), Graduate School of Education

Recommended Level
Grade 5

Topic Focus
Earth and Space Sciences

Disciplinary Core Idea
ESS1: Earth's place in the universe

Time Frame

Engage Phase
40 minutes (Activity 1)

Explore Phase
80 minutes (Activity 2)

Explain Phase
40 minutes (Activity 3)

Elaborate Phase
40 minutes (Activity 4 not counting two optional activities)

Evaluate Phase
40–120 minutes (depending which Activity 5 options are used)

Objectives
As a result of these experiences, students will be able to

- understand the relative, rank order size of the Moon, Earth, and Sun system;

- understand the relative distance between the Earth and Moon using a scale model of the Earth and Moon;

- use metric measurement skills and mathematics (e.g., the equation Circumference = πd);

- to develop scale models of these three astronomical objects; and

- critically examine textbook Moon–Earth–Sun visuals to determine whether they are ever drawn to scale.

Note: This mini-unit is adapted from Activity 13: 5 E(z) Steps to Earth-Moon Scaling, in O'Brien, T. 2011. *Even more brainpowered science: Teaching and learning with discrepant events.* Arlington, VA: NSTA Press.

TABLE 7G.1 CORRELATION TO THE *NEXT GENERATION SCIENCE STANDARDS*

5. Space system: Stars and the solar system
5-ESS1-1. Support an argument that the apparent brightness of the Sun and stars is due to their relative distances from the Earth.
Note: This mini-unit focuses on the smaller, more easily modeled scale of the relative sizes of and distance between the Earth and Moon and the relatives size of the Earth and Sun. As such, it serves as a conceptual and mathematical precursor to investigating the patterns of their relative motions and the more "far-out scale" of the stars identified in the above performance standard. If desired, it could be used in a mathematics class as a real-world application of fifth grade CCSS-Mathematics practices or as a collaborative science-mathematics mini-unit.

Scientific and Engineering Practices (Dimension 1)	Disciplinary Core Ideas (Dimension 3)	Crosscutting Concepts (Dimension 2)
1. Asking questions (for science) and defining problems (for engineering)	ESS.1.B Earth and the solar system	1. Patterns
2. Developing and using models		
3. Planning and carrying out investigations		3. Scale, proportion, and quantity
4. Analyzing and interpreting data		4. Systems and system models
5. Using mathematics and computational thinking		
6. Constructing explanations (for science) and designing solutions (for engineering)		
7. Engaging in argument from evidence		
8. Obtaining, evaluating, and communicating information		

Note: ESS = Earth and space sciences

Continued

Table 7G.1. (continued)

Common Core State Standards Connections
English Language Arts –

Reading: Foundational Skills: Fluency

RF.5.4. Read (on-level text) with sufficient accuracy and fluency to support comprehension.

Reading Informational Text: Integration of Knowledge and Ideas

RI.5.7. Draw on information from multiple print or digital sources, demonstrating the ability to locate an answer to a question quickly or solve a problem efficiently.

RI.5.9. Integrate information from several texts on the same topic in order to write or speak about the subject knowledgeably.

Writing: Texts Types and Purposes

W.5.2. Write informative/explanatory texts to examine a topic and convey ideas and information clearly.

W.5.2.d. Use precise language and domain-specific vocabulary to inform about or explain the topic.

Speaking and Listening: Comprehension and Collaboration

SL.5.1. Engage effectively in a range of collaborative discussions (one-on-one, in groups, and teacher- led) with diverse partners on *grade 5 topics and texts,* building on others' ideas and expressing their own clearly.

Speaking and Listening: Presentation of Knowledge and Ideas

SL.5.4. Report on a topic or text or present an opinion, sequencing ideas logically and using appropriate facts and relevant, descriptive details to support main ideas or themes; speak clearly at an understandable pace.

SL.5.5. Include multimedia components (e.g., graphics, sound) and visual displays in presentations when appropriate to enhance the development of main ideas or themes.

Mathematics: Mathematical Practices (the first six of eight standards)

1. Make sense of problems and persevere in solving them.
2. Reason abstractly and quantitatively.
3. Construct viable arguments and critique the reasoning of others.
4. Model with mathematics.
5. Use appropriate tools strategically.
6. Attend to precision

5.MD.1: Measurement and data

Convert among different-size standard measurement units within a given measurement system, and use these conversions in solving multi-step, real-world problems.

Represent and interpret data.

Continued

Table 7G.1. (continued)

> **5.NBT**: <u>Numbers and operations in base ten</u>
> Understand the place value system:
> **1.** Recognize that in a multi-digit number, a digit in one place represents 10 times as much as it represents in the place to its right and 1/10 of what it represents in the place to its left.
> **2.** Explain patterns in the number of zeros of the product when multiplying a number by powers of 10, and explain patterns in the placement of the decimal point when a decimal is multiplied or divided by a power of 10. Use whole-number exponents to denote powers of 10.
> **3.** Read, write, and compare decimals to thousandths.
> **4.** Use place value understanding to round decimals to any place.
> Perform operations in multi-digit whole numbers and with decimals to hundredths.
>
> **Teacher note:** This 5E mini-unit invites curriculum collaboration and integration between mathematics and science via the real-world relevant context of space science.

Engage Phase

The purpose of this phase is to activate and assess students' prior knowledge, raise questions, and catalyze thinking about the meaning of *big* as a relative, rank-ordered, eyeball estimate of size and to review the importance of metric measurements and mathematics.

Materials

- Clement, R. 1994. *Counting on Frank*. New York: Houghton Mifflin Harcourt.

- Schwartz, D., and S. Kellogg. 1997. *How much is a million?* Logan, IA: Perfection Learning.

- Wells, R. 1993. *Is a blue whale the biggest thing there is?* Park Ridge, IL: Albert Whitman and Company.

- Space Posters and Models available from Sciencemall-usa (posters and models): *www.sciencemall-usa.com*. Also available from Science Posters Plus: *www.super-science-fair-projects.com/science-posters-plus.html* and Sea

and Sky: Astronomical Art: *www.seasky.org/links/skylink08.html*

- Music videos: Beethoven's *Moonlight Sonata* and Moon (photo) Montage (2 mins 48 secs): *www.youtube.com/watch?v=c1tkBNF0ghU* or Debussy's "Clair De Lune": approximately 5 mins): *www.youtube.com/watch?v=CvFH_6DNRCY* and *www.youtube.com/watch?v=ZfSV_k3MhCw*

Activity 1: Seeing Is Believing? Eyes Can Deceive What Metric Measurements Help Us Perceive

1. Ask students, "What are three of the biggest things you can think of?" Engage the students with a Think (silent individual)–Write (individual)–Pair (dyads to discuss)–Share (whole class). (Students are most likely to mention large living things and nonliving objects on Earth. Note whether any students mention the Earth itself or other astronomical bodies, or if their perspective is more Earth-bound. It

is also important to note if students confound the idea of linear and cubic (or volume) measures and meanings of the term *big*.)

2. Follow the Think-Write-Pair-Share activity with a whole-class discussion related to the following questions:

◆ How do the different things we individually thought of compare in relative size (i.e., big, bigger, biggest)? Tabulate the students' ideas about relative sizes on a blackboard or interactive white board where they can be easily moved.

◆ (**Teacher note:** In attempting to generate a size-sequence list, you are likely to encounter cases where off-scale representations in books have misled students about relative sizes.)

◆ What sources of information could we use to confirm the validity of our rank-ordered sequence or list? (Answer: Books, the internet, direct measurements, and measurements of scale models could be used.)

3. Read aloud (or use a document camera) to share select portions of the text and visuals from the trade books noted in the Materials section to get students thinking more about the relative (scale order) size of different objects on Earth. Note that these children's books introduce the big idea of scale in a playful manner that works well with kids of all ages.

4. Introduce the Earth, Moon, and Sun as examples of objects that are bigger than any objects they mentioned that are found on Earth. Display a variety of pictures of these three astronomical bodies from books and/

or the internet, as well as physical models to raise questions such as the following:

Do the two-dimensional images and three-dimensional models we use always accurately show the relative size (or scale, proportion, and quantity) of the different things we brainstormed or these three astronomical bodies? (Answer: The three same-size images of the Earth, Moon, and Sun at the end of this activity are a perfect example where visually compelling pictures can be misleading.) Consider using one of the web-based music videos listed in the Materials section to provide an aesthetic element to the lesson and to show students different-size Earth-bound images of the Moon (which can be quite deceptive, though real).

5. While pictures that are *not* drawn to a common scale can certainly "lie" (or misrepresent reality), do our eyes always correctly estimate the relative size of objects? Hint: Consider the object silhouetted in the foreground of the Moon in the music videos listed above (i.e., the actual versus perceived distance from the object to viewer matters in our size estimates).

6. Assuming that students have previously learned how to measure the circumference and diameter of a circle with a metric ruler and string, introduce the following questions.

◆ Do our eyes always correctly estimate the relative size of different objects?

◆ How can measurements help us determine the relative (and actual) size of things?

7. Challenge students to empirically answer these questions by using a metric ruler to address the questions posed in the following optical illusions (Figures 7G.1–7G.4) (used as an in-class or homework assignment).

FIGURE 7G.1

Are the dark black helicopter blades the same length? If different, which line (top or bottom) is longer?

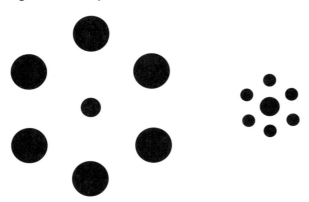

http://brainden.com/visual-illusions.htm

FIGURE 7G.2

Which central circle is bigger? The left one or the right one? Are you sure?

http://brainden.com/images/dots-big.gif

FIGURE 7G.3

Do the two checkered design balls have the same or different length diameters?

www.eyewow.com/wp-content/uploads/2011/05/circle-size-illusion.jpg

FIGURE 7G.4

Can you pick out which of the soldiers is the tallest one?

www.123opticalillusions.com/pages/opticalillusions6.php

Teacher note: The author has assembled a large number of live links to websites that feature optical illusions (*www.nsta.org/publications/press/extras/brainpoweredscience.aspx*) as part of his *Brain-Powered Science* book (Activity 5. Optical Illusions: Seeing and Cognitive Construction). Optical illusions provide a motivational context for learning mathematical and measurement skills in that they demonstrate the need for precision and the advantages of the metric system over the English system when making linear measurements.

Explore Phase

The purpose of this phase is to allow students to explore and test their prior conceptions about the relative size of the Earth we live on and the Sun and Moon as the two largest objects in our day and night skies. The Explore phase also serves as a review, application, and extension of previously learned metric measurement skills to develop scale models of the Earth and Moon.

Materials

- Black (garbage) Bag of Solar System Science filled with an assortment of sports balls (Ping-Pong ball, golf ball, handball; racquetball, tennis ball, baseball; volleyball, soccer ball, and basketball)

- Space Music such as *The Galaxy Song* (an online video version with astronomical images and subtitled lyrics can be found at *www.youtube.com/watch?v=jsgExTttJ2Y &feature=related* (2 mins, 50 secs). See also Vangelis's *Albedo 0.39* song that is set against images of the Earth–Moon space program at *www.youtube.com/watch?v=rL1oU6fH25w* (4 mins, 21 secs)

- Meterstick

Activity 2: Science, Sport Balls, and the Solar System Scale

1. If not previously discussed, briefly introduce the idea of the development and use of a model as a scientific tool that allows us to visualize, manipulate, and test an object or process that because of its size, speed, safety risks, or system level complexity, cannot be as readily directly examined and explored. Models can be conceptual (e.g., theories), mathematical (e.g., equations, graphs, and so on), computer-based (e.g., animations and simulations), or three-dimensional, to-scale physical models. Refer back to the images, posters, Earth globe models, and videos displayed in the previous lesson and ask students the following:

   > Since astronomical objects like the Earth, Moon, and Sun are too big to bring into the classroom, what everyday objects might we use as models or stand-in substitutes for the real things? What characteristics of the original objects should our models preserve and which characteristics should they ignore?

2. Introduce the Black Bag of Solar System Science with a bit of mystery by asking the students to guess what you have inside to represent the Earth, Sun, and Moon. For fun, consider playing the space music videos cited in the Materials section as an auditory background. Open up the black garbage bag and begin tossing an assortment of sports balls to randomly selected students: Ping-Pong, golf ball, and handball (alternative models for the Moon); racquetball, tennis ball, and baseball (potential models for the Earth); and volleyball, soccer ball, and basketball (the

largest balls to provisionally represent the Sun). **Teacher note:** These nine balls are listed here in three size categories to allow students to have the option of suggesting that the three astronomical objects are either all approximately the same size or clearly different in size. At this point in the lesson, you do *not* need to mention that the largest balls are not nearly large enough to accurately represent the biggest object, the Sun, at the same scale with any of the smaller balls as scale models for the Earth and Moon.

3. Ask students with the sports balls to hold them up for everyone to see. Ask all students to complete a Think (silently)–Write (their individual guesses or vote)–Pair (to discuss and change their choices if desired)–Share (whole class) as to which three balls they think best represent the correct rank ordering of sizes of the Earth, Sun, and Moon. During the Think-Write-Pair-Share, ask students to discuss (1) the source of their estimates about relative sizes; and (2) whether looking up at the day and night skies provides much help. Tally the class results on the board to see how many students correctly identified the relative size order sequence of big (Moon), bigger (Earth), and biggest (Sun).

4. Introduce information from an authoritative source that indicates that the Earth's diameter is approximately four times that of the Moon. Assign student teams to calculate and/or directly measure the diameter of the different balls to determine which two would serve as the best to-scale models of these two astronomical bodies. To measure the diameter of the balls directly, students will need a meterstick (or 12 in. long metric ruler) to place underneath two books that are used

as vertical frames to hold the ball in place on top of the metric ruler or stick. Alternatively, students can use a string (or metric tape measure) and meterstick to measure the circumference and then calculate the diameter using the equation: Circumference = $\pi \times$ diameter = 3.14d or Diameter = C/3.14. See Table 7G.2 for the measured (and calculated) values for the various sports balls.

5. This activity can be used to demonstrate that mathematics and measurements matter when making models. **Teacher note:** The more challenging task of uncovering the methods scientists have used to determine the actual diameters of astronomical objects (see Table 7G.3) must wait until later grades. Table 7G.3 shows that two different combinations of balls come close to the desired scaled ratio.

TABLE 7G.2. SPORTS BALLS DIMENSIONS

Sports Ball	Circumference	Diameter
Basketball	76.0 cm	24.2 cm
Soccer	71.0 cm	22.6 cm
Volleyball	68.6 cm	21.8 cm
Softball	30.5 cm	9.71 cm
Baseball	23.0 cm	7.32 cm
Tennis	20.9 cm	6.65 cm
Racquetball	17.9 cm	5.7 cm
Handball	15.0 cm	4.76 cm
Golf	13.4 cm	4.27 cm
Ping-Pong	12.0 cm	3.81 cm

TABLE 7G.3. EARTH-MOON DIMENSIONS AND SPORTS BALLS SCALE EQUIVALENTS

Diameter of Larger Object		Diameter of Smaller Object		Ratio Large/Small Balls
Earth	12,756 km	Moon	3,476 km	3.67/1
Basketball	24.2 cm	Tennis ball	6.65 cm	3.64/1
Volleyball	21.8 cm	Racquetball	5.7 cm	3.82/1

Explain Phase

The purpose of this phase it to review and discuss the measurements and calculations made by the various teams with the intent to clarify their understanding of the *NGSS* crosscutting concepts of scale, proportion, and quantity and system model (3 and 4). The teacher should also lead a discussion of the limitations of the sports ball models.

Materials

- Two-dimensional graphic of the Earth-Moon Scale

- Copies of books to extend the lesson (see below for an annotated selection). If available, the classroom science textbooks should also be used.

- Distribute and/or project the following two-dimensional image of the Earth-Moon scale to show students how a two-dimensional representation (or model) can sometimes make it easier to see certain aspects of a three-dimensional system. Ask students to check their science textbooks to see if the images it uses accurately represents the scale of the relative size of the Earth and Moon (i.e., diameter ratio of approximately 4:1). Discuss the importance of empirical evidence (e.g., measurements), logical arguments (e.g., mathematics and models) and skeptical review (e.g., peer review) in science and everyday life.

FIGURE 7G.5. EARTH-MOON SCALE

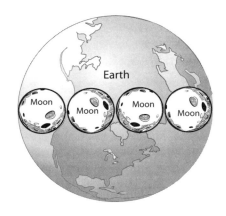

Activity 3: Metric Measurements and Moon Models

1. Discuss the relative pros and cons of two-dimensional versus three-dimensional models. Compare the Earth as a basketball model to the Earth as a globe (especially one with a three-dimensional texture to represent surface features.) Note that all models have limitations in that no model can accurately portray all the features of the real thing it represents. The sports ball models are designed to merely show the relative size of the Earth and Moon (and eventually in the next lesson, the Sun). As another example of scale models, ask students to examine various local, state and/or national road maps to see what scales are used. Discuss why having maps that are drawn to scale are important to drivers and the added advantage of GPS units that can also convey altitude (for hikers).

2. Use a document camera to share the visuals and text from one or more of the following trade books to help students better visualize and conceptualize the idea of scale.

   Banyai, I. 1995. *Zoom*. New York: Viking/Penguin Books. This picture book zooms from a farm to a ship to a city street to a desert island, constantly challenging the reader's sense of scale. See also the author's 1998 follow-up book, *Re-Zoom*, in which once again readers are shown something that turns out to be just a piece of something larger, and thus not at all what they saw (or thought they saw) in the first place. With each page, one takes a step back to see the broader view.

   Boeke, K. 1957. *Cosmic view: The universe in 40 steps*. New York: John Day Co. This innovative, black-and-white, 1950s photo essay begins with a Dutch girl holding a cat and then progressively zooms out to greater scales, and eventually reverses direction and proceeds to the microscopic level of reality. This was the original source of later versions of the powers of ten-type videos and is posted at *http://nedwww.ipac.caltech.edu/level5/Boeke/frames.html*.

   Jenkins, S. 2003. *Looking down*. San Anselmo: Sandpiper Press. The author uses cut-paper collage illustrations to take readers on a journey (without words) that starts with the Earth as seen from outer space and ends with a close-up of a ladybug.

Packard, E., and S. Mardocca. 2000. *Big numbers and pictures that show just how big they are!* Brookfield: Millbrook Press.

3. If the classroom textbook contains a chapter on the Earth-Moon system, it would be appropriate to have students work on integrating English language arts (ELA) skills and scientific and engineering practices in the context of relevant informational text.

Elaborate Phase

The purpose of this phase is to encourage students to apply and extend their understanding of the idea of scale system models to encompass the more "far out" scale of the Earth–Sun comparison (and if desired to include a preliminary look at the broader range of scales within our solar system and out to the ends of the known universe). These ideas will be further developed both mathematically and in terms of empirical scientific evidence during Earth and space science lessons in middle and high school. The Elaboration phase serves as a formative assessment to help both students and their teacher determine whether the basic objectives have been achieved prior to summative assessment that assigns grades to students.

Materials

- Exercise/Fitness balls (45–85 cm diameter, approximately $12—$18). Available from *www.simplefitnesssolutions.com/fitballs.htm* and *www.yogadirect.com/Fitness-Balls_c_1.html?gclid=CLLM-6qRy64CFYNM4Aodzg4Yiw*

- Large balloons are available from *www.balloondealer.com/skybuster.asp?gclid=CNmoqtKPy64CFUPc4AodpTNTBw*; 36 in. (91.44 cm) latex ($4) to 60 in. (152.4 cm) to 72 in. (182.88 cm) Sky Buster Balloons (approximately $20); *www.balloonsfast.com*: 17 in. (43.18 cm) Bright yellow round: 72 balloons/$16.50 72 in. (182.88 cm) Yellow latex to 96 in. (243.84 cm) Yellow latex $26

- Internet Resources

  ◆ NASA Scale Model of the Sun and Earth: *sunearthday.nasa.gov/2007/materials/solar_pizza.pdf*

  ◆ O'Brien, T. 2011. *Even more brain-powered science: Teaching and learning with discrepant events.* Arlington, VA: NSTA Press. Activity 13: 5 E(z) Steps to Earth-Moon Scaling. A large number of live links to websites that feature astronomical images and simulations (e.g., Cosmic Views, Powers of Ten and the Known Universe) are at *www.nsta.org/publications/press/extras/evenmorebrainpoweredscience.aspx*

  ◆ Suntrek: Comparing the size of the Sun to Earth (with static images and graphics): *www.suntrek.org/sun-as-a-star/sun-and-earth/comparing-size-sun-and-earth.shtml*

  ◆ YouTube: Our Solar System: Size Of Planets and Stars to Scale (begins at the scale of a parking lot and zooms to the Earth and segment 1:29 to 2:30 shows the planets in order from smallest to largest out to the Sun and beyond): *www.youtube.com/watch?v=xn8K1Zea1Sk* (segment 1:47–2:40 min) or *www.youtube.com/watch?v=ItEgD-VEExQ* (segment 1:30–2:29)

Activity 4: The Solar System Scale: It's Truly "Far Out"

1. Remind students that their explorations to date have focused on the Earth-Moon scale without considering the size of the Sun on this same scale. Holding up the Earth-Basketball model (or an Earth Globe of approximately the same size), ask students to estimate what they think the diameter of the Sun would be on this same scale. After recording their ideas (which are most likely to grossly underestimate the relative size of the Sun, use one or more of the internet sources listed in the Materials section to convey the idea that 100 Earths could fit across the diameter of the Sun! This is especially surprising to students who are used to seeing a noonday Sun that appears to be approximately the same size as a full Moon. **Teacher note:** The concept of interplanetary and astronomical distances requires a mathematical understanding of exponential notation (or powers of ten) and should be reserved for later grades. Representing both the relative size *and* relative distances within our solar system on the same scale is *not* possible within the confines of a two-page spread in a textbook (though a scale drawing of the Earth-Moon system could fit on a diagonal of a two-page spread).

2. While internet sites like Suntrek show the relative sizes of (but not the separation or orbiting distance between) the Earth and Sun in two dimensions on a relatively small scale, it is important that students experience this relationship on a larger scale that they develop in a manner similar to their previous work with the Earth-Moon model. Several options are available for them to explore:

◆ A blended two- to three-dimensional model of the relative size of the Earth-Sun can be displayed on the school football or soccer field using the Basketball/Earth (d = 24.20 cm) model and a meterstick to measure out (and mark with chalk) a solar circle that has a diameter of 24.2 m (or 2,420 cm or approximately 26.5 yds!). The whole class should distribute themselves around the circumference of this circle to get a better sense of the relative size of the Earth-Sun.

◆ A fully three-dimensional model of the relative size of the Earth-Sun can be displayed in the classroom using large exercise or fitness balls or large balloons (see Materials, p. 191) as a model of the Sun. Depending on the diameter of the ball or balloon that is selected, students should be challenged to find an everyday object (e.g., ball bearings, standard or oversized marbles, and so on) that is approximately 1/100 of that size to represent Earth on that scale. Note on this same scale, the Moon would once again be ¼ the diameter of the Earth!

◆ Optional: Depending on the availability of instructional time (i.e., if the mini-unit is taught as an integrated mathematics-science project), the Elaboration phase lesson can be further extended in one of the following ways.

3a: *Virtual Space Trips:* Use segments from one or more of the following internet simulations or supplemental activities to impress on students (1) the excitement of our journeys to the Moon and (2) how truly "far out" our solar system is even though it is only a tiny little portion of the Milky Way galaxy that is a tiny portion of the known universe.

Internet Sources

+ Exploring Planets in the Classroom (activities): *www.spacegrant.hawaii.edu/ class_acts/index.html*

+ The Known Universe (6 mins, 31 secs): *http://apod.nasa.gov/apod/ ap100120.html* and *www.youtube.com/ watch?v=17jymDn0W6U*

+ NASA Video Clip of Neil Armstrong stepping onto lunar surface: *www. hq.nasa.gov/office/pao/History/alsj/a11/ a11v_1092338.mpg*

+ Powers of Ten (slide sequence based on the original film): *http://powersof10.com*

+ Secret Worlds, the Universe Within: *http://micro.magnet.fsu.edu/primer/java/ scienceopticsu/powersof10*

+ Views of the Solar System (images, animations, and statistics): *www.solarviews. com*

+ We Choose the Moon: 40th Anniversary of Lunar Landing: *www.wechoosethemoon. org*

+ Windows to the Universe: *www.windows 2universe.org*

Teacher note: The power of ten (10^x) idea can be thought of an extension of the metric system (e.g., 1 mm (= 10^{-3} m) →10 mm = 1 cm (= 10^{-2} m) → 10 cm = 1 dm (= 10^{-1} m) → 10 dm = 1 m ... 1 km (= 10^3 m)). The concept of whole-number exponents to denote powers of ten is part of the 5th grade *CCSS, Math-ematics*, Numbers and Operations in Base Ten standards. Space science provides a natural, real-world relevant context for mathematics and science teachers to work on curriculum collaboration and integration.

3b: More Mathematics: Sun-Earth-Moon Scaled Distances: With the Earth as a basketball, Moon as a tennis ball scale, the Earth and Moon would be over 7 m apart (or approximately 30 Earth diameters) and the Sun (a ball with a diameter equal to that of approximately 100 basketballs) would be approximately 3 km away from the Earth! Interested students can use the internet to look up the relevant numbers for the average orbiting distances and calculate the actual scale model.

Evaluate Phase

This phase serves as a form of summative assessment to measure whether students (individuals and/or teams) have achieved the intended learning outcomes and to assign grades. If the results of this assessment reveal significant student misconceptions and/or conceptual holes, the teacher can decide to reteach portions of the lessons or to incorporate these same concepts and skills into the next mini-unit.

Activity 5: Summative Assessment Alternatives

Any of the activities below can be used as a form of end-of-unit summary assessment:

1. Measurements and Mathematics Mania: Students can be challenged to measure the circumference and diameter of a variety of circular or spherical objects around the classroom (coins, cans, clocks, and so on) and to calculate the value of the circumference/diameter. They should repeatedly find that irrespective of the

size of the object, this ratio is always about equal to 3 (or pi = π = 3.14 …). This pattern is one of many mathematical realities that underlie our physical universe that can be revealed through careful measurements and calculations.

2. Scientific Literacy + ELA Literacy = Synergy: Students can be asked to write a poem, informational essay, or mini-play or skit (e.g., dialogue between the Moon-Earth-Sun) that summarizes what they have learned in this series of lessons. Terms to include in their writing are *circumference*, *diameter*, *model*, and *scale*.

3. Public Performances: Teams of students can prepare presentations on what they have learned for audiences of parents and/or younger students at their school. Such performances could include physical models, multimedia, reading, and explanations of select portions of trade books, and so on.

4. Paper-and-Pencil Tests: Students can be provided with the numeric values of the equatorial diameters of other planets in our solar system and be challenged to (1) list the planets in order from smallest to largest; (2) determine how many Earths could line up across the diameter of the biggest planet, Jupiter (142,800 km/12,756 km = 11/1); and (3) develop another scale model.

5. Testing Texts: Student teams can examine a variety of science textbooks (including those from higher grade levels), trade books, and internet sites to see how many (if any) depict the Earth-Moon scale correctly. This idea can be extended to include the idea that approximately 30 Earth diameters separate the Earth from the Moon. Given that both the relative size and separation distance could be represented on a two-page diagonal, write letters to the publishers to ask them why they use visuals that underestimate how "far out" science really is!

6. Moon Trips and Mathematics: Math skills could be further tested by asking students to calculate the time it would take to travel to the moon (assuming escaping Earth's gravity was not an issue) at peak human running speeds (44.72 km/h or 27.79 mph), legal highway driving speed limit (105 km/h or 65 mph) … rocket (40,806 km/h or 25, 300 mph for Earth escape velocity).

Teacher Materials

FIGURE 7G.6. IMAGE OF THE EARTH (TO LAMINATE)

FIGURE 7G.7. IMAGE OF THE SUN (TO LAMINATE)

FIGURE 7G.8. IMAGE OF THE MOON (TO LAMINATE)

V

THE NEW SCIENCE OF LEARNING

INTRODUCTION

Illuminating Minds

Michael S. Gazzaniga, PhD
Director, SAGE Center for the Study of the Mind
University of California, Santa Barbara

I cannot imagine a more important role in education than opening up young students' eyes to the fact we humans can understand why things work the way they do.

People forget that social networking through media such as Facebook is only eight years old; cell phones are only about 20 years old. The discovery of DNA as the chemical basis for heredity is only 55 years old. How did that happen?

It is science that opens up horizons, teaches us to honor our environment, and sets us ready to conquer the ills of the world—from black holes to horrific disease. Every passing day, month, and year, science opens our eyes to what might be because of what we learn now. Teachers in the primary grades begin the process of illuminating the minds of our young children, and inspired teachers in subsequent years perpetuate our children's desire to understand the world in which we all live.

CHAPTER 8

How We Model the Complexities of the World
LEARNING AND MEMORY, SYSTEMS AND FUNCTION

Anthony J. Greene, PhD
Associate Professor of Psychology and Neuroscience
University of Wisconsin, Milwaukee

Traditional ways of thinking about learning and memory are largely incorrect, and frankly, have reached the limitation of their usefulness. We have conceived of memory as a modular storage device to be filled with data. A more fruitful approach, as we shall see, is to consider all of the systems of our brain—perceptual, motor, conceptual and problem solving, motivation, creativity, emotions, and basic drives—as adaptive systems that are constantly revised, expanded, and fine-tuned by experience. The fundamental mechanism of learning is modification by association, and it is a property of the entire brain, not memory modules.

Learning is achieved by apprehending connections among items, people, and events in ways that are meaningful, pertinent, and relevant, in ways that predict more favorable outcomes. Three implications are straightforward, but far-reaching: (1) learning is the adaptive malleability of thought and behavior; (2) learning is not mere information storage and retrieval;

and (3) learning is part-and-parcel to all aspects of our being, especially thought and creativity. By better understanding learning and memory, a cornucopia of implications for education will become readily evident. Our learning systems are designed to explore and to understand the world in increasing measure to its stunning complexity such that we become more and more effective in negotiating our lives; education is central and indispensable for our intellectual adaptivity and as such perhaps the noblest endeavor of humanity.

We've recently seen a dramatic ascendancy of "brain-based" learning. But the reasons it should be of such interest are not always obvious. After all, one can use a computer to great effect without any significant knowledge of the machine itself. Why should the brain be any different? Don't we all have some expertise on our own learning? And hasn't that been the case irrespective of the fairly recent advent of neuroscience? The answer is yes, we have a great deal of expert knowledge about ourselves and

> **Learning should be construed as the adaptive malleability of behavior. As such, it is what sets human beings apart from all other species. Our success, as individuals and as a society, depends squarely on the efficacy of our learning.**

our learning, but it is precisely things we don't know, and things we may think we know that aren't so, that are presently holding us back. As with all scientific revolutions, we are poised for a big leap in theory and application.

Where We've Been. Prior to about one hundred years ago, what we thought we knew of the brain was intermingled with much gibberish, based on introspection and misunderstanding. In fairness, the brain with hundreds of billions of neurons, and multitrillions of synapses, is still largely beyond comprehension, but was even more so then. A significant leap in our understanding of learning first came by first disposing of what we thought we knew of the brain and mind. The behaviorists in the first half of the 20th century set out to apply strict science to behavioral adaptivity and rejected psychoanalytic, philosophical, and religious accounts of the mind and brain. At the time, there were simply no good methods for observing or testing what was going on inside the head, so it couldn't be scientific. They argued that to be constrained to observables, the science of behavior should examine lawful relationships between the organism and the environment and that, therefore, it was not necessary to specify exactly what the brain does. People like B.F. Skinner argued that specifying the adaptive nature of an organism to its environment would tell us all we need to know about learning. For behaviorists then, the brain was simply a black box—with inputs that predicted outputs—for which they would offer no speculation because it was not observable. Sometimes it is most fruitful to clear away failed attempts and start afresh. Indeed, the behaviorists made enormous progress specifying changes in behavior as a function of experience and the environment, and most of learning theory is built upon their seminal discoveries. But nature is quirky, and it wasn't very long before people

began to realize that we couldn't fully understand learning and memory by abstracting from just input and output.

In the latter half of the 20th century, due in large part to backlash against behaviorism, cognitive science emerged to put the mind back into the formulation. Oddly, they weren't at first very interested in how the brain worked, only the mind. To cognitive scientists at the time, one could view the mind as something like a computer program, and the particular machine that runs the program is not particularly relevant. For example, as can be seen in Figure 8.1, the modal model of memory proposed distinct storage sites for short- and long-term memory, but it turns out the brain has no such locations. This mind-brain distinction seems strange now because we no longer think of mind and brain as distinct (as we will see, there is no software of the brain, it's all hardware), but cognitive science was relatively unconcerned with this variant of mind-matter Cartesian dualism. But a very serious problem arose in the endeavor: The theories were simply too unconstrained, and there was no convincing way to test between competing theories. Theories proliferated that were highly speculative and nondisprovable. Theories in cognitive science became like toothbrushes—everyone had his own and nobody used anyone else's. For a brief time, some feared that the days of wanton introspection and unconstrained theorizing were back. But the brain itself would become the arbiter among competing theories, and cognitive science rapidly evolved into cognitive neuroscience. The brain was back, but this time with the force of science. Referring back to Figure 8.1, we still recognize that short- and long-term memory have different characteristics, but we recognize there are no such modules in the brain; each cortical neuron has a short- and long-term memory capacity. Disregarding the brain might seem now like a silly

FIGURE 8.1. THE MODAL MODEL OF MEMORY

The difficulty was that no brain regions correspond to the proposed modules. It turns out that each cortical neuron has a short-term and a long-term memory capacity.

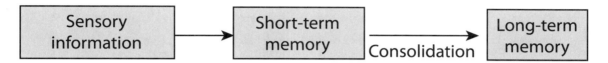

mistake for behaviorism and cognitive science, but not as much so when we consider the technological limitations of the time made studying the brain itself an impossibility. Moreover, the result was that a lot of old-world fictions about the mind and brain were cleared, allowing a better understanding enough room to eventually take root.

Breakthroughs toward the end of the 20th century made the study of the brain, in all its incredible complexity, more possible: from arrays of single-cell recordings to noninvasive imaging of neurons in the act of learning, we now have at least a start and a way to proceed. Indeed, neuroscience is the fastest growing of all scientific disciplines, and just keeping up requires all the brainpower we can muster. While we've read much about "brain-based teaching" these accounts often leave out very much mention of the brain. In this chapter, we will discuss the brain so that you can fully understand how advances in neuroscience apply to education. But don't worry; this is a survey, and there's no exam. The target audience is you, the science teacher. The chapter assumes interest and intelligence but no prior knowledge.

Brains Are Not Like Storage Devices. We are always learning. Self-modification is a constant activity of the brain; everything a neuron does alters it and the neurons connected to it. The

question is whether the learning is optimally effective. Particularly with the task of educating our children, it is important to understand that learning is not simply a matter of presenting the facts to necessarily receptive or logical minds. All learners are quirky, particularly children, and it is an understanding of the biology that opens doors to understanding the quirky mind. A principle change in thinking since the era of the behaviorists is that we have to understand the highly idiosyncratic nature of our learning mechanisms in order to have any hope of implementing them to full advantage.

The brain changes everything; that is to say, brain considerations must change our entire approach. The most central and important aspect of brain-based learning is to understand that learning and memory are not storage modules of the brain; they are facets of every neuron. Memory isn't filling a file cabinet (or a junk drawer) in the mind. Learning is modifying the brain; it is training the brain. All systems and functions of the brain are modified by learning. As teachers, we're not just stuffing encyclopedic information into a vault for students to later think upon; we're modifying thought (and working hard to ensure that what they're learning is not that they dislike school). Nor is it sufficient for teachers to consider themselves mere conduits of information. We must train thought itself with lots of practice, using the most central and important examples as prototypes.

Your memory is not like a terra-byte hard-drive; it is much better than that as a means of adaptation. When people ask me what I do for a living and I tell them I'm a cognitive neuroscientist studying memory formation (assuming I don't get a blank stare), the most frequent follow-up question is, "Can you tell me what's the matter with my memory?" I know what they mean. I forget things all the time. Why isn't memory more like a storage device? The simple answer is frankly that storage devices aren't very adaptive. Filing cabinets and hard drives just sit there and store data. They don't prioritize it, integrate it, conceptualize it, determine which parts are useful (and which aren't), or figure out how to act on it. Fortunately, for storage of data we have the foresight to write things down or enter them into some electronic device, so that we don't have to remember everything. Your memory systems may not be particularly good at remembering every detail, but neither is a notepad very good at adapting to its environment.

What's Your Learning Approach? Imagine you've just moved to a new city and you decide to take your first walk around the new neighborhood. You decide to start finding your way around with the idea that you're definitely going to need to know this, and sooner is definitely better. How do you go about it? Do you make up mnemonic devices to memorize street names, intersections, and places you'll be frequenting? Or do you go out and explore, to try to get your bearings, to figure out where things are in relation to one another, to fit important details into the context of the big picture? Chances are you take the explorer-relational approach rather than the rote-memorization approach. It turns out that the explorer-relational approach generally provides for faster, better, and longer-lasting learning, and provides a firmer foundation for future learning.

Preview: How the Brain Learns Best

Learning evolved for exploring the environment. Learning will always be an act of exploration, seeking more quality information to have better founded expectations and predicted outcomes.

New associations (synapses) are formed by altering and adding to existing associations (synapses). Every new topic is learned best when richly connected to existing knowledge.

For each learner, there is an individual optima for combining new information with existing knowledge. Likewise, individual misconceptions must be identified and redirected. Each learner has unique abilities and limitations and benefits most from an attentive, involved, and knowledgeable teacher.

Motivation is the simultaneous interaction of intrinsic and extrinsic. As important as biological drives is the exploratory drive, curiosity.

Effective learning requires interaction, feedback, and reinforcement, and takes time to sink in.

Children in particular are not ready to make commitments to long-term payoffs, instead preferring immediate gratification. This is a hard-wired phenomenon, not a lack of willingness to be rational.

Learning is a whole-brain phenomenon. Optimal learning should engage the whole student: all the senses, language, problem solving and reasoning, devising, and sociability.

Why? Because the memory systems of our brains find it fun to explore and are optimally geared towards detecting relationships and comprehension. In the environment of evolutionary adaptation, there was simply no selection pressure for rote memorization, but plenty of demand for a system that could learn and understand things to negotiate the environment. Memory is not merely a record of the past; it's a self-adapting system that uses past information for better success in the present and future. To the brain, learning and memory are not storage; they're a change to the way your brain works, to the way you process information, and a change in expected outcomes. In fact, the greatest mark of comprehension, as we shall see, is the ability to make accurate predictions. In our navigation example, correctly negotiating novel, more direct routes would be an excellent test of comprehension because you wouldn't be simply retracing your past steps, you'd be inferring a better predicted route.

We need rote sometimes, especially for new information that might have arbitrary aspects. You can use a mnemonic device to help you bring the idea back and hold on to it while you go about the work of adhering some true connections to hold it. When you're first learning the major bones in the human body, for example, some mnemonic device might be helpful. At first, they're just words that are easily forgotten, but with time and thought they become concepts, structures, machines, and their names are part of a great deal of knowledge you have about them. As an aside, it is also worth noting that the better mnemonic devices are the ones that come closest to actually learning relations. To illustrate the limitations of rote learning, suppose you broke your ankle. When the orthopedic surgeon came to see you, imagine that he started humming to himself a mnemonic device "the hip-bone's connected to

the thigh-bone, the thigh-bone's connected to the knee bone … ." It wouldn't instill any confidence, that's for sure. In fact you'd probably be looking for your crutches to make a mad-hobble out of there to find a more knowledgeable doctor. So a rote strategy might be okay as a first pass for some things, but you can't pass it off as anything resembling knowledge or comprehension. Similarly, those who know how to read sheet music for piano might know that "Every-Good-Boy-Does-Fine" is a mnemonic device to help beginners remember which line in the treble clef belongs to which note on the piano (EGBDF). But that mnemonic gets abandoned in short order as the relations between sheet and keyboard sink in. And it's a good thing, because nobody could play the piano while indexing through such a clunky and time-consuming mnemonics in his or her head; it could take minutes to get through a few bars of music. Mnemonic devices are like training wheels; they might be useful at first to get the idea without toppling over, but later they simply slow you down and obstruct future learning. This is such a truth in learning that we define the extent of learning as absolute novice if still relying on any form of mnemonic device. Knowledge that you can build on is richly associated, and it is those associations that not only bring things to mind; they eventually support inference and constitute expert knowledge.

An Overview of Cortical Plasticity. What has changed in our understanding of the brain? Well, perhaps the biggest change in thinking resulted from numerous discoveries that every region and every neuron in the cerebral cortex is involved in learning. For example, if I ask you to tell me how many windows are in your living room, you'll probably pause for a second (not having the number memorized), picture your living room in your mind's eye, and count them, much

FIGURE 8.2A. CLASSICAL CONDITIONING

One item or event (a sound) can be learned to predict another (food). Sometimes called stimulus-stimulus learning.

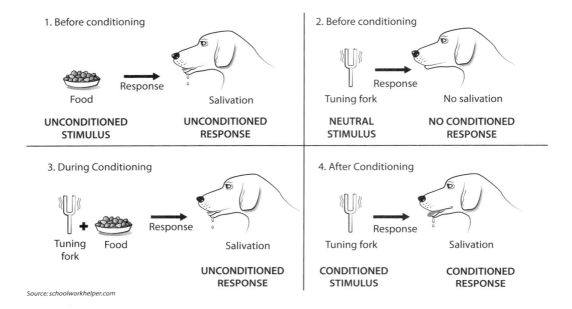

Source: schoolworkhelper.com

the way you'd count them if you were actually standing there. Interestingly, if I were monitoring your brain activity during that task, we'd see that your visual cortex (not previously implicated in memory per se) is among the most active regions of your brain. And it is active in much the same way that it would be if you were actually viewing your living room. In other words, visual memory is replayed in the visual system; activity in the mind's eye, involved in memory or imagination, is actually activity in the visual system not much different than activity observed during vision.

Furthermore, perceptual systems become more fluent at perceiving as experience increases. For instance, if you view a given object several times, each subsequent identification comes with fewer errors and in less time. In the visual system, this type of learning can be observed by less

metabolic activity required for the perception. Your perceptual systems become faster and more accurate and do so with less effort. This is thought to occur because more optimal perceptual pathways are selected, and the connections along that pathway become primed for greater use.

There are innumerable ways in which synapses modify in accordance with experience. But let's just start with two of the best understood mechanisms. The first way was discovered somewhat accidentally by Ivan Pavlov over one hundred years ago. He was studying digestion, using dogs as his model system, and realized that the dogs were learning to anticipate food (which he initially considered a nuisance to his investigation). But he had a well-prepared mind, and he quickly realized that this anticipation was a phenomenon unto itself. In Figure 8.2A, we can see the basic paradigm wherein a dog learns that a tone predicts food. One can readily imagine all the daily instances where it is entirely adaptive to know that a given event predicts another. The sound of a car horn might alert you to an impending accident, or the early signs of smoke might tell you that your dinner is close to burning on the stove. The list is endless.

But we know that the foundational purpose of learning is to better mediate between incoming sensory information and the outgoing course of action. In the previous examples, it's hugely beneficial to know in advance that a car accident might occur, or that your dinner is near burning, but even more important is what you then do about it. In operant conditioning, an action is added into the equation. B.F. Skinner developed and expanded the notion that learning is about action. As with classical conditioning, a predictor stimulus is learned, but the mechanism of consideration is that an action yields an outcome. In Figure 8.2B, you can see that a light coming on indicates that the stage is set; then pressing a bar (the operant) is reinforced by being paired with a food pellet. Returning to our examples, a car horn may indicate to you that an accident is imminent, but your application of the brakes and some quick steering are the operants that allow you to avoid the accident.

Skinner was also a central figure in understanding how higher-order associations can be formed. Much of what we learn is not absolute, but conditional. For instance, a particular manner of speech might be appropriate and reinforcing in one circumstance and completely inappropriate in another. Many a young person has returned home from military service for a holiday and asked his mother to please hold the (bleep) door

FIGURE 8.2B. OPERANT CONDITIONING

On item or event (a light) indicates that conditions are right so that an action (pressing a bar) results in an outcome (food pellet). Sometimes called stimulus-response learning.

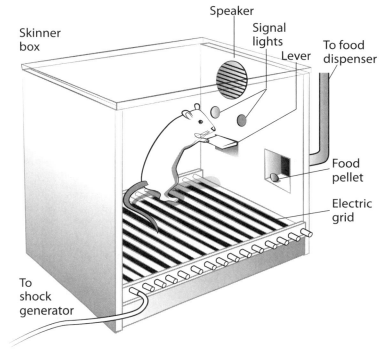

open. Not to worry. Experience quickly trains us that what may be reinforced in one circumstance is absolutely not reinforced in another. And these complex associations can become more complex and nuanced. If you're good at avoiding traffic jams on the way to work, consider what might be involved. The time of day is one predictor of the best path, but the weather is a second, to include the time of the year, and recent experience of road repairs is a third factor.

Connections among people, events, and things in the world are learned by physical connections among neurons, which represent those things. Learning that a particular sight and sound

FIGURE 8.3. SYNAPTIC MODIFICATION

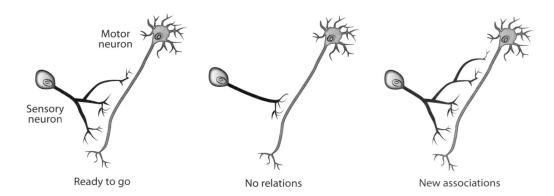

Ready to go   No relations   New associations

go together—such as a telephone ringing—is accomplished by connections between visual and auditory regions of the cortex that perceive those items. The neural mechanisms underlying classical and operant associative learning are increasingly well understood. While each instance involves distinct neural systems (for example an auditory stimulus would necessarily modify auditory neurons) the generic idea is illustrated in Figure 8.3. In this instance, in a very simple nervous system, a sea snail, a sensory neuron, and a motor neuron have a modest amount of initial connectivity. If experience teaches the organism that the incoming stimulus that activates the sensory neuron is completely unrelated to an action initiated by the motor neuron, then the synaptic connections are pruned or altogether eliminated. On the other hand, if there is a relationship between the sensation and the action, then the synaptic connections are strengthened and multiplied. In fact, neurons in proximity to one another with no initial connections may sprout connections if those neurons have correlated activity.

That kind of synaptic modification can explain a lot about how very local circuits in the brain modify. However, most connections of that sort are limited to just 1 or 2 mm. In a large brain,

what if you need to associate a sight—occipital lobe in the back of the brain—with a sound—temporal lobe on the side of the brain? The distance that has to be spanned is 5 or 6 cm, about 50 times too far. Moreover, what if a sight, a sound, an emotion, a thought, some words, and an action all have to be associated? This type of learning spans the whole cerebral cortex, and we do this 1,000 times a day. For example, any event that you can remember involves neurons from various senses, areas for emotion, and if you remember a narrative, language areas as well. All of these systems are not just very far apart; they also require an almost incomprehensible intricacy among synapses in order for us to remember them.

In very small brains, it might be possible to connect every neuron with every other neuron. But mammalian brains and in particular human brains are much, much too large for that. A given neuron might have somewhere between 3,000 and 5,000 synaptic connections, but the human brain has hundreds of billions of neurons. It just isn't remotely possible for them all to be directly connected. Consider an analogy. If you lived in an isolated community of say 20 homes (and no outside connections needed), it would be possible to simply run a phone line to and from each home

(200 connections for 20 nodes). But as the number of homes gets larger, and the physical distance greater, it quickly becomes more practical to have a central switchboard which can connect any home to any other. You could make local connections, but to make any long-distance connection, you would have to connect to the central switchboard. This is essentially how evolution solved the problem of large brains. We have a brain structure that functions like a central switchboard, which is located in the middle of our temporal lobes, situated well for central connectivity. The hippocampus serves as a central switchboard for long-distance connections across the whole brain. Local synaptic modification can occur between neurons as much as a few millimeters apart, but with hundreds of billions of neurons in the human brain, not all neurons can be directly connected. The active regions vary from task to task but the hippocampus mediates by detecting relations and indexing the regions involved. The hippocampus has direct connections to all cortical regions. It was once thought that the hippocampus was the site of long-term memory, but now we know that it doesn't store memory. It simply facilitates long-distance associations. The memory itself is stored in cortical regions for vision, audition, emotion, action, planning, language, and so on, and the hippocampus indexes their coactivity. Whole-brain learning integrates all aspects of experience.

What we know about the hippocampus has given us critical information on optimal learning.

(1) Hippocampal learning requires some time. The hippocampus appears to have two modes, one where information is actively absorbed, another where the learning is permanently consolidated in cortical synapses. The consolidation phase takes place during sleep and during daydreamy times of the day. There's very much a sort of Yin and Yang to hippocampal learning. It pays to deliberately learn, and then let it settle for a while, or sleep on it.

(2) The hippocampus is not very active when we are altogether familiar with what's going on. It is optimally active when we have some degree of familiarity, but something is new, or unexpected. This makes some intuitive sense, but the picture becomes even clearer if we understand that the hippocampus evolved principally for the purpose of foraging and exploring.

Foraging is a life-sustaining task that has some stable aspects and other aspects that are highly dependent upon particular conditions. For instance, while learning, the lay of the land doesn't change very much, but if you've recently depleted a given source of food, you would be better off not returning for some period of time. In addition, you have to navigate to varying food sources—optimized by novel finding—without ever getting lost (getting lost has a high risk of death), and without often repeating the same pattern. In spring, some food patches will be more plentiful than those that are plentiful in the summer or in the fall. A learning system designed for optimal foraging requires navigational learning, a sense of the passage of time, knowledge that some things are true under some complex conditions and not true otherwise, memory for objects, and memory for events. What's more, it requires that all these sources of information can be simultaneously integrated and associated with actions and then updated with outcomes and reinforcement. It's very tricky, very complex, and life depends upon it. The hippocampus mediates the complexities and scope of the learning, but all areas of the brain are in on it.

Even the cerebellum (noncortical) is in on the game. It was previously thought that the cerebellum is required only for coordinated muscle movements, but it turns out that it is equally important for learning precise and coordinated movements, particularly when exact timing is part of what needs to be learned. It could be involved in enticing a fish to take your hook or playing a musical instrument. It doesn't just time the coordination; the cerebellum permanently self-modifies so that you can learn and subsequently execute precisely timed activities. It accomplishes this with ladder-like circuits that can change the length of a circuit and thereby change the precise timing of any response.

This whole-brain learning is what affords us the greatest adaptive flexibility and is the basis for how we model the complexities of the world. We already know that this sort of learning is engaged when we learn new things in the context of existing knowledge. What are some other ways to engage whole-brain learning? Well, consistent with the idea that our learning systems are exploration devices, they are keyed into violations of expectations; those violations are detected, and an active process of rectification takes place. I had a science fair project in eighth grade wherein I learned, for the first time, that heavier objects do not in fact fall faster than lighter objects. Shortly after I learned it, I set about trying to explain it to classmates. Ultimately, some people were not convinced until we got permission to drop a basketball and a tennis ball from a second floor window. Despite my own advocacy, I was somewhat surprised that they landed at exactly the same time. Of course, Galileo proved the same thing by dropping two cannonballs from the Leaning Tower of Pisa (but he did it first). The notion that heavy and light objects fall at the same speed was to everyone a blatant violation of casual observation; under usual conditions, a feather falls more slowly than a hammer. Astronaut David Scott of Apollo 15 was filmed on the Moon dropping a hammer and a feather and showing they fell at exactly the same speed, in the absence of air; objects of different mass do fall at the same rate, but some objects resist air more than others. So a violation of expectations, coupled with sensible new facts, paves the way for a considerably broader understanding of how things work. This is how science works, and how learning works, both fundamentally exploratory processes.

Modifications and additions to existing learning mean new associations, which mean new synapses. At any stage of life, new learning stimulates significantly more axonal and dendritic branching and more synapses. According to estimates, synapses can increase 30% or more in a relatively short period of time. It's like powerlifting for your brain. The more you learn, the sharper you become. Most of what we know well, we know because we've learned similar things in many different guises, and we've learned exceptions to rules and probabilities of outcomes. When we're young, we have a lot of vague notions about seemingly everything, and the more we work at it, the more specific and refined those ideas become. In most cases, revisions and additions to existing learning and memory are beneficial processes; new knowledge is woven neatly in with what previously established learning and memory, and it functions as a unified understanding.

With eyewitness testimony, this can be counterproductive. The more often you discuss a given event, the more likely it is that new information (perhaps erroneous) will be integrated into what you initially observed. Then it is all but impossible to distinguish what you actually saw from embellishments. The best strategy for accurate testimony is to get a statement as soon as possible, without any possibility of discussing or rehearsing the event. That memory is malleable and constructive are entirely adaptive in all but rare instances. Research clearly shows that every time you think about something, it can be modified, and this most often strengthens and expands the memory. All that we may better model the complexities of the world.

Whole-brain learning is accomplished when whole-brain associations have to take place. As discussed earlier, these can involve multiple sensory inputs, coupled with language, coupled with emotion, reinforcement value, and so on. As with all learning, the more richly associated, the more deeply woven into the brain. This is particularly true for emotions. In fact, emotions do more than demand expression and bind us to one another (or against one another); they also mark the most significant events in life and give them more associative strength. Events like the birth of a child are the most remembered days because they are the most infused with emotion. Most of our emotions evolved as social-regulatory mechanisms (and no, that does not diminish the meaning of love). We are tribe animals and predictably our emotions have a lot to do with keeping the tribe together, even at the expense of some individual expression. Does that mean that a lot of our learning is social learning? Absolutely. In fact, the most prominent theories of brain evolution suggest that language and our particularly large brains evolved as they did in order to manage our complex social environments. For humans, work, play, commuting, and eating are all high-potential social activities. And now that I think of it, social activities for me now include sleep—our toddlers cannot be convinced for the whole night that they will sleep better in their own beds, and we just don't feel right locking them out. And waking up

to my daughter's angelic smile feels better to both of us than waking up to her crying in a lonely crib down the hall.

In fact, it's difficult to think up human activities that aren't social or that don't play well for a select audience. The two pinnacles of human behavior, learning and sociability, are indeed so intertwined as to be sometimes indistinguishable. And humans are particularly good at problem-solving and creativity as a group endeavor. In some instances, the synergy is explicit, like with the Wright Brothers, Watson and Crick, Lennon and McCartney, Generals Grant and Sherman. In other instances, individual creativity is observed within a community of like-minded individuals. For example, Emerson, Thoreau, Melville, Alcott, Hawthorne, and Whitman all knew each other (and were sometimes friends) and were strongly influenced by each other, and to some extent competed with one another. And of course, Leonardo, Michelangelo, and Raphael were contemporaneous artists and competed with and influenced one another. And, speck-on-the-map Athens, Georgia, has long been a hub of new music, to include the B52s, Widespread Panic, and REM, all of whom erupted during the alternative music era of the 1980s. Harnessing this explosive group creative energy has long been a central goal of education. The word *college* comes from the Latin *collegium*, which simply means group. A group of scholars brought together to work together, compete, interact, and hopefully generate a wellspring of new thought.

Good teachers have always recognized the social aspect of teaching and sought to engage students as intellectual persons and dwell with them there for a time. The teacher-student relationship is optimized in small class settings and all but lost in large classes and lecture halls. But equally important is the student-peer relationship in the classroom. When not managed properly, peer pressures can cause a digression to the lowest common denominator. When harnessed effectively, social factors multiply the teacher's efforts: Students reinforce one another's inputs, and one student's idea sparks that of the next. Learners benefit from reconfiguring newly learned information, elaborating upon it, and restating it in their own words. And there is nothing that drives home and test-drives learning like teaching it to someone else. We can encourage the positive aspects of student-peer relationships by establishing a dynamic, invigorating classroom culture based on trust and mutual respect. This requires small classrooms and considerable social skills from the teacher. There are certainly times to convey information directly to students, but no classroom should be an ongoing monologue (see Figure 8.5). Every classroom should have exploratory activities that engage students in discovery, the way nature devised. And every classroom should make learning a social activity, to include humor, brainstorming, elaboration, questions, clarifications, examples, and discussion. The younger the child, the less they can be relied on to invent their own way to be interested. Imbuing learning with exploration and social importance can make even the most remote topic into a relevant, intellectually stimulating event and gives it a life of its own. What's more, such strategies more fully engage the student—their whole brain—and make retention more likely.

When a given behavior is reinforced (see operant conditioning on p. 207) the so-called pleasure center of the brain becomes wired into the circuitry. The ventral tegmentum (VT) is critically implicated in all pleasure-related and reinforced behavior. A seminal study some years ago surgically inserted stimulating electrodes into the VT of rats, and the rats could press a bar to deliver mild electrical stimulation. The rats behaved rather oddly: They continued to press the bar as rapidly as possible until they lost consciousness. When they recovered consciousness, they'd immediately resume incessant bar-pressing. They would forgo food or water, even if severely deprived, and they'd forgo sexual intercourse. The rats would simply continue this until they were dead. Under normal circumstances, engaging in some rewarding activity engages the VT to a modest extent, and the involvement of the VT permanently increases the probability of engaging in that behavior. A foraging animal might discover a food patch, the reinforcing value of which would rewire its brain to come back to that patch somewhat more frequently. The VT is an integral part of the systems evolved for the purpose of optimal foraging. The same thing happens when a student receives social praise; she will be moderately more likely to repeat the desired behavior or learning. But direct stimulation of the VT cranks up the probability of that behavior to 100%. It's not an issue of free will; the mechanisms of behavior have been hijacked. The exact same principle applies to addiction. Most drugs with addictive properties mimic in some way the neurotransmitters that affect the VT. Drugs of addiction compel behavior by ramping up the requisite learned behaviors to such an extent that they become in effect compulsory. With addiction, it is not that people are simply making bad choices; the drugs have altered the systems used to make choices. The normal mechanisms of exploration, discovery, and reinforcement are laid to waste as drugs of addiction hijack the reinforcement systems to crank up the gain immeasurably in this horribly maladaptive behavior.

The bright side of understanding motivation is that we can discover how to better motivate desired outcomes in learning. There is a somewhat erroneous distinction between "intrinsic" and "extrinsic" motivations[1]. In point of fact, all behaviors that occur are motivated, and all motivations are linked by association to internal or principle motivations. Principle reinforcement comes from things like food, water, sex, social success, and other pleasures. That does not mean that we have to give students an M&M every time they perform. Nor does it mean students perform just for the love of knowledge (natural curiosity as we'll see momentarily). All behaviors result from a complex mix of motivations, which ultimately link external factors to various sources of pleasure (or at least the avoidance of aversive outcomes). Certainly teachers have sometimes copped-out of the love-of-knowledge routine and tried instead to link academic performance to career success, which leads to more money, which as we saw above has reinforcing value by association. The problem with that approach is that while it is certainly true that a good education will lead to a better career, that's a long time to wait for a first grader to get a payoff. People are never entirely rational, and this is particularly true of children. The frontal lobes are the last cortical area to become fully connected (mature). These frontal lobes allow us to weigh our options and restrain the impulsivity that would have us select the immediate but lesser rewards. Children have a great deal of difficulty choosing the option

1. There is a somewhat pervasive myth out there that reinforcing behaviors can diminish the intrinsic value of that behavior. For instance, providing any reward—praise or otherwise—for creating art might somehow diminish the love of art as a child might engage in art to obtain reward. This myth is behind all sorts of misguided neglect of good behavior, like failing to reward teachers with satisfactory salaries since they should do it for the love of teaching alone. Oddly, this diminished value myth is selectively implemented. Rewarding a behavior, then removing your reward may temporarily suspend the spontaneous occurrence of the behavior, but it does not diminish the value of the behavior, and rewarded behaviors are more often undertaken than unrewarded behaviors, irrespective of intrinsic value.

that has the better long-term gains when any immediate alternative reward is present. And this is to be expected, as a seven-year-old knows nothing of the distant future.

Fortunately, as a substitute for maturity and long-term career goals, nature has imbued us with a very healthy, very adaptive curiosity: The desire to explore things and understand their dynamics, which is valuable for the future, in sometimes unknown ways. Curiosity is an adaptive motivation because learning is not really so much about the past as about better negotiating the present and future. I would venture to guess that everyone interested in teaching science got there by at some point being thrilled during the process of discovery, and that this has paid innumerable benefits that could never have been foreseen. As an aside, note that it might have taken decades for non–brain-based learning theories to make some speculations about how to optimize classroom learning, but one look at two regions of the brain (the hippocampus and the ventral tegmentum), and their functions in closely related species makes it abundantly obvious that learning is all about exploration, and discovery; learning your way around (and learning how to learn your way around) is infinitely more important than simply being shown a path to payoff.

For me, this realization about natural curiosity came when I was a college freshman, assigned to read Stephen Jay Gould's *The Panda's Thumb*. I realized about 40 pages in that I had been completely transfixed by a discussion of the evolution of sea snails. Gould had the unquestioned ability to engage with readers at an extraordinary level of intellectual prowess, by enthusiastically bringing the reader along with him on the journey of discovery, explaining in vivid detail why the stuff is so interesting (and to be sure, the reasons were not previously obvious to me). That's the real trick: making it interesting by making it a discovery, and part of the thrill (not to mention the utility) is not knowing where it is going to lead. Nobody knew that George Boole's interest in philosophy and mathematics would lead to the development of symbolic logic, and nobody knew that Alan Turing's later interest in Boolean symbolic logic and electrical engineering would lead him to develop the modern computer. To this day, every computer on Earth does nothing more than perform the basic Boolean operations on electric circuits, discovered by two instances of curiosity. In retrospect, these were two fairly simple connections, with fairly profound implications. Quirky interests forever altered the world. Thank goodness for natural curiosity, for where would we be without it?

The term *natural curiosity* might lead us to think that it works well on its own. Young, idle brains certainly seem to have a way of discovering and exponentiating mischief. But mischief itself is just the exercise of possibilities. Immediate gratifications are driven by the same fundamental motivations that result in long-term health, wealth, and wisdom. Because short-term payoffs often come at the expense of long-term payoffs, it is our job as educators to constantly direct young minds toward greater long-term outcomes. To do this we have to understand and quite frankly manipulate motivation toward desired goals. You might ask, "What's wrong with a more laissez-faire approach wherein natural curiosity leads to learning and adapting?" The answer is that we live in a world so large that the process of learning to adult levels takes so long that one cannot possibly stumble through the path without trained guides and good maps. We've got the hardware in place to more than adequately motivate more distal goals like learning calculus, literature, European history, and so on. The

trick for successful teaching is to capitalize on students' natural motivations, especially curiosity, by directing them in ways the students do not understand well enough to do on their own. Similarly, reinforcement may push them one way or the other, but it is not indiscriminant; it must follow the lines laid by natural motivations. It all amounts to an impossible miasma to navigate without good teaching.

Given the vastness of what we must learn and teach, it is natural to ask when and if we are up against natural limitations to learning. We don't know how much information the human brain can hold. The number of possible brain states easily exceeds the number of particles in the entire universe, so the amount a healthy brain can hold is large enough to last anyone a lifetime without getting full. What's more, we've already seen that as one learns more, the brain forms brand-new connections; as such, the more you learn, the more you can learn. On the other hand altogether, there are very well known limits to how much can be learned in any single day, as we have already discussed, and that limit is lower if you concentrate all your learning on just one topic. It is therefore clearly best to space learning out over the entire course of the learning period. It would scarcely be possible to ensure that time spent engaged in academic pursuits is more ineffective than by cramming. We certainly understand why people cram—procrastination—and simply telling students to stop cramming is about as effective as any exhortation to stop procrastinating. A straightforward solution exists. Test (quiz) incrementally, and then have a larger, more cumulative exam (as you normally would). Recent research shows unequivocally that incremental testing dramatically improves all aspects of performance. It's the practice of formative and summative assessment. What's more, the student is more frequently engaged and has more imme-diate performance feedback. Yes, it takes time to implement this, but it is time well spent when you consider that the entire enterprise of educa-tion is a waste of time if students don't learn very much. And in the age of ubiquitous computer access, it is possible to have some quizzes done outside of class, on the students' own time and schedule, rather like homework. It doesn't solve every problem, and it is not entirely simple to implement, but it does ameliorate what is clearly the biggest limitation to education—students not studying daily.

Perhaps most importantly for our discus-sion, better learning leads to better predictions. If we have correctly modeled the relevant con-tingencies, we should be in a position to infer outcomes we have not witnessed. Note again that the value of predictive inference is mirrored in both good science and good individual learn-ing. For example, if I asked you how your best friend would react to news that you'd crashed his car (but you are fine) you could probably provide a fairly accurate prediction, despite hav-ing never encountered this particular scenario. Over the course of years, you've gathered, bit-by-bit, information that is relevant to making this prediction. You've seen him under stress, you've seen him react to the loss or damage of something valuable, you know well whether he's someone who's funny about his car, you've seen him display trust and confidence in you, and you've broken bad news to him before. You probably even know the best way to deliver bad news, and the best time for it. It's an easy predic-tion, for you. Modeling complex contingencies doesn't just mean better learning, it means better predictions, which mean better outcomes. The reason we lug around these large, metaboli-cally expensive brains is to optimize behavioral

flexibility, adaptivity, and prediction, through learning.

Now We Know: Why Do I Need to Know This? Anyone who has taught for long enough has heard this question. And if you're like me, you've gotten irritated with the question—as it seems like impertinence, not a real question—and then given a sub-optimal answer. But I asked the same questions when I was a young student. I distinctly remember asking a math teacher (and I very much liked math), "Why do I have to learn trigonom-etry?" and I was told something about it being useful if I ever needed to figure out how tall a flagpole is. I asked, "Why do we have to learn his-tory?" and I got the old chestnut about repeating the errors of history if we won't learn from them. Ugh. And let's face it, a lot of students are told that they need an education because without one they'll have no hope of a good job. It is then just natural that they would wonder what job require-ments specify the knowledge they're being asked to learn. So let's take a step back. Perhaps history is one of the harder academic subjects to validate for students, but for those who understand, the reasons are obvious. We all want to understand human nature; we all need to understand human nature. The here-and-now is but one slight sliver of possible examples, and it doesn't begin to give examples of all the scenarios that elicit different aspects of our nature. If we want to extrapolate to events that have not yet occurred, we need more examples than how people are acting in the immediate present. By close scrutiny of the past, we can better understand the fullness of human nature, in such contexts as world war, monarchy, plague, peasantry, and so on. To the properly educated mind, the question, "When will I have to know this?" has a clear answer. It will be indispensable to your thinking about just about everything; you'll always need to know it. The snag is that students don't know yet how their learning will help them. This is exacerbated by the fact that many of their parents don't know, or can't articulate the reasons for learning, and that teachers likewise sometimes fail to communicate the reasons students should endeavor. Therefore, those who ask, "When will I ever have to know this?" have unfortunately missed the point entirely, since learning done properly permeates all aspects of our mental lives. But indeed, if learning is not done properly, when it is done by rote, crammed, or when the goal is to improve standardized test scores, then it does not permeate, and it is therefore not used. Thus when an adult (or worse, a parent) says, "You'll never have to use that," they are right in the sense that they have never used it, but wrong in the sense that others would not use it. It is simple to identify a properly educated person: Simply ask them when you would ever use x (fill in appropriate topic) and if they shrug or say "never," their education hasn't truly taken hold. But if they reply that they use it all the time as it is part of their thinking, then their education did indeed take hold and has borne fruit.

The current complaint about standardized testing is that teachers will have to teach to the test. The problem is not that measurement is not necessary, but rather that the current standardized test is bland—meant to address things that can reasonably be expected to be common to all curricula—so that many teachers could improve standardized test performance by teaching less, solely on what is on the test; students could focus more on a smaller set of tasks. Admittedly, some classrooms would be better off if the teachers taught all that is on the test. What is required, and what would satisfy critics, is a test that is highly correlated with the curriculum. Part of it would have to be that multiple-choice tests be replaced with better testing, as multiple choice does not test the material in the way it's taught, or in the way the material would be used in the students' life. Multiple choice has very little to do with any aspect of performance as very little learning gets expressed in multiple choice–like situations.

The universality of knowledge is an outcome of a proper education, but problematically it is also a prerequisite for deep learning. This is perhaps the greatest challenge a teacher faces, to convey effectively, in advance, why any given topic is important. If students already knew that, they'd be better educated than a lot of graduates. The process must therefore be recursive and incremental, using each individual discovery, and its importance, as a foundation

> **The role of science is to extend and advance knowledge so that we may better understand and negotiate the world. The role of education is to disseminate knowledge, which is the extant prerequisite for all of life's callings. The role of science education is to perpetuate the advancement of knowledge so that the betterment of humanity may continue.**

Highlights and Summary: Tips for Teachers

- Make all learning an act of exploration. When we explore, we naturally hone our ability to produce a desired outcome. Accordingly, making predictions and testing them is how we become better explorers.

- Build new learning upon well-founded existing learning. Play to the student's strengths, and build those strengths all the way over to their weaknesses.

- There is no substitute for knowing the student. An effective teacher must know what the student knows, must know the student's misconceptions, and must know how quickly the student can integrate new learning into existing learning. Learning must be tailor-made for each individual. Resist any temptation to apply a one-size-fits-all approach.

- The successful teacher makes all learning satisfying and relevant. Understand and capitalize upon motivation, especially natural curiosity.

- Assess and provide feedback frequently, and do all that you can to discourage cramming.

- The younger the child, the more immediate the goals of learning should be.

- Engage all the senses, engage emotions, make learning sociable, involve them in the reasoning and the discussion, and most importantly, get them to explore, to discover, to make predictions and to act upon what they're learning.

for the subsequent ones. Many teachers (myself often included) need to do a better job of this; and it won't work for every single student on every single subject. Gone should be the days where you have to learn trigonometry just in case you might have to figure out the height of a flagpole, or learn history just so as not to be doomed to repeat its mistakes. To be clear, I am absolutely not suggesting that if a student doesn't know why he or she is there, that it's the teachers fault, but if few or none of the students know why they are there then some remediation from the teacher is in order. As we have seen, the human brain is very good at filtering out confusing, irrelevant information, and if material to be learned is not motivating, made relevant, and made interesting, students have a much lower chance of learning that material in truly useful ways. Some students will have some ability to do this on their own,

but if education is going to expand its efficacy, we must do more than bring the horse to water. We must take it upon ourselves to figure out how to make the horse drink. Indeed, doing so will create a recursively generated upward spiral wherein each generation is imbued by their parents with greater curiosity and depth of reasoning, rather than the current mode wherein each generation is impaired by their parents with greater skepticism about the use of education. The use of education is only there when fully absorbed. Finally, we must go well beyond the notion that education is justified by getting a better job. The rewards are too distant to be effective. Education is not just about preparing a workforce; education is about preparing adaptive and flexible minds to manage and enjoy life amid the complexities of the world. To paraphrase Alexander Pope, we must drink deeply to taste the fountain of knowledge.

Further Reading

Cohen, N. J., and H. Eichenbaum. 2004. *From conditioning to conscious recollection: Memory systems of the brain.* New York: Oxford University Press.

Greene, A. J. 2010. Making connections: The essence of memory is linking one thought to another. *Scientific American Mind* 21: 21–29.

Greene, A. J., W. L. Gross, C. L. Elsinger, and S. M. Rao. 2006. An fMRI analysis of the human hippocampus: Inference, context, and task awareness. *Journal of Cognitive Neuroscience* 18: 1156–1173.

Weller, J. A., B. Suchan, and I. Daum. 2009. Foreseeing the future: Occurrence probability of imagined future events modulates hippocampal activation. *Hippocampus* 20: 685–690.

VI

THE NEW SCIENCE OF LEARNING IN THE CLASSROOM

INTRODUCTION

Science Is Fun

Chuck Niederriter, PhD
Professor of Physics and Director of the Nobel Conference
Gustavus Adolphus College

There are many good reasons to teach science in the earliest grades, including improved long-term performance in all areas of education. But, in my opinion, the most important reason is to illustrate that learning science is fun. Students should develop an appreciation for learning that grows into a lifelong enthusiasm for gaining knowledge and understanding of ourselves and the world around us. Indeed for the entire universe. And, since science is intrinsically fun, learning it will be as well.

Even very young children are curious about the world around them, often driving their parents mad with a continuous stream of questions, "Why, why, why?" The best preschool, kindergarten, and grade school teachers are those who have the patience and enthusiasm to help children find the answers to their questions. Sometimes that means saying, "I don't know, let's find out." In the process of helping the students find the answers, teachers are teaching the process of learning and in some cases the scientific process, as well. Those lucky students will find an enjoyment in exploring the vast base of knowledge that humans have developed over the centuries.

One only needs to eavesdrop at an event like family day at the American Association for the Advancement of Science (AAAS) annual meeting, or at youth science days, or science on Saturday, or at any science museum to observe the excitement that young children exhibit when the wonders of the world around them are brought to their attention. Be those wonders biological, chemical, geological, or physical, the reaction is often something like, "Wow, that's neat." Followed by, "Let's see more," or "Let's do that again and see if it comes out the same." Of course, the smellier, louder, or more surprising, the better. There is nothing like blowing up a balloon full of hydrogen to get students' attention before talking about where it comes from and making some more with electrolysis or chemical processes.

Learning science is fun, or at least it should be. So should teaching science. I suspect that we have all experienced the odd teacher who didn't enjoy teaching, or at least a particular subject. And we recognize the effect that has on the students. My hope is that every young student will have the opportunity to learn science with a teacher who loves science and isn't afraid to show it. I think that means that those of us teaching the teachers need to model that enthusiastic love of science. Maybe it isn't possible for all science education classes to consist of only flashy demonstrations, but they certainly should be a substantial part.

Young children, like adults, will do what they really enjoy. If we truly believe that learning and learning science is important, we need to ensure that students' learning experiences are fun and enjoyable. Young students will work harder learning subjects that they enjoy than those they do not. They will also retain those habits for the rest of their lives. What better way to get started on a scientific career or lifelong quest for knowledge than with firsthand experience of the fun of science in grade school, kindergarten, or even preschool.

CHAPTER 9

What Teachers Do to Engage Their Students in Learning

By Abby Bergman, EdD
Educational Program Consultant and Former Regional Science Coordinator
Putman-Northern Westchester BOCES

Science education is changing! The sequential release of *A Framework for K–12 Science Education* (NRC 2012) and the *Next Generation Science Standards* represents a historic opportunity to rethink both *what* and *how* science is taught *and learned* in our nation's schools. In this chapter time-honored approaches, best practices, and new thinking about the teaching and learning of science provide common-sense strategies and assistance for teachers in their efforts to implement the *Framework* and the *NGSS* in their classrooms.

Setting the Stage for Learning

As teachers, we all want our students to be involved and engaged in their learning. Few moments in a teacher's day are as rewarding as observing the active involvement of students—when something clicks, and our students want to learn more about the topic or process before them. Then there are those "aha" moments when students seem to forget everything else around them and their excitement and thirst in the learning process seems insatiable.

Some might say that those moments are few and far between, but just imagine if we could structure our classrooms and our instructional practices to maximize the emotional, social, and cognitive engagement of *all* students in learning science!

There exists a body of knowledge that we can draw upon to plan logical sequences of learning experiences that will excite and inspire our students and maximize learning. To begin, we all know that there is a difference between teaching and learning. Sometimes teachers feel that when they have taught something, the obligation for learning (absorbing) lies with the student. Researchers in brain-based learning have provided new understandings for how students can become engaged in their learning and remember, extend, and transfer what they have learned to new contexts. As cognitive science has evolved into cognitive neuroscience, we understand more about what works to enhance learning and what does not. Students literally have to *create* the neuronal connections in their brain in order to understand the knowledge (concept) the teacher is explaining. The role of the teacher is to facilitate the creation of these connections. There is no automatic absorption simply because the teacher has presented material; students must actively create the knowledge (Greene 2010, pp. 24–26) (see Chapter 8).

Where to Begin?

First things first—know your students! Students learn when they are *engaged* and feel valued as individuals and learners. Knowledge of your students can be superficial—their names, general personality traits, and perhaps their friendships. But to *really* know students is a more complex and dynamic process. We can learn a lot through informal conversations with them—their history as learners, their family lives and role within those families, their interests outside of school. We can also obtain insights into the way they think. Metacognition is often referred to as the process of thinking about thinking. When we ask students to express (in oral, written, and/or artistic forms) how and why they know something, they are revealing their thought patterns, concept constructs, and approaches to gaining knowledge. Asking students to explain their thinking or how they know something can provide a window into their thought processes and how they deal with perceived realities.

When students feel that you *know who they are* and show interest in their interests, they are more likely to be comfortable, willing to take risks, and engage in their learning. When students know that their teacher took the time to get to know them, they are more likely to feel that their teacher cares about both them and their learning. Or, more simply put, students won't care how much you know until they know how much you care. Knowing about the student also gives the teacher tools to bring the student back into the lesson or classroom experience when they are not following or paying attention.

Going Beyond "Getting to Know You"

In addition to getting to know students as people and thinkers, teachers must provide students with an environment that is conducive to learning. If students feel uncomfortable, unsafe, or not respected, then their chances of success in a classroom are compromised. Feeling that they are valued both by the teacher and their peers

also helps to create a low-threat environment and promotes a willingness to take risks (Caine and Caine 2011, p. 174). Students need to learn about each other and to gain an appreciation for the benefits of diversity that they find in their classrooms. How boring it would be if we were all alike! Our varied backgrounds and differences help to make us unique individuals. We all have strengths and weaknesses. Promoting tolerance and respect for each individual can go a long way toward creating an environment in which students feel free to learn and to acknowledge and appreciate their own individual characteristics and traits. "Acceptance is a big deal to students. When they feel valued and accepted, students are more likely to learn, be more confident, and make more valuable contributions. Resourceful teachers know this and work to build school cultures that promote the acceptance and learning of all students. In such schools, teachers certainly know a lot about their content areas, but they also have a deep understanding and appreciation of the young people they teach" (The Teaching Diverse Students Initiative n.d.).

Learning about students also helps a teacher differentiate instruction, a topic that will be dealt with later in this chapter. To really understand students' readiness for instruction, as well as to find out about some of their background experiences, preassessment is the next step (see discussion on the Engage phase in Chapter 4 and curriculum examples in Chapters 5–7). Teachers want to know about students' learning preferences, their readiness for instruction in a particular topic (not their ability, but rather prior experiences), and interests that will guide them as they chart instructional priorities (Strickland 2009). Teachers who collect and use such information demonstrate to their students that they care about them as individuals and plan learning experiences accordingly.

Beyond this, teachers can model for students respect for one another's ideas and opinions. Ensuring that students have flexible mental frames allows them to accept and indeed value dissenting ideas. They should be helped to understand that a variety of viewpoints is not only valued, but exciting. Encouraging young students to be open, respectful members of a classroom community helps all students feel valued and models essential science and engineering practices (i.e., *Framework* and *NGSS* identified practices 6–8).

When students know that their teacher has taken the time to get to know them, they will feel more comfortable in the classroom; they will know that their teacher cares about them and cares about what they learn. Knowing their students also gives teachers the tools they need to motivate them and inspire their time at school, their intellectual lives, and their fulfillment and potential contributions as individuals and citizens.

Research Informs Instruction

Teachers rarely have time to sift through volumes of research, searching for something that will positively impact classroom instruction. Yet there is research out there on elementary science that has great importance for educational practice (e.g., NRC 2007 and Michaels, Shouse, and Schweingruber 2008; both available for free online reading and downloading). Some of the practical implications of this research for everyday classroom instruction are highlighted below.

Learning Is a Social Process

The majority of what we learn occurs within a social context. From our very beginnings and throughout our lives, our interactions with others shape our understanding of the world. As young children interact with others (and even with objects), they are interacting with the world as they know it.

The Russian psychologist Lev Vygotsky advanced a theory of learning that defined the ways in which social and linguistic environments influence the learning process. Learning and development take place in the interactions children have with peers as well as with teachers and other adults. Learning is derived from language and if language is social, then using language to explain or convey meaning results in an interactive exchange that is on some level social in nature. These social interactions develop language—which supports thinking—and they provide feedback and assistance that support ongoing learning and verbalizations to bring them into their realm of knowing (Vygotsky 1978).

Educators have long recognized that children do not learn in isolation. They are exposed to a physical (e.g., science equipment and supplies) as well as a social environment. As they explore new material, they need to share their thoughts, ideas, and emerging notions. Listening to what others are thinking helps to broaden understanding and see other points of view.

Continuing studies have reaffirmed the critical nature of learning in a social context. In a recent article by Meltzoff et al., it was affirmed that children readily learn through social interactions with other people. Three social skills are foundational to human development: imitation, shared attention, and empathic understanding (Meltzoff et al. 2009).

In many ways social learning is one of the most important and least emphasized aspects of school life. When students practice communicating with one another, they begin to develop one of life's most important skills. It is thought that teenagers text constantly because they do not have the confidence and skill to communicate face to face. It is much easier to press buttons then deal with how a person is responding to what you are saying in person. Younger students generally enjoy interacting with others, but this is a process in intellectual discourse that must be taught; it cannot be assumed. This is especially true when students are asked to construct, defend and/or refute explanatory, scientific arguments based on empirical evidence (i.e., science and engineering practices 6–8).

Social cues from other students highlight what and when to learn. When learning and social interaction are combined, brain circuits link perceptions to actions. These interactions require continuous adaptation and also result in the mental plasticity that promotes learning (Meltzoff et al. 2009, p. 285).

So what can teachers do to foster a positive environment in which learning as a social process can take place? There are distinct strategies for how teachers can foster productive interactions in the classroom. First of all, we need to create a respectful learning environment by withholding premature judgment (and eliminating personal attacks) on students' ideas, notions, and opinions. Teachers can help students learn structures to work well in groups. Students need to explain their emerging ideas to one another so that they can benefit from the questions and alternative ideas they receive from others. Teachers can build on the ways children learn from each other by creating a learning environment where there are ample opportunities for student-to-student discussion, collaboration, and feedback. Students share their observations and explanations for phenomena as well as the evidence for their findings and assertions in ways that mirror the practices of scientists and engineers.

Teachers can assist and assess student learning by structuring classroom discussions with purposeful questions and listening carefully to what students say as a means to guide the instructional conversation toward deeper understanding. By managing the dialogue in large- and small-group discussions, the teacher can learn where students are in their understanding and can provide timely assistance though questions, clarifications, references to prior learning, and additional tailored, just-in-time learning activities.

Cooperative learning, a very popular technique in schools, is a process that students learn over time. Teachers help students negotiate the various roles that they assume in such groupings. Learning in this way is more engaging and motivating and more reflective of the kind of creative, group problem solving that is highly valued in adult life, in the workplace, and especially by scientists and engineers.

Seminars or colloquia are other techniques for promoting social learning. These are well-planned opportunities for students to engage in intelligent discussions in which ideals, values, social issues, and principles are critically scrutinized in nonthreatening environments. They can be used to promote critical thinking, listening, communicating, and wonder. Socratic seminars are fashioned after the instruction-through-questioning methods of Socrates. These seminars focus on a wide range of topics, including specific readings, scientific demonstrations, and the arts (Tredway 1995). They are often used to share reactions to a book, article, or investigation.

Students need to be instructed in the format and process of the Socratic seminar. They are helped to

- discuss with teachers serving as facilitators, and become responsible for learning groups;

- develop an atmosphere of trust, intellectual engagement, and cooperation;

- become tolerant of a variety of viewpoints and opinions;

- build upon and react to one another's ideas, but do so in a respectful manner;

- seek to answer questions, but also to generate new ones;

- explore differences of opinion as valuable learning opportunities;

- critique ideas, not people; and

- use argumentation as a means to develop the best provisional explanation for a given phenomenon (rather than to win an argument).

It is important to emphasize the critical nature of social communication in the learning process. Effective dialogue and communication are skills that must be deliberately taught in all subjects and at all levels of school life. This is emphasized in the *Common Core State Standards, English Language Arts* (*CCSS ELA*) Speaking and Listening Standards (1–6) and *CCSS, Mathematics'* Mathematical Practice 3 (Construct viable arguments and critique the reasoning of others), as well as in the *Next Generation Science Standards* (*NGSS*) science and engineering practices (6–8). Civil, social dialogue is also a critical skill set to develop in social studies courses. Throughout their lives, students will use oral and written language for effective communication with a wide variety of individuals. As readers and listeners, they will use the social communication skills that they develop to enrich their understanding of ideas, people, and their views.

Making the Learning Interesting, Contextual, and Relevant

Young children are natural scientists. As they poke, pry, and otherwise explore their worlds, they are expressing this curiosity with a natural desire to make sense of things. Some say that this innate curiosity is often extinguished by the time students reach middle school. This curiosity must be nourished, and perhaps one of the best ways is to for parents and teachers to be curious *along* with their children. Sit at the level where the children are working; crouch down beside them. Ask questions to promote thinking. It is not difficult to capitalize upon and support the natural curiosity of young children, but it must be done in a deliberate manner. A very simple, but extremely important contribution that parents and teachers can make is to provide a model of curious, inquisitive behavior that children can imitate and emulate. In other words, they too should act like scientists!

Making Connections

Current research has demonstrated that memory and learning are dependent upon connections that we make between new stimuli and what we already know (Greene 2011; see also Chapter 8 of this book). There are neurological models that demonstrate how neurons can fire to allow learning to proceed when new evidence occurs, but at the simplest level we need to create hooks to grab students' attention and provide the scaffolding that allows them to link new material to previous learning. This process may not occur spontaneously and teachers may have to help students make the relevant connections. Children may need assistance in making a web of associations. This is why concept mapping and word webbing is such a brain-rich activity when a teacher presents new material.

This harkens back to the seminal work of noted Swiss psychologist Jean Piaget who affirmed that it was through a process of progressive assimilations and accommodations that cognitive development occurs. Piaget's landmark studies, conducted in the 1950s and 1960s, established the groundwork for later theories and research in intellectual development. Assimilation is the process by which an individual deals with the environment in terms of current mental structures. It is how individuals use their present repertoire of skills and knowledge to incorporate external events or new ideas into existing cognitive structures. Accommodation is the tendency (ability) of individuals to change in response to environmental demands to accommodate new information. It is modification in response to external events. Assimilation and accommodation go together; you can't have one without the other. When these two processes are in balance, equilibration occurs and learning proceeds. "One way of putting the matter is to say that interest and learning are facilitated if the experience presented to the child bears some relevance to what he already knows but at the same time is sufficiently novel to present incongruities and conflicts" (Ginsburg and Opper 1969, p. 223). These complementary processes are used throughout life for learning and cognitive development to extend what we know and to deal initially with seemingly anomalous events.

Several educational researchers have sought to summarize the educational implications of Piaget's work:

- Children learn through action.

- Children are born with and acquire schemas, or operational, cognitive roadmaps for how to act and respond to the world.

- As children explore their world, they form and reform ideas in their minds.

- Children construct their own knowledge, a knowledge that is a work in progress and is likely quite different from that of an adult.

- A child's stage of development reflects concepts as the child has constructed them through his or her actions in the physical environment.

Learning is a social process. This helps students become less egocentric and view things from the perspectives of others.

Engaging the Brain

Engaging all areas of the brain is another technique that can help to promote learning. Neurolinguistic findings about the brain's functions show that in the integrated brain, the functions of one hemisphere are immediately available to the other. Also, some students have preferred modalities for learning, so teaching to the whole brain provides a better chance of reaching all students. Whole-brain teaching emphasizes active minds-on learning in which the learner makes connections that tap both hemispheres.

Another key aspect of whole-brain teaching is managing the emotional climate. When students feel stressed or threatened, their brains cognitively downshift and result in the flight or fight syndrome that reduces students' abilities to learn at optimal levels (Goleman 1995 and Jensen 1998). Such downshifting can occur in response to the instructor, the academic content being taught, various coping strategies of students (i.e., social networks, stereotypes of classmates), and physical and emotional environments created within the confinements of the classroom (Kaufman et al. 2008). Playing music during learning episodes or displaying soothing colors in the classroom may also enhance the learning experience by creating a relaxed, low threat, multisensory-enriched atmosphere.

Beyond this, a goal of learning is for ideas to jump from short-term memory into long-term memory. In order for ideas to make this transition, learners must process information into another format to manipulate it. Short-term memory is brought into working memory. For working memory to create more enduring understandings, an application or association must take place. If something else does not happen, "it is likely to fade from working memory" (Sousa 2011, p. 51). In order for students to use these understandings or make associations, they can make notes, draw pictures and charts, talk to a neighbor, and in other ways to work on actively processing the new items.

Learning Is Multisensory

We know that learning involves the entire brain. The more senses involved in a hands-on learning experience and the more social interaction (sharing ideas, asking questions and most of all, communicating among each other in small groups), the better. Students need to fully experience the concept being taught in as many ways as possible. Hands-on science activities are especially memorable when placed in a logical learning progression (e.g., as advocated across grade levels by the *NGSS* and within a given grade level unit, by the 5E Teaching Cycle described in Chapter 4).

In the introduction to his guide on multisensory learning, Lawrence Bains makes the case for the importance of this approach:

> Two of the greatest challenges for teachers in the years ahead will be student engagement and achievement. Multisensory learning techniques provide an effective, highly adaptable method for addressing both. The premise of multisensory learning is simple. When

students invoke more than one sense, simultaneously over a period of time, they tend to interact with the material more intensely and thereby retain what they have learned for longer periods of time. In multisensory learning, a teacher engages students in hands-on, visual, auditory, and olfactory stimuli, and then links the activity to relevant academic objectives. It is through the reciprocal relationship between sensory input and thinking that multisensory techniques gain their power. (2008, p. x).

Variety Is the Spice of Life—and Learning

Another way to engage learners is to use a variety of instructional techniques and strategies. Variety is the essence of good teaching. Teachers who use a variety of approaches in science (and all subject areas) will have a classroom full of questioners seeking information and testing ideas—the essence of learning. Activities and other learning episodes should be varied with active exploration alternating with reflection and discussion. Learning episodes should also be very interactive—many say in 15–20 minute segments for maximum engagement. Discussions, punctuated by asking students to turn and talk to a partner, take notes, or make a graphic representation (e.g., charts, tables, graphs, and so on) of an understanding, all help to make the time spent in learning new material more dynamic and associative. As such, science activities provide a rich context for simultaneously addressing standards from the *CCSS ELA* (e.g., Cervetti et al; and see Chapter 10 of this book) and *CCSS Mathematics* (e.g., Metric Measurement, Models, and Moon Matters, the 5E mini-unit by O'Brien in Chapter 7).

Approaches to teaching should be consistent with the discipline in which the students are engaged. In science learning, for example, ideas should be tested through collecting empirical evidence: "Does it work when we try it?" The nature of the systems being studied should be considered. Hypotheses should be used as intellectual tools in the study of questions and problems. When possible, controlled experiments should be carried out. There should also be ample opportunity for criticism and an exchange of ideas, as well as seeking possible sources of error in their work. Teachers can model searching for errors and thus demonstrate the real work of doing science. For example, if students are asked to measure the length, width, and thickness of a class set of textbooks in three trials, they may find that their findings are not consistent. What might have accounted for the variations? Perhaps it was how worn the book was or maybe the ruler had an indented zero. Discussion of such findings helps students to practice the work that scientists do. When students compare their findings and build upon the ideas of those who came before them, they gain some experience in the iterative, cumulative nature of scientific knowledge.

Several approaches to science instruction each have their own level of appropriateness. For instance, interactive lecture/demonstration, the laboratory approach, and cooperative projects can all be effectively used as classroom approaches. Such variety will maintain interest and stimulation on the part of the students (Jacobson and Bergman 1980).

Making Learning Vivid

Learning comes alive for students when it is vivid and memorable. Motivational, discrepant event demonstrations (Friedl and Koontz 2004; O'Brien 2010), vivid simulations, compelling tasks, and stimulating framing of questions and challenges—all make learning come alive for students. Students must be cognitively and emotionally engaged from the very beginning of each instructional unit (i.e., Engage phase of a 5E cycle in Chapter 4). Good teachers create hooks to grab students' attention. Students need to see patterns to help make connections, and once they are with you, you can focus them on the essential elements of learning.

Scaffolding is often used as a technique to support and promote learning when teachers first introduce a concept or skill. This technique helps students link their new learning to prior experiences and see the relevance of the new learning. Reminders of past associations, organizing frameworks for ideas, principles, or information—all serve to promote elaboration in student learning. When teachers help students make connections explicit, they move their students closer to independence.

Storytelling telling is another important technique for making learning vivid for students. Stories that have a point, that demonstrate an idea or a way of understanding, engage students, capture their imagination, and make learning interesting. They remain on the edge of their seats. Whether the story is a personal one of how the teacher was inspired to research a topic or a professional writer recounting how an idea incubated and became a tool or device that we use every day, or how someone led a life that made a difference—these stories engage students, infuse a literary component, and motivate students to go further. Science stories also provide a context for highlighting the *NGSS* dimension 2, crosscutting concepts (i.e., patterns, cause and effect, and stability and change).

Seeking Relevance and Application

Students need to know that what they are learning is useful to them in their everyday lives. Whenever possible, help them establish this relevance by creating a context for how the new learning can be used. "If the connections between subject matter and students are relevant and personal to them, the learned material becomes part of their beings" (Greene 2010, p. 29; see also Chapter 8 of this book).

Students also need to learn how they can apply new learning to new situations. Effective teachers plan stimulating applications that link lesson content to the students' world. Always ask, what is the relevance? Students need to process new information in a way that makes sense to them. Help children look for patterns (*NGSS* crosscutting concept 1). Help them reflect upon and learn from their observations. Help them make generalizations. All of these techniques will serve to make learning relevant and help students apply their new learning to novel situations.

Theory Into Practice: Planning Instruction

Research into best practices in teaching and learning is a constantly evolving process. As new evidence from neurological, psychometric, and practical (anecdotal) studies emerges, the list of best and promising practices develops apace.

Although best practices are generally applicable across disciplines in terms of instructional effectiveness, science has its own set of strategies and approaches that are particular to science.

What sets science apart from other disciplines is that ideas and experiences are based upon logical arguments and skeptical review tied to empirical evidence. *A Framework for K–12 Science Education* defines eight practices considered essential elements of a K–12 science curriculum (NRC 2012):

- Asking questions (for science) and defining problems (for engineering)

- Developing and using models

- Planning and carrying out investigations

- Analyzing and interpreting data

- Using mathematics and computational thinking

- Constructing explanations (for science) and designing solutions (for engineering)

- Engaging in argument from evidence

- Obtaining, evaluating, and communicating information

These practices are fairly straightforward and suggestions for how to promote the practices are outlined in the *Framework* and the *NGSS* documents. They are not linear, as science in the real world is not conducted in a linear fashion; there are many entry points into an investigation. There are, however, some general strategies that teachers can use to realize these effective guidelines and practices.

Preassessment

At the beginning any instructional unit, it is important to elicit what students already know (or believe to be so) about a topic or concept. This provides an opportunity to guide instruction and also to activate and challenge any misconceptions students may have. It is also important to recognize prior knowledge so students can engage in questioning, thinking, and theorizing in order to construct new knowledge appropriate to their level. Teachers use a variety of diagnostic tools that serve as preinstructional assessment probes. Some of these include KWL charts, concept webs, drawings, POE discrepant event demonstrations, questioning, small quizzes, and the like. (See Chapters 4–7 for more discussion and examples of the Engage phase of the 5E Teaching Cycle.)

Once preassessments have been conducted, teachers design lessons that take students from their current level of knowledge to new understandings. Students need to process new information in a way that makes sense to them. So, as mentioned previously, they seek connections to what they already know. In the case of misconceptions, students will need to make revisions in their prior misunderstandings to accommodate new phenomena.

Asking Questions

Helping students to develop, refine, and investigate their own questions is another practice that teachers use in planning instruction. Developing investigable questions is a skill that teachers can model and then assist students in generating possible and practical questions for investigation. Student questions can be refined by asking follow-up questions and prompting students to think further about their interests and investigations. Students need to consider whether data can be collected for a particular question or whether they have the tools and the means to measure a phenomenon (science and engineering practices 1 and 3). Asking investigable questions is the key component to the Explore phase of the 5E Teaching Cycle. (See Chapters 4–7.)

Start With the End in Mind

Simply put, this popular planning strategy assumes that teachers pose essential questions for which students will have answers after a lesson or unit. What do you want students to know and be able to do? Teachers need to be clear about their goals for teaching as well as the intended outcomes; the *Framework* and *NGSS* are critical resources at the school district, school and classroom levels. Once these outcomes are clarified, the backward design begins by laying out the understandings that students are expected to achieve as well as the assessment tools that measure whether that understanding has occurred. Grant Wiggins and Jay McTighe, who have done some of the best work in this area, admit that the term *understand* can be difficult to capture. They assert:

> The word *understanding* turns out to be a complex and confusing target despite the fact that we aim for it all the time. The word naturally deserves clarification and elaboration … to *understand* is to make connections and bind together our knowledge into something that makes sense of things, whereas without understanding we might see unclear, isolated, and unhelpful facts. (Wiggins and McTighe 2005, pp. 6–7)

Assess Learning and Instruction

What is instruction unless we know that the learner has actually achieved some of the outcomes that are defined? Many forms of assessment help to determine the extent of student learning and also provide information to guide instructional decisions. Preassessments are usually employed to plan instruction. Once instruction has begun, three forms of assessment can provide the feedback that teachers need. Formative assessments occupy the bulk of teacher assessment time. Formative assessments require that both teachers and students are clear about the learning objectives. Assessments should be constructed in advance so that teachers can make midcourse adjustments during or between lessons. Examples of formative assessments include student self-assessments, rubrics, checking for understanding during lessons, handheld polling, individual whiteboards, quizzes, and examination of student work. Formative assessments also inform teachers about instructional decisions and serve as the basis for feedback to help students improve their learning,

Interim assessments are given periodically (often every six to eight weeks) and are designed to monitor student proficiency and provide teachers with information for re-teaching and following up on students. Teachers often use interim assessments to motivate and provide feedback to students about their learning and to assess their own pacing. These assessments can also help to determine the effectiveness of distinct instructional approaches, as well as whether students are on track for fulfillment of the anticipated outcomes.

Summative assessments are most often given when instruction in a group of lessons or a unit is finished, often for report cards or grades. These include unit tests, performance tasks, final exams, and, of course, high-stakes state tests. They can be end-of-year state examinations in prescribed areas, or they may be locally adopted commercial tests that supplement the information obtained on state assessments.

Teacher note: Diagnostic (Engage), formative (Explore, Explain, and Elaborate) and summative

(Evaluate phase) assessments are built into the design of the 5E Teaching Cycle (see Chapters 4–7).

Differentiated Instruction

Differentiated instruction capitalizes on student learning preferences, interests, and readiness for instruction. After a careful diagnosis, teachers create different pathways to ensure that learning activities have the best promise of success for the diverse learners that are found in any classroom. Usually, the objectives and anticipated outcomes for any lesson or unit remain the same for all learners, but lessons can be *tiered* so that students will be engaged at a level best suited for their learning strengths and needs. For example, in a unit on exploring water cycles (*NGSS*, disciplinary core idea ESS2), a variety of instructional activities can be outlined to demonstrate student fulfillment of the goals of the lesson. Some might draw a diagram of a water cycle, label it, and explain the characteristics of each segment of the cycle. Other students might design an investigation to determine factors that affect evaporation, create a chart illustrating the findings, and write a summary report. Still others might create a travel brochure describing in detail the benefits of taking a vacation on a cloud, using illustrations, photos, and charts, and finally writing a commercial to advertise this vacation. It is evident that each of these alternative activities lead to the same understandings, but students arrive there in different ways.

In planning for activities or investigations, it is also helpful to consider that not all students will inquire deeply into every topic that is a part of a unit. Students can become experts in a particular area by delving deeply into a specific aspect or understanding within a unit. Then, by practicing and capitalizing the essential skill of communicating in science, they can impart their special skill and knowledge to the others in the group. When teachers employ a variety of strategies, assignments, approaches, and experiences, they increase the chances of reaching all of the students in a class.

Science Instruction Is Unique

The acquisition of knowledge and methods of conducting investigations in science are somewhat distinct from other forms of learning. There is an emphasis on observation and gathering evidence. Observation skills can be taught in context using the classroom and the natural environment as the laboratory. Students can make observations and measurements, but the data will have little meaning unless they analyze the data for patterns that emerge. They can then communicate their new insights and understandings to their peers.

In science *what we teach* and *how we teach* it are equally important. Science should be taught in a manner that is consistent with the nature and structure of science in our lives, in industry, and its many applications (*NGSS* disciplinary core ideas ETS 1 and 2). There should be openness to new ideas, concern for possible consequences of proposed actions, and a willingness to submit ideas to empirical tests. Teachers can facilitate this kind of scaffolded, scientific approach to learning science by using 5E cycle (see Chapters 4–7) that enable students to Engage (with), Explore, Explain, Elaborate, and be Evaluated on an intentionally sequenced, integrated subset of Scientific and engineering practices, crosscutting concepts, and disciplinary core ideas (NRC 2012, p. 3).

Writing in science is another skill that students need to learn. Scientists read, write, and speak somewhat differently from scholars and practitioners in other fields. In science, students must develop precision in their description of their observations and build their arguments

largely from the evidence they have gathered. Engaging science explorations offer a natural motivational context for developing the *CCSS ELA* skills for informational text reading and nonfiction writing, while simultaneously developing the *NGSS* science and engineering practices 7–8.

One of the challenges teachers face is to help their students develop the habits of mind that characterize adult scientists. That means teachers have to nurture students' tendencies to analyze and interpret data and suggest patterns to explain data; to put forth models to explain observations; to view phenomena from different frames of reference; to use symbols and abstract ideas; to consider possible consequences for proposed actions; and to learn how to learn from experience (Jacobson and Bergman 1980, p.13). They need to look for sources of error in their investigations and always be asked to provide evidence for their claims and assertions. Instruction that is intentionally focused on having students actively using the eight science and engineering practices is the key to developing scientific habits of mind from the earliest stages of formal science instruction in elementary classrooms.

Students also need to gain experiences in the broad assumptions and generalizations of science. Helping them to develop systems thinking (crosscutting concept 4) in which they see the connections between what they do and its application is also essential. Students need to use new knowledge to solve real-life problems, use community resources, and work toward the development of a world view. Simply put, when students demonstrate and deepen their understanding of knowledge and skills, they can apply them to other situations. For example, once students learn how to measure accurately and learn the algorithm for determining the area of a room, they can be asked to apply that skill by determining how many square feet of carpeting must be ordered to cover the floor of the classroom. Furthermore, applied learning skills help students see the connections to their work in other disciplines. The ability to use these skills will greatly influence students' success in school, in the workplace, and in the community.

Interdisciplinary Learning: Crosscutting Concepts and Science and Engineering Practices

We know that students do not artificially break up their learning into the subject blocks that often characterize the typical school day. For example, when confronted with new concepts, they do not think, "Now I am doing an activity about plants; now I am doing reading about plants; now I am drawing plants." Children learn in a more holistic fashion. Unfortunately, the compartmentalization of learning is something that many schools and their schedules do to students! In order to capitalize on how the brain works, students can benefit from exposure to science concepts throughout the day—when they are reading, when they are doing math, when they are drawing, and so on. Such curriculum integration has benefits not only for students, but can also help elementary teachers cope with the common frustration of curriculum overload. When students experience concepts in a variety of settings and subject areas, those concepts are more likely to be internalized and learned than if the concepts are presented in an isolated format. The field of science is a whole, just as life is a whole!

It is for these reasons that *A Framework for K–12 Science Education* and *NGSS* emphasize an interdisciplinary, coherent teaching approach as exemplified in the seven crosscutting concepts. These are concepts that "bridge disciplinary boundaries, having explanatory value throughout much of science and engineering" (NRC 2012, p. 83). The idea of interdisciplinary thinking is also evident in the *CCSS ELA* and *Mathematics* and the *NGSS* include explicit *CCSS* connections to both ELA and Mathematics for the science standard at each grade level.

The seven crosscutting concepts identified in the *Framework* and *NGSS* documents include

- Patterns

- Cause and effect: Mechanism and explanation

- Scale, proportion, and quantity

- Systems and system models

- Energy and matter: Flows, cycles, and conservation

- Structure and function

- Stability and change

The authors of the *Framework* acknowledge that these crosscutting concepts have been featured in previous science standards documents as (four) "common themes" or (five) "unifying concepts and processes" (NRC, 2012, p. 85). It is beyond the scope of this chapter to go into further detail about these crosscutting concepts, but they do demonstrate the relevant connections that teachers should make within and across disciplines and engineering practices as they plan and assess student learning.

Communicating New and Emergent Learning

Science is a public undertaking. Scientists discuss their work with their colleagues, testing their ideas and getting help with their problems. They communicate the results of their investigations in informal discussions, journals, blogs, and conference presentations. Scientific work has to withstand the test of criticism by one's peers. Many scientists also believe that they have an obligation to communicate their work in such a way that it can be understood by the educated public and used in making personal and social decisions. Thus, communication is an essential dimension of work in science (science and engineering practice 8).

So, too, should our students have ongoing opportunities to discuss their investigations with their classmates, communicate their results, and test their ideas in public discussion. Teachers often require students to report on the problems, methods, and findings of their investigations and to entertain comments and questions from their peers. Students benefit from explaining what they know and their emerging notions to other students. This can help students to clarify and organize their own thinking. This also promotes the important nature of learning as a social activity. During investigations, it is beneficial to have students verbalize what they are thinking and what they know so that teachers can understand what they are thinking and also help to get to the root of possible misconceptions.

Teachers can help students prepare for these discussions by providing multiple opportunities for them to discuss their work in the classroom. Students should be encouraged to share their learning, explorations, and results and benefit from the reactions/critiques of others. In presenting their work to others, students should incorporate the use of various media, including charts, tables, graphs, diagrams, displays, and Power-Point or interactive white board presentations.

Teachers mediate such events in a variety of ways—usually beginning with the development of a schedule for students to share their work.

It is useful for students to take notes during the presentations so that they can ask questions for clarification. Sometimes these presentations are given to grade-level colleagues, and teachers often invite parents, guests, or experts in the field to attend as well. Part of the teacher's role is to help students understand the importance of communication in a scientific community, to feel comfortable in responding to questions from their peers, and to accept legitimate criticism. Students need to understand that this happens in science all the time and that they can benefit from collaborative reaction and thinking.

In the end, science is the investigation and interpretation of events in the natural and physical environment and within our bodies. In addition to every child's quest to know, science is also humanity's quest to know about the natural world of matter, energy, and their interactions. Scientists have studied the stars above our heads and the rocks at our feet. They have probed the atom and peered into and replicated the living cell. To a large extent, they are asking the same kinds of questions as the curious child. As Isaac Newton once declared, "If I see further, it is by standing on the shoulders of giants." In their reciprocal inquiries in science teaching and learning, all teachers and children can stand upon the shoulders of giants.

References

Achieve Inc. 2013. *Next generation science standards.* www.nextgenscience.org.

Baines, L. 2008. *A teacher's guide to multisensory learning.* Alexandria, VA: ASCD.

Caine, R. N., and G. Caine. 2011. *Natural learning for a connected world—education, technology, and the human brain.* New York: Teachers College Press.

Friedl, A. E., and T. Yourst Koontz. 2004. *Teaching science to children: An inquiry approach.* 6th ed. Boston: McGraw-Hill.

Ginsburg, H. and S. Opper. 1969. *Piaget's theory of intellectual development.* Englewood Cliffs, NJ: Prentice-Hall.

Goleman, D. 1995. *Emotional intelligence.* New York: Bantam Books.

Greene, A. J. 2010. Making connections. *Scientific American Mind* (July): 22–26.

Jacobson, W. J., and A. B. Bergman. 1980. *Science for children—A book for teachers.* 3rd ed. Englewood Cliffs, NJ: Prentice-Hall.

Jensen, E. 1998. *Teaching with the brain in mind.* Alexandria, VA: ASCD.

Kaufman, E., J. S. Robinson, K. A. Bellah, C. Akers, P. Haase-Wittler, and L. Martindale. 2008. Engaging students with brain-based learning. *Techniques* 83: 50–55. *www.acteonline.org/tech_archive. aspx.*

Meltzoff, A. N., P. K. Kuhl, J. Movellan, and T. J. Sejnowski. 2009. Foundations for a new science of learning. *Science* 325: 284–288.

Michaels, S., A. W. Shouse, and H. A. Schweingruber. 2008. *Ready, set, science! Putting research to work in K–8 science classrooms.* Washington, DC: National Academies Press.

National Research Council (NRC). 2007. *Taking science to school: Learning and teaching science in grades K–8.* Committee on Science Learning, Kindergarten Through Eighth Grade. R. Duschl, H. A. Schweingruber, and A. W. Shouse, eds. Washington, DC: National Academies Press.

National Research Council (NRC). 2012. *A framework for K–12 science education: Practices, crosscutting concepts, and core ideas.* Washington, DC: National Academies Press.

O'Brien, T. 2010. *Brain-powered science: Teaching and learning with discrepant events.* Arlington, VA: NSTA Press. (Author demonstration: *www. youtube.com/watch?v=-P_h8Fyf_-c*)

Sousa, D. 2011. *How the brain learns.* Thousand Oaks, CA: Corwin.

Strickland, C. A. 2009. *Professional development for differentiated instruction.* Alexandria, VA: ASCD.

The Teaching Diverse Students Initiative, A Project of the Southern Poverty Law Center. n.d. *Ten steps to implementing a teacher team initiative at your school. www.tolerance.org/tdsi/asset/ ten-steps-implementing-teacher-team-init*

Tredway, L. 1995. Socratic seminars: Engaging students in intellectual discourse. *Educational Leadership* 53 (1): 26–29.

Vygotsky, L. S. 1978. *Mind in society: The development of higher psychological processes.* Cambridge, MA: Harvard University Press.

Wiggins, G., and J. McTighe. 2005. *Understanding by design.* 2nd ed. Alexandria, VA: ASCD.

VII

LITERACY AND SCIENCE

INTRODUCTION

The Importance of Science in Elementary School

Dudley R. Herschbach, PhD
Emeritus Professor of Science, Harvard University
Nobel Prize in Chemistry 1986

Anyone observing young kids at play is struck by their alert curiosity and inventive impulses. Kids love hands-on opportunities to see what happens when they put together or take apart things, and they are eager to report what they discover. Many also take great pleasure in drawing or making music. These qualities seem to be innate, regardless of gender and ethnic or cultural backgrounds. At least in their first few years, most kids are naturally both fledgling scientists and artists.

Sadly, once youngsters start school, these fledgling instincts seem, more often than not, to wither away rather than flourish. The importance of providing good science education early on, from preschool and into the earliest grades, is now widely recognized. Much research has brought out compelling evidence for the feasibility and benefits. In response, there are accelerating efforts to supply professional development and teaching resources for preschool and early-grade teachers.

Another practical challenge to making science a major part of early education is the time needed for other subjects. However, properly taught, science fosters the habit of self-generated questioning and thinking, assessing evidence, and drawing conclusions from observations. These aims, and the impetus to share ideas with others, mesh well with skills nurtured by language learning and social interactions. For instance, the *Scientific Literacy Project* at Purdue University has developed an approach for kindergarten teaching that integrates science with language learning. The results proved mutually enhancing, as well as "effective for children of diverse ethnic and social backgrounds … and eliminated the gender gap in attitudes" (Mantzicopoulos 2005). A similar project at the University of Illinois at Chicago, titled *Integrated Science-Literacy Enactments*, has been developed for grades 1 through 3 (Varelas and Pappas 2012). Chapter 10 by Cervetti et al., describes a number of other projects that integrate science and English language arts.

From personal experience, I am convinced that teaching science in elementary school, in the inquiry mode, can greatly help launch students toward a genuine liberal arts education. For several decades, I've had the opportunity to talk with a wide variety of college students and alumni, many of them regretful that they became alienated from science early on in their academic trajectory. I've also had the opportunity to meet many middle school and high school students taking part in top-flight science fairs. Those students nearly always testify to inspiration received from teachers, often extending to elementary school.

In my view, looking back on more than 70 years as a student and teacher, the key question for education in any field, mode, or level is, "Does it enable the student to take ownership of the subject?" Whether in art or science, inspiring or acquiring ownership usually involves much outside or beyond school, including parental encouragement and many other factors. Yet, because roots and wings implanted in early childhood are especially important, so is what happens in elementary schools.

References

Mantzicopoulos, P., H. Patrick, and A. Samarapungavan. 2005–2008. The scientific literacy project: Enhancing young children's scientific literacy through reading and inquiry-centered adult-child dialog. *www.purduescientificliteracyproject.org*

Varelas, M., and C. C. Pappas. 2012. *Children's ways with science and literacy: Integrated multimodal enactments in urban elementary classrooms.* New York: Routledge.

CHAPTER 10
Science? Literacy? Synergy![1]

Gina N. Cervetti
University of Michigan, Ann Arbor

P. David Pearson
University of California, Berkeley

Cynthia L. Greenleaf
WestEd

Elizabeth Birr Moje
University of Michigan, Ann Arbor

In the introductory chapter of his career-crowning work, *Consilience: The Unity of Knowledge* (1998), eminent biologist E. O. Wilson describes an incident that transformed his intellectual world and fundamentally reshaped his understanding of natural science. A new university student chattering enthusiastically about the ants of Alabama to an assistant professor at Cornell University, Wilson was suddenly thrust a copy of Ernst Mayr's 1942 *Systematics and the Origin of Species*. "Read it," said his mentor, "if you want to become a real biologist."

This thin volume united Darwinian theory and modern genetics and gave an expanded theoretical structure to natural history. Wilson continues, "A tumbler fell somewhere in my mind, and a door opened to a new world." The role that reading played in Wilson's subsequent development is not the topic of his book, but this anecdote dramatizes the point we want to make in this chapter regarding the role of literacy in the work of learning and practicing science: Reading and writing are integral to the work of science. While it is probably perilous to draw too many parallels between the science practiced by professionals and science learning in elementary classrooms, the connection we propose is modest: We suggest that reading and writing are integral to the work of learning and practicing science at every level. Thus, if educators are serious about developing strong understandings of science for all learners, whether or not students intend to become professional scientists, then reading and writing science should also be viewed as supporting rather than supplanting the development of knowledge and inquiry in science from the earliest years of schooling.

What Is the Literacy in Scientific Literacy?

Scientific literacy has been the rallying cry for science education reform for the last twenty years, as many different groups have sought to enhance science learning for all children and youth. Yet this phrase has had multiple, and sometimes conflicting, meanings. Does the *literacy* in scientific literacy refer to a general facility with science concepts needed to understand science for everyday life? Does the *literacy* in scientific literacy have anything to do with the reading and

[1] This chapter is based in part on Pearson, Moje, and Greenleaf 2010.

writing of science texts? Is literacy as reading and writing even an aspect of scientific inquiry? Or does scientific literacy refer to the ability to think and practice like a professional scientist? Equally important, why does scientific literacy in any of these senses matter?

The professional literature reveals multiple ways of thinking about scientific literacy, but at least two conceptualizations dominate. The first focuses on general familiarity with the workings of the natural world and with key science concepts, principles, and ways of thinking (Rutherford and Ahlgren 1989). This perspective on scientific literacy is what Norris and Phillips (2002) refer to as a definition of scientific literacy based on a derived sense of literacy, as captured here by Rutherford and Ahlgren in the introduction to the 1989 American Association for the Advancement of Science's first Project 2061 document, *Science for All Americans*:

> [Scientific literacy involves] *being familiar with the natural world* and respect for its unity; being aware of some of the important ways in which mathematics, technology, and the sciences depend upon one another; *understanding some of the key concepts and principles of science; having a capacity for scientific ways of thinking*; knowing that science, mathematics, and technology are human enterprises, and knowing what that implies about their strengths and limitations; and being able to use scientific knowledge and ways of thinking for personal social purposes. (Rutherford and Ahlgren 1989, p. x) (italics added)

What is noteworthy about this view of scientific literacy is that nowhere in the definition is the reading or writing of print texts—or any other texts—mentioned. The importance of having facility with texts *is* discussed in the *Science for All Americans*, to be sure, but when defining scientific literacy, the focus is generally on useable science knowledge for active participation in the world.

The second dominant perspective on scientific literacy makes an explicit connection between the language of science, how science concepts are rendered in various text forms, and access to both science knowledge and participation (Norris and Phillips 2002). This conceptualization is what Norris and Phillips refer to as the *fundamental* sense of science literacy:

> If scientific literacy is conceived only as knowledge of the substantive content of science, there is a risk that striving to learn the elements of that content will define our goals without any appreciation *for the interconnection among the elements of content, their sources, and their implications* … .When it is also recognized that *science is in part constituted by text and the resources that text makes available*, and that the primary access to scientific knowledge is through the reading of texts, then it is easy to see that *in learning how to read such texts a great deal will be learned about both substantive science content and the epistemology of science*. (Norris and Phillips 2002, pp. 236–237) (italics added)

Here in these quotes, we see—particularly in the italicized sections—that the emphasis is on how science knowledge is constituted by the tools used to communicate that knowledge. Researchers and teachers guided by the more fundamental view of scientific literacy are concerned not only with how students develop the proficiencies needed to engage in science inquiry and acquire science understandings but also the role of representation (in words, arguments, texts, and images) in coming to understand and practice science. That is, they are concerned with how students develop the abilities necessary to access and produce science knowledge by reading, writing, and reasoning with the language and texts.

In this chapter, we focus on the fundamental view of scientific literacy. As such, we will suggest that the ability to make meaning of oral, written, and visual language representations is central to robust science knowledge, to participation in scientific inquiry, and to meaningful engagement in public discourse about science (Yore 2009). We will further argue that, when students learn how to read and write about science, they also learn about the substantive, epistemological, and methodological bases of science. We will push against the false dichotomy between scientific literacy and science inquiry: If science literacy is conceptualized as itself a form of literacy and if literate practices are used to advance scientific inquiry, rather than as a substitute for inquiry, attempts to extricate literacy from inquiry are counterproductive for students. And, we will argue that scientific literacy in the fundamental sense should be a focus of instruction from the earliest years of schooling.

Changing Views of Literacy and Science

The division between the derived and fundamental perspectives on scientific literacy as it is manifested in school instruction can be traced to an historical division between text-based science instruction and inquiry-based science instruction that arose in the middle of the last century. Although John Dewey and others had advocated the teaching of inquiry in science education as early as 1910, those designing school science programs emphasized textbook-driven instruction and focused on the products of science—scientific knowledge—rather than the process of science—at least until a half-century later, when Sputnik came along in 1957. Following the Soviet Union's coup, the National Science Foundation (NSF) took an interest in reforming science education to better prepare students for careers in science. The NSF began to fund professional development and curriculum development efforts that positioned inquiry as an essential part of the content of science instruction and as an essential means of developing scientific understanding and scientific habits of mind (Bybee 1997; Rutherford 1964).

The best of intentions aside, the NSF-funded curriculum efforts of the 1960s underestimated the magnitude of the change required to transform the dominant, incredibly resistant, textbook-driven science curriculum into inquiry-driven, firsthand science. Implementing inquiry-based science brought with it many challenges, foremost the lack of teacher knowledge and experience with inquiry and its pedagogical entailments, but including materials management, time, and orchestrating activity (Anderson 2002; Bybee 1997). Further, the 1960s inquiry-based science curricula were more focused on teaching than on learning and thus did not anticipate the need for teachers to modify instruction according to the prior knowledge and responses of students (Duschl, Schweingruber, and Shouse 2007). By the 1980s, many schools and school districts had returned to textbook-driven teaching practices (Weiss et al. 2003). In the decades that followed, two divergent approaches to science education came to dominate—mainly textbook-based and mainly experience-based science instruction. Textbook science programs included few firsthand experiences for students, focusing instead on the use of reading textbooks and completing textbook and/or worksheet problems. Inquiry-based science programs supported by the NSF included little reading or writing, focusing instead on firsthand experiences with materials and models.

Current research on science learning demonstrates that students learn best through a *combination* of firsthand experience and ample opportunities for reflection and rich talk about their work. This combination allows students to connect new information to what they already know, increasing the likelihood that they will learn and remember it (Bransford, Brown, and Cocking 2000; Brown and Campione 1994; Metz 2000; NRC 2000). In addition, conceptions of proficiency in science are expanding to include dispositions and practices of science beyond factual knowledge and inquiry skills. The recent National Research Council (NRC) brought together a Committee on Science Learning, Kindergarten through Eighth Grade, composed of experts in cognitive and developmental psychology, educational policy and implementation, classroom-based science education research, the natural sciences, the practice of science teaching, and science learning in informal environments. Together, they produced a report called *Taking Science to School* (Duschl, Schweingruber, and Shouse 2007), which set a new bar for students' science proficiency. It calls for students to (1)

know, use, and interpret scientific explanations of the natural world; (2) generate and evaluate scientific evidence and explanations; (3) understand the nature and development of scientific knowledge; and (4) participate productively in scientific practices and discourse.

The expanded conceptualization of science proficiency has been associated with the fundamental view of scientific literacy, in which reading and writing are seen as necessary tools for achieving this expanded skill set (see, for example, Yore and Treagust 2006; Yore et al. 2004). In addition, whereas the 1990 *Science for All Americans* document described earlier largely defined scientific literacy in terms of possessing scientific knowledge about the natural world (NRC 1990), more recent standards and policy documents in science have attended more to the role of reading and writing in scientific literacy. The NRC's (2012, pp. 74–77) *Framework for K–12 Science Education* is even more explicit about the role of reading and writing as fundamental to the practice of science and engineering.

Literacy as a Tool for Scientific Inquiry

One key to navigating the historical divide between textbook and inquiry science is the appropriate positioning of reading and writing as tools for engaging in science inquiry, rather than as ends unto themselves. In a comprehensive survey about elementary science instruction, less than half the teachers reported that learning inquiry skills was a major objective of their classroom instruction and only about half of the teachers reported engaging students in firsthand experiences on a weekly basis (Fulp 2002). It is this kind of inattention to inquiry at the elementary level that has made inquiry-based science educators wary of increasing attention to reading and writing of texts in science. However, it is possible to use literacy instruction and activities in ways that increase and deepen students' involvement in inquiry. Literacy activity and instruction in science should engage children and youth in making sense of scientific texts in the service of inquiry informed by the ways that scientists' use reading and writing to inquire about natural phenomena. Although scientists often engage in unstructured explorations of the natural world, formal investigations are always framed by other investigations. No scientist simply walks into a lab and starts manipulating materials, tools, and phenomena. Scientists situate their work in that of other scientists, and they learn about the work of others largely through reading. Texts are the artifacts of past investigations and are used for inductive reasoning about scientific phenomena. Scientists use texts to generate questions that advance the design and enactment of new lines of investigation or to provide the background necessary for replication. Most scientists also write regularly to keep track of their investigations and, later, to go public with their work.

In light of the centrality of reading and writing to the work of inquiring in science, it is clear that the attempt to protect inquiry-based science from the incursion of text is both inauthentic and unproductive. Science instruction can engage children and youth in making sense of and producing scientific texts as an integral part of scientific inquiries. Both firsthand experiences and text-based work can be viewed as part of *investigations* when they are positioned as methods of answering meaningful scientific questions. In such contexts, literate practice is not simply the passive receipt of information about science, but rather a process of actively making meaning of science. When science literacy is conceptualized as a set of tools for inquiry and situated in

the context of ongoing investigations, children and youth can engage in authentic disciplinary practices such as

- reading to find out what other scientists know about a topic in order to formulate questions for investigation;

- reading to find evidence to support and/or refute their own or others' explanations with data;

- reading to learn about methods of inquiry that they can use in their own investigations;

- reading to gather information that can inform their investigations along the way;

- writing to document their methods, observations, and results;

- reading to follow curiosities that may someday lead to more formal investigations;

- reading to learn about how scientists think about the natural world, how they shape inquiries, and how they interpret evidence;

- writing to make sense of their results and wrestle with complicated ideas;

- engaging in discussions with colleagues (classmates) to plan and make sense of their investigations;

- writing to communicate their findings and connect their investigations to a wider world of scientific phenomena, knowledge, and research;

- engaging with public discourses on topics that concern science;

- reading and writing to imagine science identities and lives; and

- reading and writing as part of inquiries that address problems in their communities that concern science.

We want to emphasize that although reading is often privileged over writing in discussions of scientific literacy, constructing texts is as important as understanding them. Writing plays a critical role in documenting investigations, and it is a critical tool of sense-making and communication. Curwen et al. (2010) report on a professional development program designed to help teachers use the Read-Write Cycle to develop students' metacognition in science. Teachers engaged third-through fifth-grade students in learning about and using a variety of reading comprehension strategies in their science and in using graphic representation and writing to organize their ideas about the content after reading. The students also used writing to synthesize and reorganize their knowledge over time. Teachers involved in a design experiment reported that students who participated in the project became more deliberate and conscious as they approached the cognitive demands of content area texts and were better able to build conceptual generalizations across texts.

In addition to supporting the development of science understandings within and across texts and firsthand experiences, producing one's own representations (e.g., in notebooks, diagrams, charts, and reports for others to read) helps students understand how and why scientists think and write the way they do (Miller and Calfee 2004). For example, in work with middle and high school youth in Detroit (Moje et al. 2004), teachers regularly ask students to evaluate whether their written representations refer back to the hypotheses they made, whether they made the data evident, and whether they have provided valid reasoning to support their claims.

When students have to defend their claims to one another, they begin to recognize the value of clear and explicit representations of what they found (Osborne 2010).

Science as a Site for Enhancing Literacy

The most important reason to engage with a more fundamental perspective on scientific literacy is that it is a better reflection of scientific practice than either the memorization of scientific facts or firsthand inquiry alone. It is also important to note, however, that such a view also represents a significant advance for literacy learning. Just as literacy tools and artifacts can enhance the acquisition of knowledge and inquiry in science, so too can science provide an ideal context for acquiring and refining literacy tools.

For decades reading instruction was grounded in a "generalist notion of reading" (Shanahan and Shanahan 2008, p. 41). In a generalist view, reading is understood as a set of skills that can be applied to different texts for different purposes. The implicit assumption in this view is that students who are taught to read texts (mainly narratives) that they encounter in basal readers will later fluidly transfer their reading skills to content-area texts. This view has been called into question—particularly in recent years—by reading educators who, motivated in part by a robust body of research that indicates that reading comprehension is shaped by literacy experiences with particular text genres, disciplines, and discourses, have expressed concern that the emphasis on fictional literature to the exclusion of nonfiction text genres has failed to prepare students for the texts and tests of later schooling (Alvermann 1991; Alvermann, Moore, and Conley 1987; Herber 1978; RAND Reading Study Group 2002; Santa and Alvermann 1991). Those who study the use of informational text have argued that the balance of texts in early reading should better reflect the balance of texts that students will encounter in later grades and in their lives outside of school—contexts dominated by nonfiction text genres (e.g., Duke and Bennett-Armistead 2003). Several recent reports on reading and adolescent literacy have also called this generalist view of reading into question, arguing for more attention to text- and discipline-specific reading practices (e.g., Alliance for Excellent Education 2010; Heller and Greenleaf 2007; RAND Reading Study Group 2002). These reports point to the need not only to get started early with discipline-specific reading and writing but also to continue to support students' development of literacy skills beyond the early elementary years. The emphasis here is not simply about helping students decode or comprehend content-area textbooks; it is about supporting students in learning to read and write in ways that will specifically foster involvement in disciplinary learning (Carnegie Council on Advancing Adolescent Literacy 2010; NGAC and CCSSO 2010; Lee and Spratley 2010).

Several scholars (e.g., Duke 2000; Moje 2007; Schoenbach and Greenleaf 2009; Shanahan and Shanahan 2008) have argued that without systematic attention to reading and writing within subjects like science and history, students will leave schools with an impoverished sense of what it means to use the tools of literacy for learning or even to reason within various disciplines (see *CCSS ELA's* focus on informational texts in its standards for ELA and Literacy in History/Social Studies, Science and Technical Subjects). Science provides a setting in which students are intellectually obligated to draw inferences, construct arguments based on evidence, infer word meanings, construct meaning from text, and use their reading and writing from within and across texts

to make sense of observations in the world—the very skills required as good readers and writers. Students fine-tune their literacy tools not only when they read and write science texts but also when they engage in science investigations precisely because so many of the sense-making tools of science are consistent with, if not identical to, those of literacy (Goldman and Bisanz 2002).

In spite of the many calls to begin instruction with disciplinary literacies in the elementary years, there are some significant obstacles. Perhaps the most significant obstacle to the development of scientific literacy in the early years of schooling is the scarcity of any form of science teaching at the elementary level. Elementary students too often are excluded from developing scientific literacy in *either* the derived or fundamental senses. The status of science teaching in elementary classrooms has been severely influenced by the zeal with which the No Child Left Behind (NCLB) initiative promoted reading and math over science and other subjects, leaving precious little time for science (McMurrer 2008; Tugel 2004). This has changed the landscape of the school day, prompting some educators to suggest that elementary science has fallen into a "quiet crisis" (Feller 2004; Toppo 2004). Even before changes to elementary classrooms prompted in part by NCLB legislation, elementary teachers devoted an average of less than two hours per week of instructional time to science (Fulp 2002). And there were indications that time devoted to science was declining. In a large-scale survey study of the impact of NCLB on elementary classroom instruction, 29% of the districts surveyed reported that they had reduced instructional time devoted to science in order to allocate more time to reading and mathematics (Rentner et al 2006). A 2008 national survey revealed that a majority of elementary schools decreased the time allotted to science by 15 minutes per day whereas time for reading and math was increased by a like amount (McMurrer 2008). In a study of teachers in Northern California, Dorph and colleagues (2007) found that 80% of the 923 elementary teachers surveyed reported that they spent less than one hour per week teaching science.

The renewed emphasis on language arts and mathematics and the onset of yearly, multiple-choice testing in those subject areas make it difficult for schools to promote science teaching at all, much less inquiry-based teaching. The science assessments that have been added to the state assessment batteries at the elementary level, like the literacy assessments before them, are multiple-choice tests that privilege the assessment of facts over concepts or knowledge frameworks. The combination of high stakes (rewards and sanctions based on performance) and low intellectual challenge (the factual character of the vast majority of test items) will compel teachers to eschew deep inquiry in favor of content coverage (Weiss et al. 2003). As a result, *the status of science instruction at the elementary level should be a major concern for all literacy and science educators*. If we want to make progress toward the goal of scientific literacy for college, career, and citizenship, we need to start earlier, when students' curiosities about the natural world are first ignited.

Getting Started Early

While there are still many impediments to increasing attention to literacy in middle and high school science classrooms, secondary science initiatives are beginning to attend to fundamental scientific literacy development for adolescents. Recent policy initiatives have supported interventions for struggling reading and efforts to develop the ability of secondary teachers to support students' literacy development (Moje 2008). However, few science educators, literacy researchers, policy makers, or practitioners are attending to the development of fundamental scientific literacy for elementary students, though there is ample evidence that they should.

In this section, we will describe several programs of instruction that enable students to get started early in school with scientific literacy. We will focus mainly on the instructional routines employed in each, though it is important to note that all of these programs come with the virtue of having experimental evidence of their efficacy in supporting students' learning in both literacy and science. The instructional programs described below share key ingredients: They are embedded in inquiry-based science instruction and are driven by significant questions about the natural world; they engage learners in using text and firsthand experiences to answer these questions; and they provide explicit instruction in the reading and/or writing of science texts in the context of these investigations.

Concept-Oriented Reading Instruction (CORI: *www.cori.umd.edu*)

For more than 20 years, Guthrie and colleagues have been refining and studying CORI, an elementary-level program designed to promote a number of literacy goals through the use of broad interdisciplinary themes (Guthrie and Ozgungor 2002), primarily drawn from science curricula, such as exploring the impact of humans on animal habitats. CORI instruction begins with content knowledge goals within a conceptual theme. Firsthand experiences related to the theme are typically used to generate interest in the topic. Students generate questions about the theme and use reading and firsthand investigations to answer their questions. As students engage in these investigations, CORI teachers provide explicit instruction in reading strategies, such as questioning, activating background knowledge, searching for information, summarizing, and synthesizing information in order to communicate with others. One goal of the CORI program is for students to experience how the information they obtain from firsthand activities and the information they acquire from reading can work together to deepen their understanding of a science topic (Guthrie 2001; Wigfield et al. 2004). For example, during a unit about how animals survive in different environments, CORI students dissect owl pellets to learn what owls eat. As they do this, the teacher encourages them to ask questions about owls and other birds. The students record their questions in their science journals and seek out books to help answer the questions. As students engage with the texts, the teacher explains how the features of informational books—such as indices and headings—can help them find answers to their questions. The teacher guides students to understand the organization of the text at the paragraph level, as well, explaining that paragraphs in informational texts often begin with a general principle and then provide details and examples. Students share their questions and answers as a class, and the teacher helps the students form links back to the theme of survival in different environments.

Of particular interest in the CORI program is the pivotal role of motivation supports, such as student choice (about tasks and texts) and collaboration (sharing questions, texts, and information), in advancing students' learning in both science and literacy. CORI has been shown to increase students' concept learning in science, their reading motivation, their use of productive inquiry strategies, and their overall text comprehension compared to control classrooms with separate science and literacy instruction (Guthrie et al. 2004).

Guided Inquiry Supporting Multiple Literacies (GIsML: *www.umich. edu/~gisml*)

Palincsar and Magnusson (2001) engaged in a multiyear program of research on the ways that hands-on (firsthand) experiences and text-based (secondhand) experiences can together support students' conceptual understandings and scientific reasoning. In GIsML professional development, elementary teachers learn to engage students in cycles of investigation guided by specific conceptual questions, establishing the classroom as a community of inquiry. GIsML emphasizes sustained involvement in investigations of significant questions in science—e.g., What influences the motion of a ball down a ramp? How does light interact with objects? What changes make sounds different? (Palincsar and Magnusson 2002a, 2002b, 2002c). Within an investigation, students engage in an inquiry sequence in which they prepare to investigate, collect, and analyze data, prepare to report their findings, and report (Hapgood, Magnusson, and Palincsar 2004). The investigations combine firsthand explorations of the natural world with secondhand experiences through the use of a fictional working scientist's notebooks. The notebook texts, which include exposition, narration, and representations of data, are a kind of think-aloud by a scientist as she engages in her own investigation of the guiding questions (Hapgood, Magnusson, and Palincsar 2004). After students investigate scientific questions firsthand, they consult text to learn how the scientist has interpreted similar evidence. The notebooks engage students in interpreting data along with the scientist and inform students' answers to the guiding questions by adding confirming evidence, new ideas, and, sometimes, contradictory evidence that students must reconcile with their own observations. Students use discussion and further investigation to make sense of similarities and differences. The texts also model a scientist using secondhand materials, reading and interpreting with a critical stance, and drawing conclusions from multiple sources of evidence. The notebook texts provide many opportunities to engage with different kinds of representations of data, such as tables and diagrams. In one GIsML unit described by Hapgood et al., second graders investigated factors that influence the motion of an object on an inclined plane. In this unit, the scientist's notebook text took the form of a big book. The book described how the fictional scientist, Lesley Park, came to wonder about motion through her experiences in the world and how she followed up her wonderings with investigations using ramps and balls. The students were encouraged to engage with the text in a highly interactive manner, making predictions and claims, critiquing the scientist's reasoning, and using Lesley's tests as a model for their own firsthand investigations. Over the course of the unit, which involved the reading of two scientists' notebooks and engaging in several firsthand experiences, students developed important skills of scientific literacy, including interpreting firsthand and secondhand data and leveraging those data as evidence and making sense of multiple forms of representation. In a separate quasi-experiment comparing fourth graders studying light in either a GIsML or a "considerate text" (i.e., especially well-written, cohesive text) treatment, GIsML researchers found that students learned more in the GIsML instruction than in the considerate text condition, concluding that the notebooks promoted talk that led to greater engagement and, ultimately, improved understanding (Palincsar and Magnusson 2001).

In-Depth Expanded Applications of Science (Science IDEAS)

Romance and Vitale (1992, 2001) developed the IDEAS model of integrated science and language instruction for elementary students which replaces the time allocated for traditional literacy instruction with a two-hour block of science that includes literacy skills. The science instruction is concept-focused and involves firsthand experiences, attention to science-process skills, discussion, reading comprehension, concept mapping, and journal writing. Particularly notable in the Science IDEAS model is the planning process that teachers use to create IDEAS units. The teacher begins by creating a concept map around a core science concept, such as evaporation (see *http://cmap.ihmc. us* for free CMap program). Often, the teacher will write ideas related to the key concept on sticky notes and move them around until they form a network of related ideas. The resulting concept map serves as the blueprint for the design of the unit. The teacher uses the concept maps to plan instructional experiences, taking into account what the students know and how the concepts connect to students' everyday experiences. IDEAS teachers annotate the concept map with ideas for firsthand investigation, writing opportunities, and reading opportunities—all in the interest of building students' conceptual understanding. For example, in an evaporation unit, students might learn that heat is a factor in speeding up evaporation by observing that a wet paper towel placed near a heat source will dry more quickly than a paper towel placed away from the heat. The students might write in their journals throughout the unit, documenting the results of their firsthand investigations, and explaining how each of the firsthand experiments helped them understand something new about evaporation. Students might read a text to learn more about the process of evaporation at the molecular level, engaging in a careful sentence-by-sentence discussion of the ideas and of how the text communicates those ideas. The students might reorganize ideas from text using manipulable concept maps. In doing so, they come to better understand both the organization of the concepts and the ways that concepts are encoded—and can be decoded—in science text. Several multiyear efforts with students in grades 1–5 show that Science IDEAS students outperform students receiving segregated language arts and science instruction on standardized reading and science tests.

Seeds of Science/Roots of Reading (Seeds/Roots: *www. scienceandliteracy.org*)

Seeds/Roots (see Cervetti et al. 2006) began as an attempt to embed inquiry-oriented reading, writing, and language activities within the already successful Great Explorations in Math and Science (GEMS) K–8 inquiry-based science program. The program is based on the fundamental principle that reading, writing, and discourse are best enacted in science as tools of inquiry. Students use firsthand experiences, reading, writing, and discussion to answer meaningful science questions. For example, in one unit about light for third and fourth graders, students investigate the question, "How does light interact with different materials?" by

- investigating with flashlights and materials;

- using their growing knowledge of text features to search a reference book with data on light's interactions with other materials;

- recording their evidence from both firsthand and text sources; and

- engaging in discussions about their evidence.

As they engage in this investigation, they also read a book about why communication among scientists in general and disagreement in particular are important for moving science ahead. In another unit, students conduct an inquiry into the best ingredients to use in designing a mixture that will serve as glue. As they conduct their hands-on investigation, they read a book entitled *Jess Makes Hair Gel*, in which the protagonist demonstrates stamina and persistence in trying to find the right set of ingredients to make hair gel to control his unruly hair. The lesson they take away from the reading (you have to be systematic and persistent when you are engaged in design research) applies directly to their ongoing glue-making investigation. They also encounter "models" of how to record their ongoing methods and observations; those skills will prove useful in completing their unit assignment.

Across two experiments comparing Seeds/Roots with a content-controlled inquiry science comparison group, the curriculum-based Seeds/Roots program demonstrated advantages on measures of science understanding and vocabulary acquisition, with a less consistent advantage for reading comprehension for students in grades 2–4 (Cervetti et al. forthcoming; Wang and Herman 2005). In the more recent of these studies, fourth-grade students using the Seeds/Roots curriculum also made significantly greater gains in their science writing than did students in a control condition.

Lessons From Adolescent Programs

It is no secret that much more work has been completed on issues of integration in middle and high schools than in elementary, if for no other reason than there is much more science curriculum and pedagogy available in those settings. And there are lessons to be learned—or at least hypotheses to be tested empirically—for those of us in elementary science and literacy. For example, Greenleaf and colleagues at the Strategic Literacy Initiative at WestEd have been developing models of discipline-based literacy instruction and professional development (under the rubric of Reading Apprenticeship) to foster more engaged academic learning for underprepared students in secondary and post-secondary settings (Greenleaf, Brown, and Litman 2004). In this apprenticeship model, science teachers inquire deeply into what they do as readers and thinkers to derive meaning with complex science texts of varied kinds—including science explanation and exposition in scholarly journals as well as the diagrams, data arrays, mathematical expressions, and graphs that convey information. Teachers then learn classroom routines for engaging students in active inquiry and sense-making with such texts: routines for modeling and mentoring students in productive reasoning processes; fostering metacognitive awareness of comprehension problems and problem-solving processes; and for promoting collaborative discussions of science texts. A second example of an adolescent program that can inform fundamental scientific literacy instruction at the elementary level is the work of Moje and her colleagues with middle and high school youth in Detroit (Moje et al. 2004; Sutherland et al. 2003; Textual Tools Study Group 2006). Teachers involved in the project engage students in reading both scientific and lay-audience texts related to phenomena under study. The teachers also engage students in translating across multiple forms of representation, particularly as they gather data and formulate explanations to communicate their findings. When writing explanations from scientific investigations, students engage in peer review to evaluate whether their written explanations refer back to the hypotheses

they made, to what extent they made the data evident, and the quality of reasoning they have provided for their claims. Writing in this way supports students in developing stronger science conceptual knowledge and better scientific explanations.

Summary

This body of evidence demonstrates the promise of approaches to literacy and science instruction that are integrated in the service of inquiry, showing that it is possible to improve the instructional quality of both science and literacy teaching and learning. We are encouraged by the fact that other groups have found similar results (e.g., Anderson et al. 1997; Miller and Calfee 2004; Gomez and Gomez 2007; Pappas et al. 2002) documenting the efficacy of text and literacy activity within science curricula.

Planning Instruction That Supports Fundamental Scientific Literacy

Increasingly, there are published curricula designed to support elementary students' development of scientific literacy. However, it is also possible to get started without the support of a comprehensive integrated curriculum. In this section, we outline a planning process that you might use to infuse an existing inquiry-based program with opportunities for scientific literacy development, using examples from a gravity unit.

1. Begin by mapping the inquiry-based science unit's goals and inquiry experiences in a list or a concept map. A map for a weeklong unit on gravity might look something like what is shown in Figure 10.1.

2. Look through the unit's inquiry experiences and associate each with concepts in the map.

FIGURE 10.1. INQUIRY-BASED WEEKLONG SCIENCE UNIT MAP ON GRAVITY

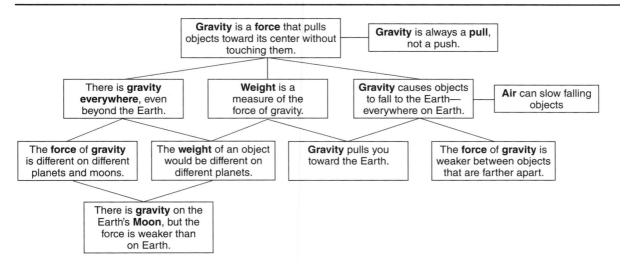

For example, in order to understand how weight and gravity are related, the unit might follow a period of open exploration with an activity in which students investigate the question, "Is there gravity on the Moon?" by engaging in activities such as weighing different objects and using an internet-based calculator to figure out how much these same objects would weigh on the Moon (*www.exploratorium.edu/ronh/weight*). Try to ensure that every concept on the map is associated with firsthand experiences and that students have several opportunities with more extended inquiries in which they pose a question, gather evidence, and make sense of the evidence. You may wish to use web resources to augment your unit. NASA offers many resources for teachers and students, including the following sites.

- *www.nasa.gov/audience/foreducators/ topnav/materials/listbytype/ Gravity_on_Earth_Versus.html*

- *www.nasa.gov/audience/forstudents/k-4/ stories/what-is-microgravity-k4.html*

- *www.nasa.gov/audience/foreducators/ topnav/materials/listbytype/Why_Do_ Astronauts_Float.html*

- *www.nasa.gov/audience/foreducators/ topnav/materials/listbytype/The_Con- stant_Pull_of_Gravity.html*

- *www.nasa.gov/audience/foreducators/ microgravity/home/toys-in-space.html*

3. Review your grade-level science standards and augment the unit's goals so that it includes attention to science concepts, science inquiry skills, and understandings about the nature of science. For example, the gravity unit might include goals such as observing and formulating questions based on observations, comparing and contrasting, and understanding that science knowledge is based on evidence. Identify opportunities in

the unit to develop each of these skills and understandings. For example, as students read and engage in firsthand investigations, record evidence for key questions, such as "Does gravity pull on all objects with the same force?" on chart paper. Point out to students that scientists also gather evidence from different sources to answer important questions and build scientific knowledge.

4. Next, ask yourself, "How might reading and writing be used in ways that support students' involvement in this unit?" For example, students might benefit from reading about how scientists set up fair tests and observe systematically over time. Their investigations may also be enhanced by attention to writing about observations and augmenting observations with illustrations. If you think your students will struggle with the concept of gravity as an invisible force, they may benefit from the explanations and images that a trade text like *Gravity Is a Mystery* by Branley and Miller offer. Make a list of these potential opportunities.

5. Look through your English language arts standards for learning goals that support your work in the unit (and look to *CCSS ELA/Literacy Connections* feature of the *Next Generation Science Standards*). For example, the ELA standards from the *Common Core State Standards* (*CCSS*) include many goals that can be supported through integration with an inquiry-based science unit, including goals related to integrating information gained from reading two or more texts, taking notes, organizing information, and writing explanations. You might also include goals related to students' use of informational text features, such as headings, glossaries, and images. Look through your unit map with

an eye to opportunities to infuse reading, writing, and talking. Add these experiences to your unit map.

6. Begin to identify science trade texts that fit with the themes of the unit. Look for texts that provide insight into the dispositions and processes of science (e.g., scientist biographies and discover narratives), as well as books that explain and illustrate science concepts. The following articles and National Science Teachers Association (NSTA) website offer lists of excellent science trade books on a wide variety of topics.

   ◆ Bircher, L. S. 2009. Reading aloud: A springboard to inquiry. *Science Teacher* 76 (5): 29–33.

   ◆ Brassell, D. 2006. Inspiring young scientists with great books. *Reading Teacher* 60 (4): 336–342.

   ◆ Morrison, J. A., and T. A. Young. 2008. Using science trade books to support inquiry in the elementary classroom. *Childhood Education* 84 (4): 204.

   ◆ NSTA Outstanding Science Trade Books: *www.nsta.org/publications/ostb*

7. Read and reflect on what you do to make sense of the reading materials you collect. Think about how you can model and mentor students in these same reading and reasoning processes. How can you share strategies for recording observations, overcoming the obstacle of unknown words in texts, or quickly determining whether a text will help answer a particular question?

8. Develop assessments that will help you track students' progress toward the unit's goals.

Moving Forward

The path toward greater proficiency in science reading, writing, and inquiry for all students will necessarily travel through the classrooms of knowledgeable teachers who understand the vital role literacy plays in enhancing rather than replacing science learning and who can mentor their students in these practices. Teacher knowledge is the key to advancing student achievement. A number of programs are changing the ways that teachers are prepared and changing the instructional materials that are available to practicing teachers to invite stronger attention to language and literacy in science. Many of the efforts we describe in this section are situated in secondary education, but the insights gained from these programs are applicable to teachers across the K–12 spectrum.

Initial Teacher Preparation

Initial teacher preparation has often virtually guaranteed isolation between literacy and science instruction by teaching literacy methods and science methods separately. Moje and colleagues (Bain and Moje 2012; Moje and Bain 2011) have redesigned the secondary teacher education program at the University of Michigan to focus on building new teachers' understanding of the disciplinary practices supported by reading, writing, and reasoning, rather than treating literacy methods as a separate subject for teachers preparing to teach science or any other secondary school discipline. This redesign has afforded the opportunity for teaching interns to examine the texts of science, to plan instruction that integrates complex uses of text into inquiry, and to learn how to teach young people how to think, read, and write like scientists so that they can either pursue additional science training or act as responsible citizens in a world shaped by scientific decisions.

Persuaded by the argument that such attention to the role of language and literacy in the disciplines should begin at the earliest levels of instruction, the university also recently funded the hiring of a cluster of elementary-level subject-area scholars who specialize in literacy instruction integrated into science and social studies.

Other projects to reconceive the approach to literacy instruction in teacher preparation programs are noteworthy. For example, Donahue (2003) and Braunger and colleagues (2004) describe a discipline-centered approach to courses for literacy methods, required for secondary teaching credentials. In dramatic contrast to traditional teacher preparation courses that maintain separate offerings for science and literacy teaching methods and offer literacy methods as a set of instructional strategies to help students access science content from texts, literacy in these programs is promoted as a tool for active, inquiry-based science learning that can support students in acquiring science understandings and reasoning processes and a deeper appreciation for the nature of science investigation and knowledge.

Ongoing Professional Development

Because teaching is a professional enterprise, teachers continue to develop knowledge and craft of the profession as they teach, in part through their association with science colleagues or professional organizations, and in part through professional learning opportunities such as seminars and institutes. Although professional offerings available to learn new science content and approaches to inquiry abound, opportunities to learn to support students' development of science reading and writing skills and strategies are slim. Greenleaf and colleagues (e.g., Greenleaf and Schoenbach 2004) offer a model of what such professional development opportunities might look like. They have developed programs specifically designed to support teachers in developing more robust conceptions of science reading and its role in learning.

Merely teaching science teachers a collection of literacy strategies does not help and may actually hurt. Instead, teaching literacy in scientifically specific ways requires conceptual change for teachers. The challenge facing professional developers is to help teachers move to new ways of thinking and acting in the classroom to promote deep thinking and reasoning around texts and investigations and to learn to implement instructional routines that support scientific reasoning no matter the data of classroom reasoning—text or phenomenon or investigation.

Promoting deep thinking and reasoning among teachers (and their students) is facilitated when professional development appropriates inquiry processes, making the literacy and science connection and reasoning processes of inquiry themselves the object of ongoing professional inquiry. Central questions driving these professional inquiries for teachers include the following.

- For what purposes do scientists read and write?

- What counts as text in science?

- What do we know and do as skillful readers and writers of scientific texts?

- How can we make this knowledge and these processes apparent to our students?

- How can we provide students with opportunities to practice and the mentoring and guidance they need to acquire these vital science literacy proficiencies?

By taking an inquiry stance as they investigate their own science literacy practices, teachers can simultaneously develop the insights and pedagogical moves they will need to mentor their students. A recent study affirms that these kinds of carefully designed learning opportunities for teachers can and do translate into increased achievement for students (Greenleaf et al. 2011).

One common misconception secondary science teachers hold about reading originates in the "expert blind spot" phenomena. Because these teachers are themselves disciplinary experts, instructional texts meant for students hold no mysteries or challenges for them. The ease with which science teachers are able to comprehend traditional science textbooks blinds them to the difficulties students may have. But when such teachers have an opportunity to dig into science writing that poses challenges for them, they begin to see that reading complex science text is neither automatic nor straightforward. Challenging texts require even knowledgeable science readers to put into play their many skillful problem-solving strategies, to marshal stamina and effort for the undertaking, and to maintain a high level of self-motivation to stay with the task in order to gain new understandings (their first love). Teachers emerge from such engagements with new eyes for the challenges their students face with science texts, as well as a deeper appreciation of their own capabilities as science readers, capabilities they realize they can help their students gain. Teachers who undergo this experience as temporarily "disabled" also begin to recognize how poorly many of our textbooks represent authentic reading and writing about science (Schoenbach and Greenleaf 2009) and how difficult it would be for their ELA colleagues to assume responsibility for mentoring and engaging students in the rigors and rewards of science reading. As developers of such programs of teacher preparation, Greenleaf and her colleagues have found that science teachers who are inquiry oriented can take up the text as another data source to investigate the natural world. Conversely, for science teachers who are text oriented, learning to carry out text investigations becomes a way into science reasoning and inquiry. Integrating science and literacy can thus be a back door into inquiry approaches for teachers who are not already inquiry-based science teachers. Such opportunities to investigate science literacy practices need to be made available to teachers on a broad scale.

Curriculum Development

In the past 30 years, policy makers, practitioners, and researchers have launched many inspired efforts to fundamentally reform K–12 science education with a focus on investigation and inquiry in keeping with the nature of science knowledge and activity. However, in these efforts, the quality of and role of reading and writing in inquiry are often overlooked, with primary attention placed on shaping hands-on investigations for students that will result in strong conceptual understanding. As discussed earlier, most of the NSF-funded, inquiry-based programs included little student reading material, perhaps as a reaction to the dominance of mainly textbook-based science instruction. It is clear, however, that a new movement is underway. An increasing number of inquiry-based science programs for elementary students are introducing the use of texts in the form of science "readers" and science "notebooking"—including many NSF-supported inquiry-based curricula (e.g., Lawrence Hall of Science n.d.; National Science Resource Center n.d.). These materials are grounded in the understanding that science learning entails and benefits from embedded literacy activities and that literacy learning

entails and benefits from being embedded within science inquiry. Further, some new curricula are designed to be educative for teachers, providing resources to learn needed science content, literacy practices, and pedagogies that support student learning (Cervetti et al. forthcoming). Cervetti, Pearson, and their colleagues at the University of California, Berkeley, have developed a curriculum—Seeds of Science/Roots of Reading—for elementary grades that intertwines science and literacy learning. Seeds/Roots is driven by learning goals in science, including understanding science concepts, the nature of science, and inquiry, and by goals in literacy, such as understanding and using science text to support inquiry at every step of the inquiry cycle.

Similarly, Greenleaf and colleagues have developed discipline-based inquiry units to support ninth-grade struggling readers to develop academic literacy proficiencies that explicitly model and support the ways of reading and reasoning vital to science learning and understanding. In a 10-week unit designed to mentor and engage students in science reading and reasoning processes, students investigate the factors contributing to the epidemic increase in obesity and diabetes among American youth and ways to reverse these alarming trends. As they investigate these factors, students learn how to make sense of varied science representations—data tables, demographic statistics, nutrition labels, diagrams of the digestive and endocrine systems, graphics such as the varied food pyramids produced by the CDC over time, timelines and maps. They use a broad set of texts including textbook excerpts, science reporting in the national media, monographs from the Centers for Disease Control (CDC) and Department of Agriculture, authoritative websites from universities, NSF, and health commissions, learning to approach these texts critically as well as scientifically. As students investigate questions about risk factors related to diabetes and obesity, they keep their own diet and exercise journals, reflecting on how these factors relate to their own health and that of their family and friends, and how science understanding and literacy can affect people's ability to take charge of their own health.

Assessment

Finally, it is important to note that all the professional development in the world will have little impact if we cannot also create more balanced assessment portfolios for our accountability systems (NAE 2009). The inclusion of challenging performance tasks—tasks that involve extended inquiry (over several days), analysis of findings, and public reports of student work—would help to promote the very sort of inquiry that research documents as effective. As long as single-answer multiple-choice tests serve as the primary metric for measuring student learning and teacher quality, not only in science but in literacy as well, it will be difficult for teachers to take the risk of promoting genuine inquiry in their classes.

Inquiry as the Common Core

As a final point, we emphasize that all of our suggestions for moving ahead are really suggestions for making inquiry the common theme of reform. Teacher learning is most profound when teachers can employ the very same inquiry processes for their own professional learning that they aspire to enact with their students. By making their own learning about literacy and science pedagogy the object of inquiry, teachers can simultaneously develop the insights and pedagogical strategies they will need to mentor their students. Scientific literacy instruction of the sort supported by empirical research requires that the dispositions and practices of inquiry-based science be appropriated for inquiry in reading and writing. And finally, we must reshape our assessment systems to better reflect the nature and goals of inquiry oriented instruction in both science and literacy. If we can manage all of these initiatives, we might be able to help teachers situate literacy and science each in the service of the other as students gain tools and proficiency in both. The agenda is surely daunting, but the costs of avoiding it are high and the rewards for pursuing it are substantial.

References

Alliance for Excellent Education. 2010. *Policy brief: The federal role in confronting the crisis in adolescent literacy.* Washington, DC: Alliance for Excellent Education. *www.all4ed.org/files/ FedRoleConfrontingAdolLit.pdf.*

Alvermann, D. E. 1991. Secondary school reading. In *Handbook of reading research*, ed. R. Barr, M. L. Kamil, P. B. Mosenthal, and P. D. Pearson, 951–983. New York: Longman.

Alvermann, D. E., D. W. Moore, and M. W. Conley. 1987. *Research within reach: Secondary school reading.* Newark, DE: International Reading Association.

Anderson, R. 2002. Reforming science teaching: What research says about inquiry. *Journal of Science Teacher Education* 13 (1): 1–2.

Anderson, T. H., C. K. West, D. P. Beck, E. S. Macdonell, and D. S. Frisbie. 1997. Integrating reading and science education: On developing and evaluating WEE Science. *Journal of Curriculum Studies* 29 (6): 711–733.

Bain, R. B., and E. B. Moje. 2012. Mapping the teacher education terrain for novices. *Phi Delta Kappan* 93 (5): 62–65.

Bransford, J. D., A. L. Brown, and R. R. Cocking, eds. 2000. *How people learn: Brain, mind, experience, and school*. Washington, DC: National Academies Press.

Braunger, J., D. Donahue, K. Evans, and T. Galguera. 2004. *Rethinking preparation for content area teaching: The reading apprenticeship approach*. San Francisco: Jossey Bass.

Brown, A. L., and J. C. Campione. 1994. Guided discovery in a community of learners. In *Classroom lessons: Integrating cognitive theory and classroom practice*, ed. K. McGilly. Cambridge, MA: MIT Press.

Bybee, R. 1997. *The Sputnik era: Why is this educational reform different from all other reforms?* Paper presented at the symposium reflecting on Sputnik: Linking the Past, Present, and Future of Educational Reform. Washington, DC. October. *www.nationalacademies.org/sputnik/bybee1.htm*

Carnegie Council on Advancing Adolescent Literacy. 2010. *Time to act: An agenda for advancing literacy for college and career success*. New York: Carnegie Corporation of New York.

Cervetti, G. N., J. Barber, R. Dorph, P. D. Pearson, and P. Goldschmidt. Forthcoming. Integrating science and literacy: A value proposition? *Journal of Research in Science Teaching.*

Cervetti, G. N., P. D. Pearson, M. A. Bravo, and J. Barber. 2006. Reading and writing in the service of inquiry-based science. In *Linking science and literacy in the K–8 classroom*, ed. R. Douglas and K. Worth, 199–221. Arlington, VA: NSTA Press.

Concept-Oriented Reading Instruction (CORI). *www.cori.umd.edu.*

Curwen, M. S., R. G. Miller, K. A. White-Smith, and R. C. Calfee. 2010. Increasing teachers' metacognition develops students' higher learning during content area literacy instruction: Findings from the Read-Write Cycle Project. *Issues in Teacher Education* 19 (2): 127–151.

Donahue, D. 2003. Reading across the great divide: English and math teachers apprentice one another as readers and disciplinary insiders. *Journal of Adolescent and Adult Literacy* 47 (1): 24–37.

Dorph, R., D. Goldstein, S. Lee, K. Lepori, S. Schneider, and S. Venkatesan. 2007. *The status of science education in the Bay Area*. Berkeley, CA: Lawrence Hall of Science, University of California, Berkeley.

Duke, N. K. 2000. 3.6 minutes per day: The scarcity of informational texts in first grade. *Reading Research Quarterly* 35 (2): 202–224.

Duke, N. K., and V. W. Bennett-Armistead, eds. 2003. *Reading and writing informational text in the primary grades: Research-based practices*. New York: Scholastic.

Duschl, R. A., H. A. Schweingruber, and A. W. Shouse, eds. 2007. *Taking science to school: Learning and teaching science in grades K–8*. Washington, DC: National Academies Press.

Feller, B. *The Boston Globe*. 2004. Teachers Concerned for Science Education. July 5.

Fulp, S. L. 2002. *2000 national survey of science and mathematics education: Status of elementary school science teaching*. Chapel Hill, NC: Horizon Research.

Goldman, S. R., and G. Bisanz. 2002. Toward a functional analysis of scientific genres: Implications for understanding and learning processes. In *The psychology of science text comprehension*, ed. J. Otero, J. A. Leon, and A. C. Graesser, 19–50. Mahwah, NJ: Lawrence Erlbaum Associates.

Gomez, L., and K. Gomez. 2007. Reading for learning: Literacy supports for 21st century work. *Phi Delta Kappan* 89 (3): 224–228.

Greenleaf, C., and R. Schoenbach. 2004. Building capacity for the responsive teaching of reading in the academic disciplines: Strategic inquiry designs for middle and high school teachers' professional development. In *Improving reading* achievement through professional development, ed. D. S. Strickland and M. L. Kamil, 97–127. Norwood, MA: Christopher-Gordon Publishers.

Greenleaf, C., W. Brown, and C. Litman. 2004. Apprenticing urban youth to science literacy. In *Bridging the gap: Improving literacy learning for preadolescent and adolescent learners in grades 4–12*, ed. D. S. Strickland and D. E. Alvermann, 200–226. Newark, NJ: International Reading Association.

Greenleaf, C., C. Litman, T. L. Hanson, R. Rosen, C. K. Boscardin, J. Herman, S. A. Schneider, with S. Madden, and B. Jones. 2011. Integrating literacy and science in biology: Teaching and learning impacts of reading apprenticeship professional development. *American Educational Research Journal* 48 (3): 647–717.

Guided Inquiry Supporting Multiple Literacies (GIsML): www.umich.edu/~gisml.

Guthrie, J. T. 2001. Engagement and Motivation in Reading. Paper presented at the National Invitational Conference on Successful Reading Instruction, Washington, DC.

Guthrie, J. T., and S. Ozgungor. 2002. Instructional contexts for reading engagement. In *Comprehension instruction: Research-based best practices,* ed. C. Collins Block and M. Pressley, 275–288. New York: Guilford.

Guthrie, J. T., J. Wigfield, P. Barbosa, K. C. Perencevich, A. Taboada, M. H. Davis, N. T. Scafiddi, and S. Tonks. 2004. Increasing reading comprehension and engagement through concept-oriented reading instruction. *Journal of Educational Psychology* 96 (3): 403–423.

Hapgood, S., S. J. Magnusson, and A. S. Palincsar. 2004. Teacher, text, and experience: A case of young children's scientific inquiry. *The Journal of the Learning Sciences* 13 (4): 455–505.

Heller, R., and C. L. Greenleaf. 2007. *Literacy instruction in the content areas: Getting to the core of middle and high school improvement.* Washington, DC: Alliance for Excellent Education.

Herber, H. L. 1978. *Teaching reading in content areas.* 2nd ed. Englewood Cliffs, NJ: Prentice-Hall.

Lawrence Hall of Science. n.d. Foss Science Stories. Nashua, NH: Delta Education. *http://lhsfoss.org*.

Lee, C. D., and A. Spratley. 2010. *Reading in the disciplines and the challenges of adolescent literacy.* New York City: Carnegie Corporation of New York.

Mayr, E. 1942. *Systematics and the origin of species.* New York: Columbia University Press.

McMurrer, J. 2008. *Instructional time in elementary schools: A closer look at changes for specific subjects.* Washington, DC: Center for Education Policy. *www.cep-dc.org/index. cfm?fuseaction=document.showDocumentByID& nodeID=1&DocumentID=234*

Metz, K. E. 2000. Young children's inquiry in biology: Building the knowledge bases to empower independent inquiry. In *Inquiring into inquiry in science learning and teaching,* ed. J. Minstrell and E. van Zee, 371–404. Washington, DC: AAAS.

Miller, R. G., and R. C. Calfee. 2004. Making thinking visible: A method to encourage science writing in upper elementary grades. *Science and Children* 42 (3): 20–25.

Moje, E. B. 2007. Developing socially just subject-matter instruction: A review of the literature on disciplinary literacy. In *Review of research in education,* ed. L. Parker, 1–44. Washington, DC: American Educational Research Association.

Moje, E. B. 2008. Foregrounding the disciplines in secondary literacy teaching and learning: A call for change. *Journal of Adolescent and Adult Literacy* 52 (2): 96–107.

Moje, E. B., and R. B. Bain. 2011. *Restructuring teacher education for disciplinary literacy.* Paper presented at the annual meeting of the American Educational Research Association, New Orleans, LA.

Moje, E. B., D. Peek-Brown, L. M. Sutherland, R. W. Marx, P. Blumenfeld, and J. Krajcik. 2004. Explaining explanations: Developing scientific literacy in middle-school project-based science reforms. In *Bridging the gap: Improving literacy learning for preadolescent and adolescent learners in grades 4–12,* ed. D. Strickland and D. E. Alvermann, 227–251. New York: Carnegie Corporation.

National Academy of Education (NAE). 2009. *Standards, assessment, and accountability: Education Policy White Paper*. Washington, DC: NAE. *www.naeducation.org/Standards_ Assessments_Accountability_White_Paper.pdf*

National Governors Association Center for Best Practices (NGAC), and Council of Chief State School Officers (CCSSO). 2010. *Common Core State Standards*. Washington, DC: NGAC and CCSSO.

National Research Council (NRC). 1990. *Fulfilling the promise: Biology education in the nation's schools*. Washington, DC: National Academies Press.

National Research Council (NRC). 2000. *Inquiry and the national science education standards: A guide for teaching and learning.* Washington, DC: National Academies Press.

National Research Council (NRC). 2012. *A framework for K–12 science education: Practices, crosscutting concepts, and core ideas*. Washington, DC: National Academies Press.

National Science Resource Center. n.d. *Science and technology concepts program*. Washington, DC: National Academies Press.

No Child Left Behind Act of 2001. 20 U.S.C. § 6319 (2008).

Norris, S. P., and L. M. Phillips. 2002. How literacy in its fundamental sense is central to scientific literacy. *Science Education* 87: 224–240.

Osborne, J. 2010. Arguing to learn in science: The role of collaborative, critical discourse. *Science* 328 (5977): 463–466.

Palincsar, A. S., and S. J. Magnusson. 2001. The interplay of firsthand and text-based investigations to model and support the development of scientific knowledge and reasoning. In *Cognition and instruction: Twenty five years of progress,* ed. S. Carver and D. Klahr, 151–194. Mahwah, NJ: Lawrence Erlbaum.

Palincsar, A. S., and S. Magnusson. 2002a. *Light program of study—Interactions of light and objects overview*. Ann Arbor, MI: University of Michigan. *www.umich.edu/~gisml/light/pos-looverview.pdf*

Palincsar, A. S., and S. Magnusson. 2002b. *Motion (K–2) program of study plan*. Ann Arbor, MI: University of Michigan. *www.umich.edu/~gisml/ motionk-2/pos_plan.pdf*

Palincsar, A. S., and S. Magnusson. 2002c. *Sound program of study overview*. Ann Arbor, MI: University of Michigan. *www.umich.edu/~gisml/ sound/pos_overview.pdf*

Pappas, C. C., M. Varelas, A. Barry, and A. Rife. 2002. Dialogic inquiry around information texts: The role of intertextuality in constructing scientific understandings in urban primary classrooms. *Linguistics and Education* 13 (4): 435–482.

Pearson, P. D., E. B. Moje, and C. Greenleaf. 2010. Literacy and science: Each in the service of the other. *Science* 328 (5977): 459–463.

RAND Reading Study Group. 2002. *Reading for understanding*. Santa Monica, CA: RAND.

Rentner, D. S., C. Scott, N. Kober, N. Chudowsky, V. Chudowsky, S. Joftus, and D. Zabala. 2006. *From the capital to the classroom: Year 4 of the No Child Left Behind Act*. Washington, DC: Center for Education Policy.

Romance, N. R., and M. R. Vitale. 1992. A curriculum strategy that expands time for in-depth elementary science instruction by using science-based reading strategies: Effects of a year-long study in grade four. *Journal of Research in Science Teaching* 29 (6): 545–554.

Romance, N. R., and M. R. Vitale. 2001. Implementing an in-depth expanded science model in elementary schools: Multi-year findings, research issues, and policy implications. *International Journal of Science Education* 23 (4): 373–404.

Rutherford, F. J. 1964. The role of inquiry in science teaching. *Journal of Research in Science Teaching* 2 (2): 80–84.

Rutherford, F. J., and A. Ahlgren. 1989. *Science for all Americans.* New York: Oxford University Press. *www.project2061.org/publications/sfaa/default.htm.*

Santa, C., and D. E. Alvermann. 1991. *Science learning: Processes and applications.* Newark, DE: International Reading Association.

Schoenbach, R., and C. Greenleaf. 2009. Fostering adolescents' engaged academic literacy. In *Handbook of adolescent literacy research*, ed. L. Christenbury, R. Bomer, and P. Smagorinsky. New York: Guilford.

Seeds of Science/Roots of Reading. www. scienceandliteracy.org

Shanahan, T., and C. Shanahan. 2008. Teaching disciplinary literacy to adolescents: Rethinking content-area literacy. *Harvard Educational Review* 78 (1): 40–59.

Sutherland, L. M., E. B. Moje, R. W. Marx, P. Blumenfeld, J. Krajcik, and D. Peek-Brown. 2003. *Making scientific explanations: The development of scientific literacy in project-based science classrooms.* Paper presented at the National Reading Conference, Scottsdale, AZ. December.

Textual Tools Study Group. 2006. Developing scientific literacy through the use of literacy teaching strategies. In *Linking science and literacy in the*

K–8 classroom, ed. R. Douglas and K. Worth, 239–263. Arlington, VA: NSTA Press.

Toppo, G. *USA Today.* 2004. U.S. 8th-Graders Gain in Math, Science; 4th-Graders Weak. December 14.

Tugel, J. 2004. Time for science. *Alliance Access* 8 (2): 1–3.

Wang, J., and J. Herman. 2005. *Evaluation of seeds of science/roots of reading project: Shoreline Science and Terrarium Investigations.* Los Angeles: CRESST.

Weiss, I. R., J. D. Pasley, P. S. Smith, E. R. Banilower, and D. J. Heck. 2003. *Looking inside the classroom: A study of K–12 mathematics and science education in the United States.* Chapel Hill, NC: Horizon Research.

Wigfield, A., J. T. Guthrie, S. Tonks, and K. C. Perencevich. 2004. Children's motivation for reading: Domain specificity and instructional influences. *The Journal of Educational Research* 97 (6): 299–309.

Wilson, E. O. 1998. *Consilience: The unity of knowledge.* New York: Knopf.

Yore, L. D. 2009. *Science literacy for all — More than a logo or rally flag!* Paper presented at the International Education Conference, National Institute of Education, Singapore. November 26.

Yore, L. D., B. Hand, S. R. Goldman, G. M. Hildebrand, J. F. Osborne, D. F. Treagust, and C. S. Wallace. 2004. New directions in language and science education research. *Reading Research Quarterly* 39 (3): 347–352.

Yore, L. D., and D. F. Treagust. 2006. Current realities and future possibilities: Language and science literacy—empowering research and informing instruction. *International Journal of Science Education* 28 (2–3): 291–314.

CONCLUSION

Moving Forward

SCIENCE IS ELEMENTARY!

Alan J. McCormack
Professor Emeritus, Science Education
San Diego State University

Teachers at the elementary school level are very fortunate—their students are naturally curious. Curiosity abounds in young children—the everyday sights and sounds of the world are enticing. They watch and wonder and ask lots of questions: "Can a ladybug see me? What are clouds? Why is a marshmallow so soft and a rock so hard?" And kids aren't afraid to act on their queries—they are ready to bend, spindle, manipulate, smell, and explore materials in every way imaginable. They are natural scientists. Like scientists, they automatically observe, question, experiment, and form ideas about the natural world that offers endless fascination.

Just as actual scientists construct explanations for natural events, young children construct personal explanations for their experiences with objects they encounter in their environments. Kids are delighted to roll balls down ramps of different inclines, determine how to make dropped sheets of paper fall faster, and figure out if mealworms are more likely to spend time in light or dark places. Their explanations don't always coincide with those of scientists, but they do construct their own explanations.

Child development researchers Charlesworth and Lind (1995) found that young children begin to construct scientific concepts during their preschool years. Even as babies, they begin learning about the size, weight, and shape of objects. They grasp, taste, and throw objects into nearby space, thus developing their conceptions of the properties of material objects. Soon, they sort things by size, shape, or color. The best preschool programs encourage children to learn through interaction with their environment—the basis for all science.

Alison Gopnik (2010), Professor of Psychology at University of California, Berkeley, has been conducting groundbreaking research into how babies are far more capable of thinking than anyone ever thought. She has found considerable research evidence that young children learn in the same way that scientists do. Her research focuses on questions such as "Which objects do babies reach for or crawl to?" and "How do young children imitate the actions of people around them?"

Gopnik and her colleagues found that young children seem to have an intuitive feel for statistical regularities. In one experiment, they presented eight-month-old babies with a box full of mixed-up Ping-Pong balls, 80% white and 20% red. The researcher took out five balls, seemingly at random. The babies seemed surprised (they looked longer and harder) when the adult pulled out four red balls and one white, rather than four white balls and one red. The babies seemed aware that this was a surprising (improbable) result. In another experiment with older babies (20 months), toy green frogs and toy yellow ducks were mixed in a box. The experimenter removed mostly green frogs from the box and showed these to the subject. Each baby was asked to give the researcher a toy from a mixed group placed on the table. The babies invariably gave her a frog if she had taken mostly frogs from the box. This was interpreted that her statistically unlikely selection meant she was not acting randomly but must favor frogs.

In other studies described by Gopnik, four-year-olds were left alone with plastic-geared machines and other machines with levers and pop-up pictures. The kids turned out to be amazingly good at figuring out how the gears worked. The pop-up pictures were part of a toy that had two levers and a duck and a puppet that popped up. One group of kids was shown that the duck appeared when one lever was pressed, and the puppet appeared when the other lever was pressed. A second group was shown that when both levers were pressed at once, both toys popped up, but they were not shown what happened when each lever was pressed separately. Both groups were allowed to play with the toy. The first group played with the toy much less than the second group—the second group was left with a mystery, stimulating them to explore the toy. This is nice evidence confirming what other researchers have found in studying learning of science with older elementary grades children—*mystery* is one of our most potent human motivators! Fortunately, science is the realm of a never-ending plethora of natural mysteries, and these motivate both children *and* scientists to explore!

Unfortunately, traditional teaching tends to run counter to children's natural inclinations. Instead of allowing access to materials and time for natural exploration, preformed scientific concepts are often force-fed into children's minds, violating naturally instinctive principles of learning and the nature of science. Teaching by telling, giving notes, assigning reading, and other rote approaches have been commonplace. A direct instruction and reading approach to science became the mantra in many schools.

However, the past few decades have seen a slow-but-steady revolution in science education. We are moving toward viewing science as a hands-on (and minds-on) adventure in inquiring into the many facets of the natural universe and seeing children as constructive learners. We no longer look at science as a mass of information to be transmitted to students but aim to engage students in active construction of their own ideas and explanations within cooperative groups of collaborative investigators.

The contributors to this book have proposed that students learn science best by paralleling what scientists do as they explore phenomena. The writers dismiss the idea that there is a single scientific method; rather, there are many, many scientific *methods*. The multiplicity of diverse problems that scientists attack requires an arsenal of different methods (i.e., science and engineering practices). Scientists and students alike ask questions, formulate hypotheses, test ideas, collect data, and formulate explanations. Imagination plays a large role in these processes, and models, theories, and explanations are constructed.

This approach to scientist-paralleled learning is rightly called constructivist learning. In philosophy of science education, students are assumed to arrive at any lesson with a store of prior knowledge related to the lesson topic. Students are challenged to bring their current understandings forward to a conscious level, and participate in a variety of experiences to test, connect, and reform their understandings, thus continually reconstructing and expanding meaning for themselves.

In Chapter 8, Anthony Greene provides substantiation from the neurosciences to support the current constructivist approach to learning science. Dr. Greene points out that true learning is not "mere information storage and retrieval" but is "adaptive malleability of thought and behavior." In other words, true learning requires the learner to build his or her own conceptual categories and adjust them according to personal experiences. "Self-modification is a constant activity of the brain," Greene summarizes.

The brain tends to reject being forced to learn by rote memorization, contends Dr. Greene. Modern research into memorization finds that the brain is wired to form and interpret coherent connections, not arbitrary input. Putting ideas into context facilitates longer-term retention of information. For science learning, this suggests using historical and cultural contexts, analogies and metaphors, and relating science concepts to everyday experiences. For example, a study of air pressure would benefit from the historical context of Otto Von Guericke's 1674 experiment with the Magdeburg Hemispheres. Two large half copper spheres were fitted together with an airtight rubber gasket and the air was removed from inside the combination. At that point, the spheres could not be pulled apart, even by strong teams of horses. This provided some of the earliest evidence that air was real and exerted considerable pressure. Learning about the air pressure concept could be further promoted with a physical demonstration as a visual analogy. Two rubber plumber's plungers can be pushed together, removing much of the air between the two rubber cups. Kids will have a tough time pulling the plungers apart due to the stronger air pressure on the outside surfaces of the plungers! As a further extension into everyday experiences, students can be presented with a naturally occurring discrepant event for discus-

sion. On airplanes, bags of potato chips often appear over-filled with air; they are bloated and seem ready to burst! The reason—the chips were packaged in a factory near sea level where the air pressure is much higher than inside the cabin of a high-flying airplane. The air inside the bag has higher pressure than the cabin pressure. As Dr. Greene explains, "Tying new learning to existing associations—by engaging in contextual learning—we greatly improve results" (Greene 2010).

When connections to real things and real life experiences are made a focus, science capitalizes on kids' natural curiosity and inherent need to figure out how things work or why they are the way they are—"Why do soda cans 'whoosh' when they are opened?" "Why do plumbing pipes break when they freeze?" "Where do puddles go after a rainstorm is over?" If connections between the concepts of science are made familiar and relevant to students' personal lives, learning is permanently incorporated into connections among the brain's neurons, an idea currently designated as brain-based learning.

Teachers of elementary science are no longer viewed as disseminators of knowledge, but as facilitators designing and/or providing situations in which students create, share, compare, and assimilate their own knowledge. To be sure, teachers are still very involved in learning processes. They set the scene to encourage wonder in initiating science activities, help students form key questions for investigation, help structure experiments, and guide formation of explanations.

Why Teach Science?

Science, engineering, and technology are fundamental to living in the 21st century. Automobiles, airplanes, refrigerators, television, and computers are staples in everyday life. These devices had origins in basic scientific ideas from physics, adapted by engineers and technicians to become life-enhancing miracles. Think of the advances in the science of medicine that promote longer and disease-free lives for so many people. Without doubt, science helps create a higher quality of life. To cope with our science and engineering-constructed world requires at least a rudimentary understanding of basic concepts of electricity, matter, energy, and biology.

School programs need to be directly aimed at developing students' scientific literacy. They all need to understand their natural environment in order to make informed decisions concerning local, state, national, and global issues. Global warming, oceanic pollution, and local sanitation are just a few of the pressing issues that come to mind that will require logical analysis and decision making by all citizens. And some of our students will ultimately be involved in scientific and technological occupations for which they will require considerable scientific expertise.

Experiences within a good school science program invariably involve students in various dimensions of thinking, and science experiences can contribute much to development of both logical and creative thinking skills. A worthy science program engages students in observing, formulating good questions, constructing hypotheses, designing investigations, collecting and managing data, and building explanations (i.e., *NGSS* science and engineering practices). All of these are wonderful experiences in higher-order thinking. Much research has shown that processes of thinking develop gradually from early infancy into adulthood and that these skills improve through practice and experience. Experiences in science from the early grades are vital contributors to intellectual development.

Science can also be an excellent medium for improving children's reading and writing skills.

Though the fundamental avenue for developing understanding of natural events should be through hands-on, direct confrontation with the materials and events of the world, the use of printed materials and media as information sources cannot be denied. Children, once motivated to pursue knowledge of a scientific question, can learn much from science texts and trade books. For example, *Follow the Drinking Gourd* by Jeanette Winter is a story of Civil War–era runaway slaves who follow the Big Dipper (the "Drinking Gourd") north to freedom in Canada (for a science explanation see *http://quest.arc.nasa.gov/ltc/special/mlk/gourd2.html*). Or, Dr. Seuss authored *Bartholomew and the Oobleck*, a wonderful story about a young boy's involvement with an unusual form of matter (various websites offer recipes for hands-on experiments with "oobleck" at *www.instructables.com/id/Oobleck* and *www.livescience.com/21536-oobleck-recipe.html*). Because students become motivated to know more about science topics, they can enhance their skills in reading expository texts in search of key information. Writing skills are also improved through recording observations, keeping science journals, editing notes taken by cooperative groups, and writing creative stories and poems based on scientific explorations and discoveries.

Gina Cervetti, lead author of Chapter 10, maintains that "Reading and writing science should [be] viewed as supporting rather than supplanting development of knowledge and inquiry in science from the earliest years of schooling." Dr. Cervetti provides an extensive research basis justifying use of children's literature and science texts as key instruments for building science literacy.

New Science Standards Are Needed

The achievement in science and mathematics education by students in the United States is falling behind. As a result, both our students and our country are losing in competition in a growing global economy.

In the 2009 NAEP Science Assessment, more than one-third of U.S. eighth-graders scored below basic acceptable levels.

The United States ranked 17th in science and 25th in mathematics on the 2009 PISA assessment.

In worldwide measures of national innovation, the United States has lost its former leading position:

- More than 50% of U.S. patent applications for technological innovations in 2010 were submitted by citizens of foreign countries.

- The United States' share of high-tech exports has diminished. China has now surpassed us in the worldwide share of exports of high technology to other countries.

The evidence is clear: We need to prepare more of our students for exciting careers in science, technology, engineering, and mathematics (STEM). STEM workers are needed for global scientific and economic competitiveness and for dealing with the numerous challenges of environmental and standard-of-living challenges for the future.

For those with curious personalities, a creative and problem-solving view of the world, and other scientific inclinations, a STEM career can be the best in the world. STEM specialists get to do what they truly enjoy and at the same time contribute to the betterment of life for humanity. Scientists, engineers, inventors, and mathematicians tend to be admired by society and can enjoy the accomplishment of discovering or inventing new ideas, while also earning a decent standard of living.

The U.S. Department of Commerce produced a recent study, *STEM: Good Jobs Now and for the Future* (2009), providing evidence that STEM

workers play a key role in economic growth and stability. Results of the study are encouraging:

- STEM occupations are projected to grow by 17% from 2008 to 2018, compared to 9.8% growth for non-STEM occupations.

- STEM workers command higher wages, earning 26% more than their non-STEM counterparts.

- More than two-thirds of STEM workers have at least a college degree, compared to less than one-third of non-STEM workers.

- STEM degree holders enjoy higher earnings, regardless of whether they work in STEM or non-STEM occupations.

STEM careerists drive our nation's competiveness by generating and implementing new ideas, creating new products, and building new industries. STEM careers are the careers of the future. And these professionals have the satisfaction of knowing their work helps other people. They discover new medicines, new mechanical devices, and breakthroughs in electronics that literally change the world. STEM professionals might work in a laboratory genetically engineering bacteria to produce new antibiotics. Or they might work with an oil company in analyzing deep geologic rock strata. Perhaps the work takes place in a deep-sea submersible looking for new species of marine animals. In all cases, their careers are fulfilling and usually exciting.

Implementing the *Next Generation Science Standards*

The *NGSS* can be used to reform science education to many good effects: (1) more emphasis will be given to hands-on, discovery-oriented learning through the integration of science and engineering practices; (2) student achievement as measured by international standardized tests may rise; (3) new emphasis on engineering design is likely to increase both student motivation and creative thinking abilities; (4) attention to cross-cutting concepts will develop better connections with the true nature of the scientific enterprise; (5) more attention to applications of science and interconnectedness of scientific and engineering disciplines will bring about deeper understanding and appreciation of science and engineering in our everyday lives; and (6) the new science standards will be better coordinated with the *Common Core State Standards, English Language Arts (CCSS ELA)* and *Mathematics (CCSS Math)*.

One of the best ways to approach implementation of the new standards is to adopt the 5E Teaching Cycle as described by Thomas O'Brien in Chapter 4. The 5E Teaching Cycle synergistically integrates curriculum, instruction, and assessment via the following sequence of intentionally linked, developmentally scaffolded lessons:

- Engage

- Explore

- Explain

- Elaborate (and Extend)

- Evaluate (Summative Assessment)

This approach almost guarantees implementation of many facets of the *NGSS*.

An Exciting New Emphasis— Engineering Design

The incorporation of engineering into the *NGSS* opens up doors for highly motivational and enjoyable adventures into engineering design. Scientists deal with questions about the natural universe, while engineers confront important everyday problems and try to design mechanisms, materials, or processes to solve these problems for the improvement of everyday living for humans.

A growing number of high-tech industry leaders say that U.S. companies are focusing on short-term gains at the expense of long-term technological dominance. Trend lines show that we are not supporting creative thinking and innovativeness at a sufficient level, either in the industrial world or in education. Creativity, the crucial growth engine of the U.S. economy and one of the most sublime qualities that make us human, is at risk of stalling out. Thus, the current emphasis on engineering design by the *NGSS* is most timely and appropriate.

Engineering design can perhaps best be fostered by introducing grade level–appropriate challenges to students, inviting them to devise inventions or devices that might solve the challenges. Some samples of challenges are automatic toothpaste: Invent a device to place the right amount of toothpaste on your toothbrush, without squeezing a tube with your hand; balloon popper: Build a device that will pop an air-filled balloon (rule: you must be at least 5 feet away from the balloon when it pops.); paper clip picker-upper: Imagine that an entire box of paper clips has been spilled on the floor and create a device that will pick up the paper clips and deliver them back to their box.

Everyday construction materials (cardboard, string, scissors, glue) and junk (old tin cans, wire, discarded toy wheels, paper cups) have been found to be the best materials for construction of novel contraptions. Drawings from the famous cartoonist Rube Goldberg of zany devices are great inspirations to innovate for kids. For examples, see websites such as the following.

- *www.rubegoldberg.com*

- *www.youtube.com/watch?v=cVgcmmS0W3Q*
- *http://coolmaterial.com/roundup/
  rube-goldberg-machines*
- *www.teachingchannel.org/videos/
  rube-goldberg-contraptions*

Researchers who study thinking and learning processes often categorize thinking into two basic dimensions: convergent thinking and divergent thinking. Convergent thinking is focused and analytical: It involves thinking in terms of a set of rules as in logic and mathematics. This sort of thought is aimed at producing a single correct answer to a problem. Creative thinking involves divergent productive thinking, a process aimed at producing numerous possible solutions to an open-ended problem. Associative links are made among new combinations of objects and ideas. Certainly, both convergent and divergent thinking modes are crucial in science and engineering, but divergent thinking has generally been neglected in schools in recent years. This may be at least partly due to a trend toward a more information-based science curriculum.

As an operational model for designing creativity-nurturing science and engineering activities for students, shoot for the following outcomes in students:

- Fluency: production of lots of ideas
- Flexibility: production of ideas in lots of different categories
- Originality: production of new and different ideas (statistically uncommon ideas)

These skills can be encouraged through a wide palette of science and engineering activities: brainstorming, invention workshops, visual/spatial experiences, discrepant events, imagining future scenarios, inventing organisms adapted to given habitats, and so on. The creative process arises from a ferment of ideas in the brain, turning, twisting, and colliding until something new emerges. Frequently, this process is initiated by a perceived perplexity, an intriguing challenge, or something mysterious. Creative teachers have capitalized on these thought-provokers, providing an impressive arsenal of *NGSS*-based motivating activities, and more are sure to emerge in the future. As a nice bonus, science curriculum researchers have discovered that these sorts of learning activities are associated with a boost in motivation to learn and more positive feelings toward school in general.

Recent work by neuroscientists buttresses the idea that creative thinking skills can be nurtured. The brain has been found to be plastic, rather than static: It is marvelously responsive, adaptable, and constantly changing. In *The Creative Brain* (2006), neuroscientist Nancy Andreasen describes current research findings that indicate the brain is changed by experience, and that creativity can be induced in the plastic brain. Creativity-oriented science experiences can encourage openness to experience, curiosity, and a tolerance for uncertainty. The challenge of a more creative science program can help kids (and teachers) feel the sparks of sudden insights, flashes of inspiration, and liberated curiosity. Ideas can float, soar, and connect if we let kids have wings. For some, it is pure euphoria!

NGSS Coordinates With the Common Core State Standards

The timing of the release of the first draft of the *NGSS* is perfect—it comes on the scene just as many states are implementing the *CCSS ELA* and *CCSS Mathematics*. This will be a great boost for elementary science, since science in the early grades has been largely ignored in recent years due to the wide emphasis in standardized testing of ELA and math and the exclusion for teaching and assessment of science. Attempts are being made to align the *NGSS* with the *CCSS* so that they form a symbiotic relationship and bring back to the foreground the obvious importance of science and engineering in the intellectual experiences of children.

The *NGSS* and the contributors to this book emphasize that constructing and analyzing reasoned arguments to support a conclusion in science are basic to science and engineering practices. This conforms beautifully to the Common Core Anchor Standards for Reading (Rothman 2011, p. 85), Standard 8 under Integration of Knowledge and Ideas: "Delineate and evaluate the argument and specific claims in a text, including the validity of the reasoning as well as the relevance and the sufficiency of the evidence."

In the *CCSS* for mathematical practice we find more compatibility with *NGSS*:

1. Make sense of problems and persevere in solving them.

3. Construct viable arguments and critique the reasoning of others. (Rothman 2011, p. 94).

Governor James B. Hunt of North Carolina outlined three reasons for supporting the movement toward the *CCSS*:

> The *CCSS* promotes equity for all American students : "These new standards will ensure that a child's education is not determined by where he or she lives, rather than his or her abilities. We must close gaps in opportunity and achievement

that obstruct the success of all young people" (Rothman 2011, pp. ix–x).

"Students are competing with their peers across oceans and continents, and in an increasingly transient society, it is critical that what they learn is consistent and relevant from state to state" (Rothman 2011, p. x).

The *CCSS* derives from "the work of experts in the field, masters of the best science available about learning, teaching, English language arts, and math .... The products that emerged from these groups were tested against standards from the other nations to ensure they would meet the test of competitiveness and by other experts who could attest to their rigor, teachability, and importance" (Rothman 2011, p. x).

If we substitute *NGSS* for *CCSS* in Hunt's arguments above, the statements would be equally valid. Both sets of standards are parallel in goals, philosophy, and style and they complement each other wonderfully.

Let's Move Forward!

Although some of the changes brought forward by the *NGSS* will require major curricular changes, increased professional development for teachers, and financial support for needed learning materials, much can be done immediately by committed individual teachers. The grade band core concepts can be used as a guide for selection of science information to be emphasized. *Disciplinary Core Ideas* from science can be given focus, rather than trying to cover everything in the vast landscape of scientific knowledge. Strive for deep understanding as opposed to meaningless memorization of strange vocabulary words.

Frame science lessons around key questions, using discrepant events, mysteries, unique materials, and interesting real things (an actual fossil or plant is always better than a picture or descriptive words). The real thing is worth a thousand pictures! Find ways to stimulate students' ideas, and genuinely listen closely to them. Give some real energy to following a 5E plan of action—Engage, Explore, Explain, Elaborate (and Extend), and Evaluate. This approach will help greatly in applying the philosophy of the *NGSS*. Think of problems to attack, rather than material to cover. Consider storylines, episodes from the history of science, analogies, imagination and invention, and investigation as arrows in your exciting quiver of science teaching. Always keep in mind that to accomplish anything new or wonderful, you must risk failure! Believe, regardless of economic or cultural background, that each and every student can learn to love and do science as science is truly elementary!

References

Andreasen, N. C. 2006. *The creative brain: The science of genius.* New York: PLUME/Penguin Books.

Charlesworth, R., and K. Lind. 1995. *Math and science for young children.* 2nd ed. Albany, NY: Delmar Publications.

Gopnik, A. 2010. How babies think. *Scientific American*: 76–81.

Greene, A. J. 2010. Making connections: The essence of memory is linking one thought to another. *Scientific American*: 22–29.

McCormack, A. 1989. *Inventors workshop.* Los Angeles, CA: David Lake Publishers.

McCormack, A. *NSTA Reports.* 2011. It's Time for More Early Childhood Science. December 7.

Meltzoff, A., P. Kuhl, J. Movellan, and T. Sejnowski. 2009. Foundations for a new science of learning. *Science* 325: 284–288.

Michaels, S., A. W. Shouse, and H. Schweingruber. 2008. *Ready, set, Science!* Washington, DC: National Academies Press.

National Research Council (NRC). 2012. *A framework for K–12 science education: Practices, crosscutting concepts, and core ideas.* Washington, DC: National Academies Press.

Rothman, R. 2011. *Something in common: The common core standards and the next chapter in American education.* Cambridge, MA: Harvard University Press.

Seuss, Dr. 1949. *Bartholomew and the oobleck.* New York: Random House Publishers.

United States Department of Commerce. 2009. *STEM: Good jobs now and for the future.* Occasional Report. *www.esa.doc.gov/Reports/stem-good-jobs-now-and-future*

Winter, J. 2008. *Follow the drinking gourd.* New York: Knopf Books.

ABOUT THE EDITORS

William Banko, MD

- President of Knowing Science, LLC (*http://www.knowingscience.com*)

- Dr. Banko has been involved in medical manufacturing for over 25 years (*www.surgicaldesign.com*) and has been responsible for many innovations in small incision cataract surgery. Dr. Banko has authored over 25 publications in the field of ophthalmic surgery and holds several patents.

- Currently, Dr. Banko's primary interest is in elementary science education, and he is working closely with the Science Teachers Association of New York State (STANYS) to promote the importance of teaching science education at an early age.

Marshall L. Grant, PhD

- Senior Director, Formulation Development, MannKind Corp.

- Dr. Grant received his PhD in chemical engineering from Princeton University. Dr. Grant was assistant professor at Yale University and is currently managing a research team developing inhalable insulin.

- Due to his passion for science, he devotes part of his time to developing science curriculums designed for elementary grades.

Michael E. Jabot, PhD

- Professor, Science Education and Director, Institute for Research in Science Teaching, State University of New York at Fredonia

- Dr. Jabot's current research focuses on methods of measuring the impact of instructional interventions on student learning in science.

- He has been very active in the development of learning progressions and conceptual diagnostic assessments in science as well as frameworks for Education for Sustainability (EfS). As a member of New York State's Lead Team, he has been very active with both the development of the *Next Generation Science Standards* (*NGSS*) and the dissemination of professional development to teachers.

Alan J. McCormack, PhD

- President 2010–2011 National Science Teachers Association (NSTA)

- Professor Emeritus of Science Education, San Diego State University

- Dr. McCormack has been a committed teacher, educator, and member of the science education community for more than 40 years.

- He has authored 70 journal articles, 12 science textbooks, 3 science handbooks, and has been a presenter at several NSTA national and area conferences since 1978.

- In 1990, he was presented with the NSTA Distinguished Teaching Award. Dr. McCormack has also received the NSTA Gustav Ohaus Award for Advancement in Science Education, the NSTA-STAR Award, and the NSTA Ohaus Award for Innovations in College Science Teaching. The Wyoming Science Teachers Association (WSTA) also recognized McCormack with the Excellence in Science Teaching award in 1986.

Thomas O'Brien, PhD

- Professor of Science Education, Graduate School of Education, Binghamton University, State University of New York (SUNY)

- Author of a three-volume series from NSTA Press: *Brain-Powered Science: Teaching and Learning with Discrepant Events*: *www.nsta.org/publications/press/brainpowered.aspx*.

- For the past 26 years, he has directed the science teacher-education programs at Binghamton University. His expertise includes both curriculum development (e.g., writer and Teacher's Guide editor on the first edition of the American Chemical Society's *Chemistry in the Community* textbook) and professional development (e.g., more than 25 federal and state-funded summer institutes). He also teaches in his school's Educational Leadership program.

- He has received awards for excellence in teaching and/or service from the American Chemical Society, the New York State Association of Teacher Educators, the SUNY chancellor, and the New York State Science Education Leadership Association.

CONTRIBUTORS

Bruce Alberts, PhD
Professor Emeritus, University of California, Department of Biochemistry and Biophysics; Editor-in-Chief, AAAS SCIENCE magazine

William Banko, MD
President of Knowing Science, LLC and Surgical Design Corp.

Abby B. Bergman, EdD
Educational Program Consultant, Former Regional Service Coordinator, Putnam-Northern Westchester BOCES

Dario Capasso, PhD
Department of Physics, City College, City University of New York (CUNY)

Gina Cervetti, PhD
Assistant Professor, University of Michigan, School of Education

Steven Chu, PhD
Former U.S. Secretary of Energy; Nobel Prize in Physics 1997

Arne Duncan
U.S. Secretary of Education

Michael Gazzaniga, PhD
Director, SAGE Center for the Study of Mind, University of California, Santa Barbara

Marshall L. Grant, PhD
Senior Director, Formulation Development, MannKind Corp.

Anthony J. Greene, PhD
Associate Professor of Psychology and Neuroscience, University of Wisconsin

Cynthia Greenleaf
Co-Director, Strategic Literacy Initiative, WestEd, Oakland, California

Dudley Herschbach, PhD
Professor Emeritus of Science, Harvard University; Nobel Prize in Chemistry 1986; National Medal of Science 1991

Eric R. Kandel, MD
Columbia University Professor and Kavli Professor of Brain Science; Nobel Prize in Physiology of Medicine 2000; National Medal of Science 1988

Alan J. McCormack, PhD
President 2010–2011 NSTA; Professor Emeritus of Science Education, San Diego State University

Elizabeth Moje, PhD
Professor; Arthur F. Thurnau Professor; Associate Dean for Research, University of Michigan, School of Education

Patricia B. Molloy
Principal of Jackson Avenue School, Mineola, New York, Mineola School District

Chuck Niederriter, PhD
Professor of Physics; Director, Nobel Conference
Gustavus Adolphus College

Thomas O'Brien, PhD
Professor of Science Education, Binghamton University, Graduate School of Education

P. David Pearson, PhD
Professor of Language, Literacy, and Culture, Human Development, Graduate School of Education, University of California, Berkeley

Steven Pinker, PhD
Professor of Psychology, Harvard University; Author of *The Language Instinct and How the Mind Works*

Lesley Quattrone
Former K–12 Language Arts Coordinator for West Clermont Local Schools (Cincinnati, Ohio) and Greenwich Public Schools (Greenwich, Connecticut)

Robert Rothman
Senior Fellow, Alliance for Excellent Education (Washington, DC)

Brian Vorwald
President 2012–2013, Science Teachers Association of New York State (STANYS) and Adjunct Associate Professor of Earth and Space Sciences, Suffolk County Community College, Ammerman Campus

5E Mini-Unit Contributors

Jennifer Baxter
Palmyra-Macedon Primary School, Palmyra-Macedon Central School District, New York

Lori Farkash
Moses Y. Beach Elementary School, Wallingford, Connecticut

Jenay Sharp Leach
Woodley Hills Math and Science Focus School, Alexandria, Virginia

Annie Madden
Chappaqua Central School District, Chappaqua, New York

Thomas O'Brien, PhD
Professor of Science Education, Binghamton University, Graduate School of Education

Dr. Helen Pashley
Consultant; Putnam/Northern Westchester BOCES

INDEX

*Page numbers printed in **boldface** type refer to tables or figures.*